AFI

# The
# Development
# State

# AFRICAN ISSUES

AFRICAN ISSUES

# The Development State

**Aid, Culture & Civil Society in Tanzania**

**MAIA GREEN**
**University of Manchester**

JC JAMES CURREY

James Currey
is an imprint of
Boydell & Brewer Ltd
PO Box 9, Woodbridge
Suffolk IP12 3DF (GB)
www.jamescurrey.com
and of
Boydell & Brewer Inc.
668 Mt Hope Avenue
Rochester, NY 14620-2731 (US)
www.boydellandbrewer.com

First published 2014

1 2 3 4 5 17 16 15 14

The right of Maia Green to be identified as
the author of this work has been asserted in accordance with
sections 77 and 78 of the Copyright, Designs and Patents Act 1988

**British Library Cataloguing in Publication Data**
A catalogue record for this book is available on request from the British Library

ISBN 978-1-84701-108-4 (James Currey paper)

The publisher has no responsibility for the continued existence or accuracy of URLs for
external or third-party internet websites referred to in this book, and does not guarantee
that any content on such websites is, or will remain, accurate or appropriate.

This book is printed on acid-free paper

Typeset in 9/11 Melior with Optima display
by Avocet Typeset, Somerton, Somerset TA11 6RT

# CONTENTS

# PREFACE & ACKNOWLEDGEMENTS

This book is the outcome of successive engagements with development as an evolving social field in Tanzania and internationally. It is based on research and engagement in Tanzania carried out since 1999 in varying capacities, including work as a development consultant to several donor-financed projects. I first carried out anthropological research in Tanzania as a graduate student. Between 1989 and 1991 I conducted fieldwork in Ulanga District, Morogoro Region, on the impact of mission Christianity. In 2003 I undertook further ethnographic work in Ulanga and in neighbouring Kilombero District, exploring transformations in anti-witchcraft practices. In 2012 I was able to spend six months doing ethnographic research work examining the cultural dimensions of economic change. Between 1998 and 1999 I worked as a Social Development Adviser for the United Kingdom's Department of International Development in support of the country programme in Tanzania. I have since worked with a number of organisations, including the Foundation of Netherlands Volunteers (SNV), the Tanzania Gender Networking Programme (TGNP) and Twaweza! as a short-term consultant providing advice on diverse programmes mainly dealing with civil society and local-government reform. I undertook a consultancy for Irish Aid's district support programme in Ulanga in 1996, and was a member of the team that performed the final evaluation of the Local Government Reform Programme eleven years later.

The field research which informs this book was undertaken as part of several research programmes. Work on the modernisation of anti-witchcraft services was supported through the Global Poverty Research Group funded by the UK Economic and Social Research Council; research on the emergence of local civil society organisations was undertaken as part of the Department for International Development's Religion and Development Research Programme examining the differences between faith-based and secular non-governmental organisations (NGOs). Research on new development citizenships described in Chapter 8 was generously supported through a Fellowship at the think-tank Research on Poverty

Alleviation in Dar es Salaam, financed by the International Development Research Centre. The research on participation in development is based on work commissioned for the Irish Aid district development programmes in 1996, on an evaluation of Research on Poverty Alleviation's civil society support programme carried out in 2008, and on my involvement in the evaluation of the Local Government Support Programme (LGRP). Research in development is a collaborative endeavour. The fieldwork on transformations in anti-witchcraft services was carried out with Simeon Mesaki of the University of Dar es Salaam. The work on local NGOs in Mwanza was carried out with Simeon Mesaki and Claire Mercer. Evaluation visits to specific projects were conducted together with Lemayon Melyoki (district governance for SNV) and Susan Kayetta (the community programme of REPOA – Policy Research for Development). The evaluation of the national Participatory Poverty Assessment which informs my analysis of participatory instruments in development was conducted with Rachel Waterhouse whose inputs strongly influenced my understanding. Permission to conduct formal fieldwork was granted by the Tanzania Commission for Science and Technology and the University of Dar es Salaam with whom I was affiliated for the Religion and Development Research Programme. I am grateful to these organisations.

The arguments in the book have benefitted from discussions with the many students who have taking my course unit at the University of Manchester – Meeting the Millennium Development Goals: The Anthropology of International Development. I have also been extremely fortunate over the years to have had productive dialogues with generous colleagues working in development and in academia whose insights have informed the arguments in this book. Particular thanks are due to Simeon Mesaki and Claire Mercer as research partners. Additionally, I acknowledge the contributions of Aud Talle, James Woodburn, Kathryn Snyder, Alana Albee, Waheeda Samji, Masuma Mamdani, Valerie Leach, Joseph Semboja, Samuel Wangwe, Brian Cooksey, Marjorie Mbilinyi, Marja Liisa Swantz, Jane Guyer, Lucas Katera, Blandina Kilama, Amandus Muhairwa, Paula Tibandebage, Peter Eponda, Ophelia Mascarenhas, Lorne Larson, Emmanuel Maliti, Gepson Absalom, Peter Kichelele, Sam Maghimbi, Susanne Mueller, Steven Robins, Iddy Mayumana, John Gledhill, Erica Bornstein, Jamie Monson, Stein Sundstol Eriksen, John Hanson, Budd Hall, Hannah Brown, Richard Sherrington, Carole Rakodi, Howard Clegg, Todd Sanders, Graham Harrison, Gertrude Kihunrwa, Hassan Mshinda, Rehema Tukai, Kate Dyer, Kelly Askew, Jamie Monson, Sam Hickey, David Hulme, Diana Mitlin, Uma Kothari, Dan Brockington, Victoria Lawson, Susan Watkins, Paivi Hasu, Karen Armstrong, Lesley Saunderson, Peter Loizos, Angelique Haugerud, Usu Mallya, David Mosse , Donald Mmari, Per Tidemand, Brian van Akardie and Thea Stein.

I could not have written the book without the help and co-operation of numerous informants – some of whom I met only once in the context of group workshops or village visits – and the assistance and support of the staff of local government authorities in different parts of the country. Thank you all. Others I have known for many years and we have spent countless hours talking about development. Special thanks to the late Bernadina Kuoko and to Justin Kuoko, Clara Mkamate, Tobias Mkamate, Mbui Mlali, Rashid Henji, Eugene Chalala, Rafael Barua, Amri Shimata, Martin Malekero, Hamisa Kyelula and Shaibu Magungu.

Producing a book depends on the skilled inputs of various people. Jessica Symons and Patrick Newman helped with copy editing, Graham Bowden of Manchester University's Cartographic Unit drew the maps and Kristy Tobin prepared the index. Finally, Jaqueline Mitchell was an enthusiastic and encouraging editor.

Earlier versions of some of the chapters presented here have been published as articles. Chapters 2, 3 and 6 first appeared in *Critique of Anthropology* (www.sage.com), Chapter 4 was originally published as 'Making Development Agents: Participation as Boundary Object in International Development' in *The Journal of Development Studies*, (www.tandfonline.com). Chapter 5 was initially published in *Social Analysis*. A version of Chapter 7 originally appeared as a co-authored piece with Simeon Mesaki in *American Ethnologist*. Material from Chapter 8 features in a forthcoming piece for *Economic Anthropology*.

Maia Green

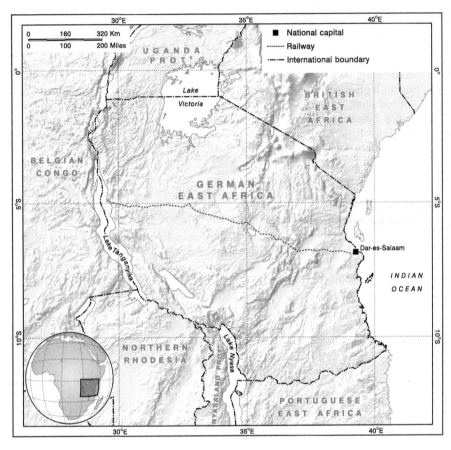

**Map 1** German East Africa, pre 1917

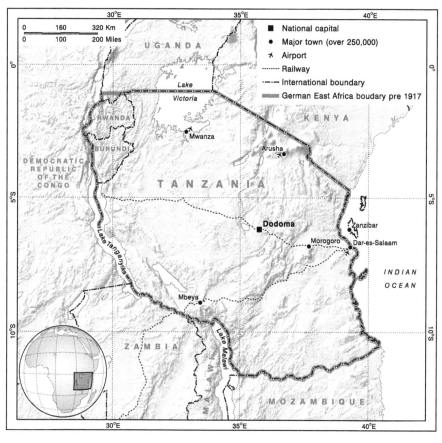

**Map 2** Tanzania, after 1964

# Introduction

International development, presented as the urgent need to end poverty and the ills associated with it, appears to be the global issue of the twenty-first century (Sachs 2005; Roy 2010; Gabay 2012). The fanfare surrounding the Millennium Development Goals (MDGs), along with the massive increase in aid from 'Western' powers in the aftermath of the Cold War, have ensured that the aspirations associated with what is categorised as 'development' have achieved prominence in countries receiving, and in countries providing, the resource transfers that comprise international development assistance. Development initiatives in support of the anti-poverty agenda extend far beyond the so-called 'failed states' subject to international efforts of reconstruction and as responses to 'humanitarian' emergencies. Development assistance is a normal component of state budgets in countries categorised as 'poor', many of which are in Sub-Saharan Africa, where foreign aid informs the design and scope of national policies. Although the scale and reach of development assistance in African countries has reached unprecedented levels since the late 1990s (O'Connell & Soludo 2001; Powell & Bird 2010; Moss et al. 2006), the imbrication of foreign development assistance and the activities it supports in the constitution of states, societies and subjectivities is long-standing. In countries constituted through development transfers and relations, development as a category of organisation and the imagination extends far beyond associations with external interventions and the formal practices associated with development agencies and institutions. It is a pervasive cultural trope that conveys understandings of modernisation, personal achievement, desired lifestyles and state power, as well as the possibilities of inclusion within a wider set of unequal but potentially transformative relations (Pigg 1992, 1993; Mercer 2002; Snyder 2002; Walley 2002, 2004).

International development is a global business, accounting for financial transfers in excess of 100 billion US dollars annually (de Haan 2009). Only a small proportion of this money goes to supplementing state

1

budgets or providing actual services for the poor. A substantial amount is spent on salaries for technical experts and officials, their travel, housing and training. Huge sums are directed towards the consolidation of development as a specialised system of knowledge and practice, through support for specialist institutions, 'capacity-building', and research (Goldman 2006; Dezalay & Garth 2002; Phillips & Ilcan 2004). Development has a tangible presence in recipient countries, in the branding of developmental infrastructure, such as schools and clinics, and the signboards advertising the offices and activities of developmental organisations. It is stridently present in the logos and vehicle liveries of project personnel traversing rural areas, in the colourful T-shirts worn by groups of people brought together to participate in what are designated community activities, and among delegates clutching marker pens and folders in the lobbies of four-star hotels in the capital cities where development workshops are held. It is evident too in the expanding support industry of development-service professionals that accompanies aid spending, providing lucrative contract opportunities for the facilitators, consultants and researchers who make development work.

International development organisations and institutions receiving development funding employ increasing numbers of 'national' staff originating within the countries where programmes are implemented. They also employ, often on short-term contracts, a large mobile pool of consultants and managers who make up a transnational professional class within the development workforce. International development is no longer predominantly characterised by relations between Western foreigners and those constituted as recipient 'Others' intermediated through the intimacies of small-scale projects in a local area. Development relations are enacted between persons within and between diverse countries and institutions at different scales. The secondary-school leaver acting as a volunteer in a village-based civil-society initiative in India stands between villagers as beneficiaries and the NGO implementing the project, which is wholly managed inside the country by national staff. This organisation in turn receives funding from several foreign organisations in Europe and the United States. Its former manager occupies the equivalent role in Malawi where the project the organisation is implementing was designed by a team of consultants from a company in South Africa. The project is supported by experts from Nepal using trainers from the United States. The circulation of personnel is matched by the circulation of ideas and practices through which development is carried out. The production of what comes to be counted as development knowledge, including the standardisation of best practices, is fundamental to the operation of the international development system (Mosse 2005a; Goldman 2006; Moore 2001; Green 2009).

In many low-income countries in the global South that have few openings for professional waged employment and a growing number of educated young people, the international development sector has become a desired destination for new graduates, and for increasing numbers of people seeking status as 'volunteers' on the periphery of paid employment (Swidler & Watkins 2009; Brown & Green forthcoming). Association with development can imply relations with funding streams and access to resources, but it also conveys a subject position of interstitiality, between project and beneficiary and between developed and less-developed status. Association with development as purveyor of the progressive future speaks powerfully to those keen to situate themselves as forward-thinking and occupying a zone of cosmopolitan commonality with professionals working in development organisations. A personal association with development is highly sought after, differentiating between those who are undeveloped, and hence in need of development, and those who are more developed and hence occupy a moral position from which to ensure their ultimate improvement (Pigg 1992). Aspiration to development implies claims to a particular subjectivity at least performatively, which can entail engagement in activities intended to bring about the development of others (Mercer & Green 2013; Mindry 2001).

This book explores the effects of international development in Tanzania, an East African country whose existence as an independent state in the half century since independence has largely been made possible through the transfers of resources, policy templates and expertise which make up development assistance. As a non-aligned state with a reputation for political stability Tanzania has played a leading role in the international development order. An exemplar of nationalist development models with experiments in African socialism in the nineteen seventies, Tanzania regained the support of Western donors in the early twenty-first century through its commitment to the World Bank Poverty Reduction Strategy approach. As a good recipient, open to the demands of public sector reform entailed by the good governance agenda, Tanzania was among the first countries to receive aid from aligned donors directly into government budgets as part of the harmonised modalities of development assistance designed to support poverty reduction strategies (Craig & Porter 2006; Gould 2005; Anders 2005; Green 2006; Wangwe 2010). (This transformation of Tanzania's aid relationships is described in more detail in Chapter 1.)

Although economic growth has reduced reliance on foreign aid in recent years Tanzania continues to receive around one third of its government expenditure from development assistance. The influence of donor agencies as 'development partners' on national political priorities is significant. The substantial financial flows that support the aid endeavour entrench a dispersed economy of intervention in which beneficiaries are those who can claim to undertake development activities. Development as national project, most recently articulated in the revised Development Vision and the reinstated Five Year National Development Plan (URT 2011), is integral to the imagination of the Tanzanian nation. Ideas about development, and practices associated with it, structure everyday life for many citizens, even where they are not formally engaged in the development sector. Development motifs inform attitudes to class and inequality, poverty and wealth, modernity and tradition. Development organisational forms such as the civil-society organisation, project proposals and the ubiquitous 'workshop' are not merely institutions through which development is practically enacted and conduits to its financial and social resources. They are an established part of the social environment.

Development in Tanzania may have had limited success in bringing about the extent of change it promised, but the institutions and relations which promote it are perceived to be a rich source of opportunity for individuals to achieve what they define as development on their own terms.[1] The focus of this book is not to evaluate the impacts of development assistance in order to determine whether aid is or is not effective. It is, rather, to explore the effects of development as it impacts on the culture, politics and society. In contrast to those studies which view development as an external order imposed on unwilling subjects, I show how development is central not only to the constitution of Tanzanian popular culture and practices of government, but to the historical constitution of the state itself as an object of international intervention.

## International development

Present day incarnations of development have origins in the strategies and approaches devised by nineteenth-century European states to deal with the problems of poverty and immiseration brought about by processes of rapid social dislocation precipitated through industrialisation. Intentional development evolved as a response to the undesirable social consequences of economic development. 'Doctrines of development', the packages of policies and initiatives, designed to manage the negative effects of economic change on populations dislocated through transformations in the agrarian economy, were exported to the colonies as strategies for governing populations and economies (Cowen & Shenton 1996). They were later taken up by independent states in Africa, Australasia, Latin America and Asia seeking to become both developers of their undeveloped populations and to be objects of development assistance (Cooper 2005). Development as a set of interventions directed at changing particular populations or the conditions which affect them implies relations of differentiation between developer and 'developee' and the invention of specialised forms of organisation, such as the project, to impose them (Hirschmann 1967; Thomas 1994).

---

[1] The failure of development as planned change is not confined to Sub-Saharan Africa. According to Cowen and Shenton, intentional development is almost predetermined to fail in ameliorating social crises because it is generally a response to, rather than a cause, of social transformation (1996: 57).

Development in various forms was integral to the colonial endeavours pursued by foreign powers through diverse instruments of government, including education, military conquest and Christian missions (Thomas 1994; Comaroff & Comaroff 1991; Beidelman 1982; Green 2003; Robbins 2004). It remains foundational to the goals and strategies of post-colonial nation states (Hardt & Negri 2000: 132). This has an international dimension, a legacy of colonialism combined with the limited resource base of poorer states, particularly in Africa, that have been reliant on grants and loans in order to meet operational costs and provide basic services. The international dimension of development implies that foreign governments and agencies retain a stake in the activities of states in receipt of development aid as well as varying degrees of financial and political influence. Influence in development is not restricted to relations between individual states. International development as a set of relations is made up of matrices of lateral and horizontal connection across policy specialisms and funding streams, within and between organisations, operating at different scales. These involve multiple actors and institutions, including multilateral agencies such as the World Bank and the United Nations Children's Fund (UNICEF), donor and recipient governments, private companies specialising in the supply of development services, and hundreds of thousands of non-governmental organisations ranging from large international operators such as Oxfam and CARE International to smaller local organisations (Mosse & Lewis 2005; Mosse, 2011, 2013). Such relations enact the imagined global of the international order (Tsing 2000, 2005; Hardt & Negri 2000, 14), (Riles 2001; Craig & Porter 1997). Verticality, in enacting scale, is a core organisational principle of the system. It is accentuated through complex chains of contracting down to the imagined beneficiary, the community, as the ultimate object of development intervention (Ferguson & Gupta 2002; Hart 2001).

## Development as national project in Tanzania

The United Republic of Tanzania is situated in East Africa, comprising a union of the island state of Zanzibar with the former British protectorate of Tanganyika. Development in the history of Tanzania is simultaneously an ideological package about trajectories of transformation and an unstable modality through which the object of intervention is situated within the political relations that seek to transform it. Development as a project of national improvement has been the prime objective of colonial and post-colonial governments and has contributed to the social improvement rationales of various colonial Christian missions (Coulson 2013; Iliffe 1979; Green 2003). Attaining independence from Britain in 1961 and union with Zanzibar three years later, the country has grown from a population of 12 million in 1967 to around 45 million in 2012 (Coulson 2013: 8). The British colonial government's attempts to institutionalise community development, a history of mission philanthropy founded on charity and self-help, and two decades of economic hardship under socialism have consolidated a national culture of development as small *miradi* – 'projects' (Kiswahili – as all foreign words unless otherwise noted) – initiated through resource transfers often brought about through highly personal patron-client relations.

Although part of the East African community of territories formerly administered by the British colonial state, Tanzania has a markedly different history from that of either Kenya or Uganda. Initially appropriated by the German East Africa Company as part of a territory encompassing also the present-day countries of Rwanda and Burundi, what was to become German East Africa was part of a colonial experiment in planned development that was cut short by the First World War. Boundaries redrawn after the German defeat, the newly demarcated territory of Tanganyika was administered by Britain as part of its East African empire subject to the requirements of a League of Nations mandate. As a protectorate not a colony it was to be governed in the interests of its resident population with a view to eventual self-government. In contrast to Uganda, there was no central political authority at the time of colonial encroachment. Tanganyika's population was widely dispersed in sparsely settled hamlets identified with over one hundred linguistic and cultural groupings.

British rule in Tanganyika was organised around the perceived need to develop rural society so that it could become 'modern' as a precondition for economic development and independence. Modernising rural production through changing the attitudes and practices of rural producers was a preoccupation shared by the first independent government under Julius Nyerere. Although there were substantial continuities between colonial and post-colonial development policy in the 1960s, notably the emphasis on community development and self-help, Nyerere's attempt to push through a wholesale policy of socialist transformation as a fast track to development was a radical departure from colonial rural development policy. Informed by an ideologically naive conceptualisation of an authentically African socialism, based on supposedly indigenous forms of rural co-operation and the absence of exploitation in 'traditional' African society, Tanzanian socialism, or *ujamaa*, involved the nationalisation of businesses and property in the major cities, a strict code that aimed to prevent leaders from profiting from their positions, and the forced resettlement of the rural population into nucleated settlements, some of which were intended to operate as collectives.

The failure of Tanzanian socialism was not only a consequence of a flawed ideological model promising unrealistic returns from rural co-operation in the absence of exploitation. Socialist villagisation was propagated by development doctrines that fetishised the capacity of 'communities' to become the engines of social and economic transformation, promoted through development agencies, including the World

Bank, that provided financial support and technical assistance to enable its implementation.[2] Problems in the agricultural sector, a flawed import substitution model, and the failure to invest in basic infrastructure accelerated economic collapse. The high cost of the war with Uganda to oust Idi Amin was blamed by politicians at the time for the economic crisis that precipitated eventual recourse to structural adjustment in the late 1980s. Inflation of almost 40 per cent, poor farm gate prices and low public-sector pay meant that for much of the first quarter century of independence Tanzanian citizens were worse off than they had been during the colonial era.[3]

The socialist period has important implications for the significance of development as cultural trope and political relation in Tanzania. First, the consolidation of poverty through economic stagnation which lead to Tanzania's resumption of relations with the international financial institutions was an entry point into the partnerships of poverty reduction in the 1990s, expanding Tanzania's development relations to include a wider set of governmental and non-governmental actors, as the aid sector became larger and more differentiated as an outcome of the new neoliberalised aid relations around poverty reduction strategies (Craig & Porter 2006; Gould & Ojanen 2005). Second, the institutional requirements of village-driven development through *ujamaa* and the discourse of self-reliance had necessitated the consolidation of a complex system of vertical organisation through which communities, as drivers and beneficiaries of development, could be integrated into the state. The socialist system of village government built on the colonial system of community development that preceded it, in which headmen were the points of integration between citizens and district offices which, under indirect rule, delegated responsibility for development to native authorities and, in the decade prior to independence, to rural residents who had to change themselves in readiness for an assumed impending modernity. Development as war waged against 'poverty, ignorance and disease' in the interests of colonial subjects was superseded by development as the responsibility of post-colonial citizens seeking socialist modernisation.[4] This incarnation of development as the responsibility of citizens persists in contemporary Tanzania, resituated within the context of relations between Tanzania

---

[2] For an account of the relationship between the World Bank and villagisation, see Payer (1983). The Bank provided the technical advice on which villagisation was based, recommending block farming and nucleated settlements. The collectivisation component came from Nyerere's socialism. World Bank finance made the implementation of Tanzanian resettlement policy viable (1983: 794).

[3] For accounts of the economic crisis in Tanzania during the 1980s and early 1990s, see Yeager (1982); Coulson (2013); Tripp (1997).

[4] The three enemies were also targets for Nyerere in the 1967 Arusha Declaration. They appear in colonial policy documents from the 1940s, perhaps originating in the 'Five Giant Evils' identified by Beveridge's (1942) report on the future of the Welfare State in Britain. These were squalor, ignorance, want, idleness and disease. Lyndon B. Johnson invoked the trilogy as 'the enemies' in his 1965 'We Shall Overcome' speech to full Congress.

and international donors legitimated in terms of multilateral agreements around poverty reduction and the MDGs.

Expectations of development as the duty of citizenship are reiterated in the devolved processes of planning for development as the primary activity of local government, an obligation that extends beyond local government officers to ordinary villagers. Village governments acting as communities must undertake projects for improvement to support national development as nation-building through citizen participation. Just as the efforts of every village contribute to developing the nation, the efforts of every citizen contribute to the development of every village, literally through the labour and cash which villagers have to make available for development initiatives and through the efforts made by individuals in striving to pursue their own personal projects of life improvement.

## Change and continuity in Tanzania's development order

Tanzanian social and political organisation, including ideas of community which remain foundational to current development imaginaries, were established through colonial policy and consolidated by successive regimes of transnational developmental intervention. At the turn of the twenty-first century these regimes underwent a decisive shift towards modalities of responsibilisation. Under this system recipient countries have increased autonomy for prioritising their own development through a country-generated poverty reduction strategy and the provision of finance to sustain it through direct budgetary support (Harrison, 2001; Lie 2011). New policy models built on and were informed by the rationales of the developmental regimes that preceded them. The poverty reduction strategy as an aid instrument was significant not so much for its focus on poverty, but for the legitimation of a move towards extensive liberalisation amounting to a radical restructuring of social and economic relations through the promotion of the private sector and the conflation of economic and political freedoms (Craig & Porter 2006; Harrison 2004). Democratisation, the reduction of core areas of state activity and an emphasis on market logics were aggressively pursued as developmental in Tanzania, along with strategies to increase local decision making and central government fiscal accountability. The emphasis on decentralisation, community participation and accountability promoted through the 'good governance' agenda undergirding this policy vision led, in Tanzania as in other post socialist settings, to an influx of donor finance to support a specific portfolio of interventions aimed at fostering the growth of local civil society and the extension of participatory approaches. Operating in a changed context of accelerating liberalisation and personal freedoms after two decades of socialist economic stagnation, development models and the resources that flow through them provide new models for citizen engagement in development as social opportunity, as well as, through donor-financed programmes of decentralisation, distributing the social institutions of development throughout the country.

Despite the triumphalist claims of Western donor agencies, echoed by their civil-society satellites, that debt relief, country 'ownership' and the ending of conditionality heralded a new era for the continent (Mercer 2003), the apparent transition in development regimes segued into long-standing incarnations of core developmental tropes and organisational forms, within and beyond Tanzania. Some of this continuity is explained by the remarkable stability of the Tanzanian political order. The same political party through which Nyerere governed has retained power since independence. During this period it has reconfigured itself from the nationalist independence party, the Tanganyika African National Union (TANU) to Chama Cha Mapinduzi (CCM), the Revolutionary Party, at the vanguard of socialist transformation. Over the past twenty years it has gradually assumed a new identity as a champion of nationalistic growth through the free market, reducing grass roots influence on policy processes and increasing the power of the senior leadership. Major changes in the allocation of political office under liberalisation notwithstanding, notably the separation of party office from positions in the administration, there are substantial continuities in the operation of power and state patronage through development. The ideological emphasis on community planning through village and ward development committees never extended to policy formation but was, and is, a means of ensuring the local implementation of priorities set at national level by party leadership.

Liberalisation did bring important changes, the most far-reaching of which were not as a result of the transition to a multi-party system of government but of inclusion within a wider set of evolving aid relations. Notable innovations during this period include the practices for community engagement promoted through international civil society organisations, as non-governmental organisations were now known, which by the late 1990s were becoming part of the standard development tool kit for stakeholder engagement and legitimacy, even in large governmental and multilateral development agencies. Precisely at the time when authoritarian structures of community co-optation associated with socialist governance in the villages were supposedly giving way to more democratic forms under liberalisation, the basic organisational structures through which community development was effected were reinvigorated through the new development models that sustained them. In addition to a process of local-government reform lasting more than a decade, the final phase of which aimed to enhance the participatory dimensions of villages as governments in their own right,[5] successive development programmes

---

[5] The Local Government Reform Programme was a multi-donor-funded programme that was 'mainstreamed' into the Prime Minister's Office of Regional Affairs and Local Government for its final phase commencing in 2008. The final phase was to focus on 'lower local government'.

implemented through state agencies and civil society organisations have relied on structures of village government to achieve the participation of beneficiaries in programmes, generally through contributions that constitute co-financing in cash or, more usually, through the supply of labour or the construction of infrastructure (Lange 2008). (These issues are addressed more fully in Chapters 2 and 3.)

This history shapes popular understandings of development in Tanzania as pertaining to certain kinds of persons, practices and relations. In popular discourse, development as *maendeleo* refers both to the actions and institutions associated with foreign interventions justified in the name of social and economic progress and to a range of local and nationally initiated endeavours directed at social transformation, endeavours that may or may not be financed through development assistance. Development is not constituted solely as an external force, although its relational quality means that it is often associated with other persons and places. It is, rather, a state to which to aspire. Development can be achieved as a result of individual effort, part of a person's struggle to 'build a life' (*kujenga maisha*) (Giblin 2005: 9). Using one's own resources, particularly one's innate qualities of drive and judgement,[6] is a starting point, but conditions in the country mean that this is often insufficient. A person's path towards development may need to be catalysed through relations with others who can in some way provide support or access to resources that can help one achieve the next step on the way. Patrons, benefactors and helpers feature strongly in popular narratives of development as a personal achievement. Achieving development therefore necessitates attention to establishing and maintaining appropriate institutional and personal relationships with persons and institutions already associated with the developmental, including those associated with development practices and organisations.

Development conveys difference between the developed and those for whom development is lacking, within virtually any set of relations. Therefore, it is often experienced in relation to its absence. Even where development is in evidence, in the form of a newly constructed road or school buildings, or in the rising skyline of a growing city, this merely highlights where it is not. Development connotes difference – between Western countries and Africa, between countries in Africa, between places within countries, between city professionals and villagers, and between rich and poorer people within a single village. Development can even delineate differentiation between members of the same family and between different stages of one's own life. Development, because it is about difference and because it is historically associated with external organisations, also conveys a sense of situation in an unequal but potentially enabling relation external to others as *wafadhili* – benefactors or helpers, providers of assistance. These others may be conceived as

---

[6] *Akili kichwani*, literally 'intelligence in one's head', but *akili* conveys more than straightforward intellect. Its meaning is more akin to a combination of cunning and cleverness.

donor organisations, NGOs, experts or patrons who have the capacity to provide the missing resource to bring about the developmental. Popular representations of development in Tanzania emphasise the centrality of the social relationships that make development outcomes possible. Agency is not ascribed to development as a reified power but to the institutions and individuals enmeshed in relations with development resources. These include persons associated with governments, donors and the civil society organisations, many of them created as a result of donor funding, who have at their command the empowering agentive attributes of 'capacity' (*uwezo*) and expertise (*utalaam*) that can render development resources productive.[7]

Contemporary discourses of development in Tanzania borrow from previous forms of development as community driven and locally owned, combined with popular capitalism's dogmas of accumulation and self-improvement in a post-socialist argument about the prioritisation of individual above collective action – an argument necessitated by the erosion of public institutions and the neoliberal politics of public-sector restructuring. If development is lacking this is because of an absence of capacity or relationships with the potential source of transformation. The argument of absence comes to assume an explanatory status for the apparent paradox of Tanzania, namely that a state conceived within and through development as a twentieth-century project remains essentially without the benefits promised by it. At the same time, development relations and organisational forms enable emergent relations of inequality, consolidating class structures and providing access to the symbolic and material capital that permits some to achieve, at least partially, their development ambitions. The 'bureaucratic bourgeoisie' identified by Issa Shivji as created by the state (1976; Samoff 1979) is now nurtured through development within and beyond it, including through the new organisational forms brought into being on the periphery of state activity, and formal development organisations through which beneficiary participation is effected.

## The organisation of the book

The chapters in this book examine the social life of development as relation, institution and form of organisation in Tanzania in the years after the end of socialism and at the height of the aid partnerships that characterised the organisation of development in the decade after the millennium. This situation is changing as Tanzania's political elite reinstate a national development plan and seek to use finance from a range of new providers, including private finance from China and global agribusiness, in a bid to pursue an aggressive agenda directed towards

---

[7] Development agency literature and handbooks translate 'capacity-building' as *kujenga uwezo* but *uwezo* also conveys notions of capability and power.

enterprise-driven growth. However, relations with established donors, or 'development partners', remain important, especially for the financing of health and education and in terms of the national vested interests in perpetuating development relations and institutions in various forms, including think tanks, policy institutes and numerous donor-created civil society organisations. Institutional architectures of project finance and participation established through the development onslaught ensure that the organisational forms perpetuated through development interventions and relationships persist, notably in the organisation of decentralised local government and its contrived relations with development-initiated civil society organisations (CSOs) – at least in the short term.

This book is written from an anthropological perspective that pays close attention to the social and cultural constitution of relations and to the moral imagination that motivates social actors. Rather like development interventions themselves, organised by sector and for a limited period, the book presents a snapshot of development practices around particular interventions in different parts of the country, rendered intelligible through the salience of ideas about development and the institutions that organise it as a national cultural frame. My focus is on how development imaginaries and interventions constitute emerging social forms, and how development as culture offers new possibilities for personal self-construction. Most studies of development produced by anthropologists have privileged either a development agency or local community as the object of supposed intervention (Mosse 2005a; Escobar 1995; Ferguson 1990). My approach, informed by engagement with development as a practitioner in various capacities, as well as by more direct ethnographic research, is deliberately interstitial, situated between development and its object. The objects of development are, I suggest, co-created through engagement with development institutions and practices. Much of the book describes the ways in which these processes are rendered workable and for what ends, by actors with situated motivations within the cultural economy of development at different scales. The book examines institutions familiar to those who have worked in development in any country, including participation, civil society and local knowledge, situating these technologies of intervention within the social universe and policy discourses accompanying liberalisation.

The chapters in this book address the development foci of international policy in Tanzania after the turn of the millennium and the new modalities for the organisation of aid that characterised development order after the Cold War, including harmonisation, poverty reduction strategies and debt relief. The institutionalisation of community, through discourses of self-help and participation, performs work of economic and social transformation for socialist and neoliberal regimes not so much creating space for achieving collective projects of economic development, as creating the basis of a perceived contrast between forced development from above and people's personal projects of development, often enabled, at least in the imagination, by an idealised relation to sources of material support that can supply what is missing to achieve it.

As Tanzania and aid have evolved during this period the final chapter considers the move towards a discourse of inclusive growth and the resurgence of a national development plan in 2011 as backdrop to new practices of self-construction and consumption, epitomised in the new social form of the supermarket as paradigmatic symbol of the progressive future.

The central argument of this book is that development in Tanzania is a modality through which state, culture and society are organised. Chapter 1 introduces the institutionalisation of development in Tanzania through an historical account of the constitution of the Tanzanian state. The Tanzanian state was, and is, constituted to implement development through its relations with citizens as villager beneficiaries. This is not a post-colonial endeavour. The precursors to the modern Tanzanian state were constituted within the ambit of relations of moral internationalism and intentional development as a consequence of German and British colonial relations. Chapters 2 and 3 explore the implementation of development through the paradoxes of participation as political institution and historical artefact in Tanzania and beyond. Participatory development introduced by donors as part of post-liberalisation development programming replicated the modalities and limitations of participation under colonial community development and Tanzanian socialism. Beneficiaries are at the same time responsible for their own development yet lack the capacity to attain it. Both state and donor conceptualisations of development as essentially collective are contrasted with widespread understandings of development as a personal project of self-improvement.

Chapter 3 explores another troubling dimension of participation: its contribution to the production of uniformity around development interventions within and beyond Tanzania. This occurs, I suggest, as an effect of some of the specialised institutional techniques through which development is organised as well as the key role of facilitation in creating the consensus that participatory techniques interpret as amounting to community legitimacy. The characteristics of participatory institutions as institutions through which communities as development objects are created is the focus of Chapter 4. Such institutions, and the techniques through which they are realised, operate as 'boundary objects' (Star & Griesemer 1989) that align common interests at the same time as they enable a differentiation between implementers and beneficiaries of development.

Chapters 5 and 6 consider the donor-driven promotion of local civil society organisations as specific institutions through which participation as beneficiary engagement is managed. New forms of CSO that have appropriated the function, at least partially, of community development in intermediating between state and beneficiary reiterate the cultural practices of enacting verticality associated with socialist developmental governance. They increasingly provide an opportunity for new forms of entrepreneurship through development. Chapter 7 explores this theme of development entrepreneurship and the circulation of its organisational forms further through the efforts of a traditional healer to adapt his services developmentally through a model of improvement derived from public-service reform. Chapter 8 examines emerging forms of development citizenship through choice and accountability practices that align with the developmental subjectivities of those seeking to identify with the middle class as the developmental citizen in readiness for Tanzania's new development incarnation as a middle-income country.

# 1

# Tanzania ▮ A Development State

The prevalence of development ideas and practices as cultural forms is characteristic of contexts in which the forms and practices of development, and the people associated with them, have economic power and cultural capital. In such contexts, idioms derived from development come to be associated with claims to situation within global and comparative frames (Wilk 1995; Pigg 1992, 1993). This extends far beyond Tanzania (Chakrabarty 2000). For countries that have been highly dependent on development relations and the resources they make available, development is more than cultural frame. It becomes constitutive of economic and political orders at different scales. Where development relations and the resources they convey come to be enmeshed with state architectures and systems of administration in addition to the provision of goods and services beyond the state, it becomes possible to characterise this particular political economic formation as the development state.[1]

Development states are those that are materially and ideologically sustained through development relations. Such states are largely dependent on aid transfers to meet recurrent budgets. Their institutional configurations are significantly determined by development relations, deriving from the kinds of developmental templates distributed through development programmes, as in the design of systems of local-government financing or organisational structures for the management of health services or the environment (e.g. West 2006). Finally, as is evident in the so-called 'governance states' produced through World Bank policies during the 2000s (Harrison 2004), development relations structure much of the content of the developmental policies and tactics claimed as the objective of government. Even where these are reframed by country governments within nationalistic developmental claims, policy content in key areas, such as around economic liberalisation, tends to be aligned with the concerns of powerful donor organisations (Hickey 2013).

[1] See also Moore (1998) on the effects of aid dependency on the state in what he calls the 'fourth world'.

The politics of authenticity and ownership may be assigned to what is actually peripheral to the interests of both parties, as for example in the articulation of nationalistic anti-homosexual positions by several African governments.[2]

## Development states

Development states are distinct from developmental states, that is, states such as China, Vietnam and Malaysia, which are organised around commitments to economic productivity and technical modernisation (Leftwich 1995). Although these are likely to be articulated aims within the development plans and strategies advocated by development states, their approaches to transformation tend to be dominated by the theorisations and policy models promoted by international development agencies. Development states, unlike developmental states, generally have weak track records of economic and social development. As states constituted largely through relations with international development organisations, they are likely to be enmeshed in unequal relations with other states that claim an interest in their development. They are therefore subject to inclusion within trajectories of social and economic reform effected through relations with international development institutions. Because development states are fiscally reliant on foreign aid, these relations determine the scale of government resources and national budgets. For much of the period immediately after the end of the Cold War up to the economic crisis of the first decade of the twenty-first century, new modalities of harmonisation among donor agencies and techniques of governing at a distance through country strategies meant that the ideological content of government policies and state practices in a number of development states were increasingly determined through development relations (Craig & Porter 2006).

The extent to which development relations determine the character of development states varies. Countries that are more aid-dependent and that have longer histories of policy subjection reveal this history in their institutional composition. Institutional templates such as civil-society organisations, water committees, or 'communities' promoted by international development organisations have been literally inserted to make up the normative institutional components of a developing economy. Village development committees, 'traditional' birth attendants (Pigg 1997), gender equality strategies and the like populate development states, along with a portfolio of standard institutions for bringing state institutions and policy content into alignment with that which is promoted as developmental good practice by donor agencies and their associates. Recent examples include sector development programmes,

---

[2] As evident in Uganda, Nigeria and Zimbabwe.

medium-term expenditure frameworks, public expenditure reviews and country assistance strategies. The legacies of state restructuring, decentralisation and public-sector reform are clearly evident in those states in Africa and Asia implicated in the poverty-reduction approach promoted by the World Bank since the late 1990s. This reliance on institutional templates for developing societies makes development states appear institutionally similar, wherever they may be, at the same time as making development expertise practically applicable across a range of developing country contexts (see also Pigg 1993; Ferguson 1990; Moore 2001). In development states national political cultures and social practices are constituted *through* development, not *by* it (Pigg 1993). Development informs cultural aspirations about self-realisation, structures relations between the successful and the excluded, and provides templates for political mobilisation.

While Tanzania, like some other aid-dependent countries in Africa, is a paradigmatic development state, its relation with international development as a system of institutions and resources is arguably more intimate than that of other states. It is generative. Tanganyika as the forerunner to the present state of Tanzania, formed through union with Zanzibar in 1964, was brought into being through relations of international diplomacy at the end of the First World War, when the greater part of what was then German East Africa was delineated as an administrative territory to be governed subject to international oversight of the emerging international order of the League of Nations. As a territory established through colonial annexation, German East Africa had been part of an explicit strategy of 'development for exploitation' (Koponen 1994). The British colonial administration that ruled Tanganyika under the League of Nations mandate adopted a succession of development strategies in order to effect a transition from indirect rule through native authorities to an embryonic system of local government, a transition entailing a move from compulsory labour in lieu of tax to compulsory labour justified as participation in community development. Development was the goal of the nationalist government that assumed responsibility for the country after gaining independence from Britain in December 1961.

As development internationalism became part of the broader policy environment of international relations during what was proclaimed by the UN General Assembly as the 'Decade of Development' in the 1960s (Morgan 1964: 5), achieving Tanzanian development was no longer only the concern of the former colonial power and the United Nations as the League's successor. It became the target of the development efforts of a number of foreign governments on both sides of the Cold War divide. Although Tanzania broke off relations with the international financial institutions for a period immediately prior to structural adjustment in the mid-1980s, it maintained wide relations with a range of donor countries, seeking bilateral support from some smaller states, as exemplified in its relations with Denmark, Norway and Sweden. China was a substantial donor during the 1970s, financing and providing technical support for the construction of the TAZARA, the Tanzania-Zambia railway (Yeager 1982: 105; Monson 2009). The impasse with the international financial institutions ended in 1986. By the time the agreement with the World Bank was reached, the country had already embarked on a programme of harsh austerity measures exceeding the conditions of adjustment in a desperate effort to revive the failing economy (Havnevik 1993, 287). Just over a decade later Tanzania became the second country to acquire decision-point status as a Highly Indebted Poor Country and hence eligibility for aid harmonisation and debt relief in 1999 (Mercer 2003).

Incorporation into the World Bank-promoted Poverty Reduction Strategy aid regime since the turn of the millennium has contributed to macro-economic stability and annual growth rates of around 6 per cent, as well as, despite the rhetoric of a shrinking state, a massive investment in public services, particularly in health and education. Tanzania perceives itself, and is claimed by donors, as something of a development success, with improved social and economic outcomes for citizens compared with the extreme poverty of the 1980s and early 1990s. Although there is clear evidence that the political elite are now striving to reclaim ownership of developmental agendas and the state through an aspirational national development plan in which private-sector growth predominates (URT 2011), development relations within and beyond Tanzania remain enormously significant. Tanzania successfully sustains its post-independence reputation as a development exemplar, whose good record on human rights and liberal constitution make it an acceptable recipient for Western donors, while the historical relationship with China permits ongoing aid and investment relations, particularly in large-scale infrastructure projects. Although an increasing proportion of public finance is raised locally, in 2010–11 Tanzania received one-third of government expenditure from international sources (Development Partners Group 2014), and its policy concerns are extensively influenced by extra-national agendas.

Development as a principle of national organisation in Tanzania is neither solely an artefact of the colonial era nor the monopoly of the post-colonial state. The organisational and categorical forms created to manage the development effort under colonialism and through socialism have not merely endured, they have become the enduring basis of social organisation within contemporary Tanzanian society. Tanzania as a nation state was not simply conceived as the nationalist reframing of a British colonial project. It was equally the product of the emerging political order of moral internationalism facilitated via the League of Nations stewardship. Tanganyika had been conceptualised by Bismarck's Germany as a project of economic and social development situated within the totality of the German colonial economy (Koponen 1994: 665). The development of the territory of German East Africa was therefore primarily oriented towards the economic development of the German state. This process was managed, ineffectively, through a centralised bureaucracy from the Reichstag (Iliffe 1969: 38). The trusteeship of the League of Nations under which Britain administered Tanganyika necessitated a different orientation of colonial development that was to be directed towards the improvement of the conditions of the population of the territory (League of Nations 1923). The British administration pursued, with variable success, a range of strategies for social and economic transformation. These were strongly influenced after 1950 by the need to rapidly prepare the territory for future self-government.

As the cornerstones of late British colonial policy in Tanganyika, agricultural modernisation, producer co-operatives and community development set the stage for the transition to socialism under the leadership of the country's first president, Julius Nyerere. Tanzanian socialism, popularised as *ujamaa*, translated the colonial infrastructure of community development into the operational modalities of socialist self-reliance, establishing the enduring institutional and social forms through which development policies and practices are enacted in the present. Moral internationalism within which development is situated as the policy objective of actors external to the Tanzanian state structures development relations and actors' expectations about what is necessary to achieve it, in the form of investment, capacity or expertise. This in turn functions within a system in which development is defined as the responsibilities of communities who are its beneficiaries but who must ultimately seek self-reliance. This chapter examines the historical evolution of the political institution of Tanzanian development. It shows how internationalism, community development, decentralisation and self-reliance came to be established as the architecture of development relations through regimes of colonial governance that constituted development as object of state policy but the responsibility of local government.

Independence in 1961 and the formation of the United Republic of Tanzania three years later did not represent a radical break with the core strands of colonial policy. The constitutive nature of development as the internal and external basis of the Tanzanian polity continues to characterise the post-colonial state. The political strategy pursued by Nyerere and the Tanganyika African National Union (TANU), the political party he led at independence, was premised on the continued need for development relationships structurally integral to the future of the Tanzanian state. Development relations profoundly influenced the direction of policy in independent Tanzania, with its emphasis on agricultural modernisation and socialist collectivisation. The Tanzanian state and its population became an experiment in the application of development models and practices imported from countries as diverse as Israel, China, the United Kingdom, Norway, Cuba and the United States (Coulson 2013: 364–66).

The centrality of development relationships to the political and economic order of the Tanzanian state informs Tanzania's continued status as a 'good recipient', perpetuating its position as a testing-ground for a portfolio of interventions justified through development (Jennings 2002, 2003, 2007) in which global policy ideas and techniques of social and institutional reform become templates for government action and for the foreign governments, multilateral organisations and international civil-society actors that support and promote it. Over the past decade Tanzania has implemented virtually all the interventions advocated by mainstream development organisations, following the World Bank's lead, including local-government and public-sector reform. It has executed policies intended to foster the proliferation of what are categorised as the 'local' civil-society organisations central to the social imaginary of donor-promoted democratic governance. (This process is described in greater detail in Chapters 5 and 6.) Like its neighbours elsewhere in Africa who have embarked on the implementation of World-Bank-designed social protection strategies Tanzania is in the process of operationalising a World-Bank-influenced social protection framework, and has involved a number of national activist-oriented civil-society organisations in the tracking of public expenditure. The country is equally open to the development innovations of non-governmental and private-sector actors. The government of Jakaya Kikwete, elected in 2005, has encouraged the expansion of micro financial services operated by not-for-profit and private-sector providers, as well as experimenting with novel forms of private business engagement in development through the recently announced Southern Agricultural Growth Corridor (SAGCOT) initiative, a donor-promoted approach replicated in a number of other African countries, including neighbouring Mozambique.

## Colonial developments

Tanzania is not only a paradigmatic development state. It is a paradigmatic modern state also, having been brought into being through the German colonial project intent on economic development, defined in terms of capitalist integration of Tanzanian agricultural production into the global economy in support of Germany's own industrial and social revolutions (Koponen 1994: 66). The territory that was to become Tanganyika was demarcated from the outset of the German colonial endeavour as a national economic project, which it was the responsibility of the colonial regime to manage for success. It was initially appropriated by the mercantile German East Africa Company under the directorship of Carl Peters in 1885, as part of Bismarck's strategy of mediated colonialism to be carried out through commercial interests acting independently of the German state. The inability of the company to attain control with its small number of men meant that the German state was forced to take over after 1891 (Iliffe 1969: 11).[3] The ultimate objective of the German colonial

[3] In 1888 the German East Africa Company had only eighty-eight men in the territory, all of whom were at the coast. (Koponen 1994: 78).

state was to develop the colonial economy through systematic modifications in the operation of production and the social organisation of labour (Koponen 1994: 170).

Initial pacification and military conquest were violently contested, most notably in the *maji maji* war, a widespread anti-colonial rising that devastated the southern part of the country. As Germany gradually consolidated its control over the colony, which was increasingly enmeshed in global markets for primary commodities in high demand, such as cotton and rubber, an explicit policy of programmatic development was pursued by the administration seeking to recoup its costs through facilitating the conditions under which private enterprise could be profitable and raise government revenues. Monetisation, the introduction of taxation, markets at which barter was forbidden, and the establishment of a system of local fiscal administrations (*communes*) within districts governed by colonial officers with clear responsibilities for collecting and spending revenue and for undertaking a range of developmental activities, including building roads, the provision of basic schooling and the introduction of new agricultural techniques, were elements of this enabling framework (Koponen 1994: 220–81). Others were the construction of a transport infrastructure, notably the central railway from Dar es Salaam to Tabora and Kigoma, and setting up regional administrations and investments in human capital, education and health.

German colonial development through an administrative state did not get very far in German East Africa. There were insufficient resources, human or capital, to proceed apace with the implementation of an imposed vision on an uncompromising and angry population. Resistance was widespread. In the years up to 1905 there had been armed uprisings and outbreaks of anti-colonial violence in several areas, including Mahenge, Njombe and Songea (Monson 1998: 99). The number of colonial staff, military and civilian, was never adequate to populate the administrative system, let alone attain control over the far reaches of the country. Concerns to keep administrative costs to a minimum worked against its extension. Settlers, initially discouraged as a matter of policy, were few in number and thinly spread.[4] The system of rule tenuously depended on locally recruited officials, *akida*, and their functionaries under the ultimate command of German soldiers or German bureaucrats (Iliffe 1979: 180; Koponen 1994: 118; Gwassa 1969: 103). At the outbreak of the First World War not all districts were under civilian rule. Iringa and Mahenge in the south were under the direct control of the military (Iliffe 1979: 119).

Military repression and scorched-earth tactics created compliance, but never consent. The German administration was itself divided over the appropriate tactics for colonial development, adopting a policy of promoting peasant production after 1907 but failing to resolve the

[4] According to Iliffe (1969: 57) there were 2,570 Europeans in total in 1906.

conflicting demands of settler farmers for more land to be alienated from local populations and for increased political control (Iliffe 1969: 93). The First World War, which put an end to Germany's colonial ambition, terminated government initiatives and disrupted the business activities of the private traders and planters on whom colonial development depended. In the aftermath of German defeat the territory was administered by Belgium prior to being divided among the allied victors. The greater part of German East Africa that became Tanganyika territory was as incorporated into the British colonial order, and a new development imaginary, that of trusteeship through indirect rule associated with 'native administrations' (Lugard 1965) and later, community development.

Despite the failure of the German colonial project in Tanganyika, with its devastating impacts on population and agricultural productivity, particularly in the south (Iliffe 1979: 454; Culwick & Culwick 1938/39), the period of German rule left a lasting legacy. It established the institutional and ideological foundations for Tanzania as a development state. *Entwicklung* (development) was a deliberate objective of German colonial policy envisaged as the rational improvement of the economy and productivity of the territory (Koponen 1994: 665). This kind of colonialism involved a move away from the extractive mercantilism founded on trade in ivory, rubber and slaves that preceded it, demanding a sustained engagement. German colonialism established the social order of development in Tanganyika, conceptually as a means of organising activities deemed developmental, and practically, in the institutions created for organising. The German colonial annexation and the administrative structure for territorial control created the national polity which would become the contemporary state. The German colonial regime introduced district-administered development through the *commune* system as a collector of revenue and as a vehicle through which developmental activities could be organised, and hence established institutions of local governance as agents of development and constitutive of the political relation between rural populations and the state. Finally, it created a skeleton cadre of individuals and institutions through whom development as both idiom and objective of governance could potentially be effected. Not all of the institutions were populated by colonial officials from Germany. Several thousand locally recruited staff occupied posts as government functionaries of one sort or another: headmen, *akida* and clerks.

Initially this organisation of development was confined within the coloniser/colony dyad of Germany and the territories it had appropriated. After the German defeat in the First World War, development as constituting a specialised purpose of colonial governance became integrated into the newly institutionalised international system. The League of Nations mandate, a supplement to the Treaty of Versailles, created the option of protectorate status for what had previously been German colonies. A brief interlude when Tanganyika was overseen by Belgian authorities led to the assumption of effective responsibility for the territory of Tanganyika by the United Kingdom government in 1920 (Callahan 1993, 461). The British mandate for East Africa was agreed in July 1922. Britain, as mandatory, was to 'be responsible for the peace, order and good government of the territory'. There were additional responsibilities. As set out in Article Three, the mandatory should 'undertake to promote to the utmost the material and moral wellbeing and the social progress of its inhabitants' (League of Nations 1923: 155). This could not be left to the goodwill of colonial governments. In response to anti-colonial pressure from the Americans, who had joined the war late (Crozier 1979) and whose government was hostile to the European imperial project (Iliffe 1979: 246), a specially appointed Mandates Commission was established to ensure, through a system of annual reporting, that the objectives of the treaty were pursued. These sought to legitimate colonial rule as a kind of 'administration in trust' of the residents of a colony who were deemed unable to deal with the exigencies of the 'modern world'. Article Twenty-two of the Covenant of the League of Nations instructs colonial powers in the following terms (in Lugard 1965: 62–3):

> To those colonies and territories which as a consequences of the late war have ceased to be under the sovereignty of the States which formerly governed them, and which are inhabited by peoples not yet able to stand by themselves under the strenuous conditions of the modern world, there should be applied the principle that the wellbeing and development of such peoples form a sacred trust of civilization, and that securities for the performance of this trust should be embodied in this Covenant.

## Development as moral internationalism

The Covenant provides an obvious rationalisation for the continuation of colonial rule in areas that had been subject to German control. It should not, however, be viewed as a continuation of European notions of colonial sovereignty, as had characterised the aftermath of the scramble in the 1890s, but as embarking on a different conceptualisation of colonial governance altogether. This new conceptualisation of colonial control was represented as serving a higher moral purpose than either meeting the material needs of the population of the colonial power or taking control of a territory as an economic resource, although these objectives were present. Importantly, the moral purpose of colonial government was to be institutionally embedded within the nascent international system. This structure, with its dual emphasis on international oversight of development processes on the one hand and the stated prioritisation of the well-being and development of subject peoples on the other, sets a precedent for the international social system through which contemporary development is organised and in which Tanzania continues to be embedded. International development as an endeavour undertaken by governments, colonial or otherwise, within the ambit of the formally constituted international community, did not begin, as Escobar maintains, with the creation of the Bretton Woods Institutions (1995: 72). It was established in nascent form through the League of Nations as forerunner to the United Nations system (Zanasi 2007). The innovation of Bretton Woods was in development financing, a model initially designed to support the post-war recovery of Western nations after 1945 and adapted to support the fragile economies of post-colonial states.

International development is distinct in some respects from colonial development, which, until the 1940s, had privileged the development of the colonial powers over the subject territory.[5] The Second World War, the new social policies in the aftermath of war and European reconstruction, and the evolution of the international system from the League of Nations after 1945, established the principles of differentiation between colonial and international development pathways, as Britain and France prepared the groundwork for the ultimate divestment of colonial territories through Acts of Parliament in which the welfare of colonial subjects appeared for the first time as the stated objectives of government policy (Eckert 2004: 469).[6] British colonial policy during this period experimented with new approaches to intentional development, notably in rural areas, including substantial changes in the native authority system, which moved gradually toward a system of territorial rather than tribal administration, the introduction of district development plans and the provision of grants for small-scale local projects as well as larger technically designed development schemes.[7] The latter, epitomised by the spectacular failure of the Groundnut Scheme (Hogendorn & Scott 1981; Rizzo 2006), were largely unsuccessful.

The period between the passing of the first British Colonial Development Act of 1929 and Tanganyikan independence in 1962 was a time of transition, from the old model of colonial development to the emerging internationalist one, in which universalist visions of human well-being and rights formally superseded the previous discourse of local exceptionalism and absence of civilisation (Cooper 2005). This vision, which prioritised the long-term economic and social development of colonial populations above the economic development of the colonial power, was

---

[5] Colonial development is not unitary either, as David Scott has argued. Using the example of British colonial government in Ceylon (now Sri Lanka) he shows how modern and colonial forms of government are not coterminous (1995: 194–5). In Ceylon, colonial government used distinct modes of governing at different periods under the same colonial regime. A similar argument is made here concerning Tanganyika in relation to both British and German colonial rule, each of which underwent different modalities of governing through development.

[6] Authors such as Eckert consider this policy shift to amount to a new form of 'developmental colonialism' (2004: 469).

[7] The transition from native authorities to modern forms of local government, and the range of hybrid institutions that ensued, is described by Iliffe (1979: 481–3).

first articulated in British colonial policy through the Colonial Development and Welfare Act of 1940, subsequently amended in 1945, 1950, 1955 and 1959 (Morgan 1964: 33). It was an approach to development as moral responsibility adopted by colonial powers and nationalist movements alike, providing a rationale for the continuation of economic influence through development assistance and the opportunity for the continuing extension and proliferation of what was termed 'technical assistance' provided by foreign agencies and the international system to newly independent nations. Independence in the 1960s for East African states coincided with the United Nations' Decade of Development. Internationalism brought other innovations in establishing the enduring institutional architecture of international development forms. These included an initial attempt at harmonisation in aligned approaches to aid in support of national priorities through 'comprehensive programmes' that was first adopted across the agencies of the United Nations system in 1956, an approach reiterated in the Comprehensive Development Framework of the World Bank and ultimately in the Poverty Reduction Strategy country plans through which recent aid relations in much of Africa have been organised.

In the case of Tanganyika, international support was not only concerned with political influence. It was essential to national functioning. In 1960, on the eve of independence from Britain, 20 per cent of the Government's capital budget came from colonial grants, while the costs of government itself in the form of administration, police and revenue collection accounted for just over one-third (35 per cent) of total budgeted expenditures (IBRD 1961: 31–8). The first national development plan had been hurriedly put together by colonial officials as a three-year transitional framework to ensure maximum stability (Jennings 2003: 165). The second national plan was to last for five years. It was an opportunity for the new leadership to be seen to set the terms of the development agenda, albeit through the utilisation of appropriate kinds of development expertise. The resulting document is a hybrid of an emergent discourse of populist nationalism with authoritative trajectories of transformation. It is during the first Five Year Plan period (the second national plan), between 1964 and 1969, that village resettlement came to be prioritised as part of a deliberate developmental move from 'improvement' to 'transformation' (Smith 1966: 380, 363). This imperative would later become articulated as the technical rationalisation justifying the need for compulsory villagisation and short-lived collectivisation (Payer 1983).

Newly independent Tanganyika was deeply enmeshed in relations with multiple governments as providers of financial and development assistance, as well as, importantly, providers of the ideas and models of how development could be achieved. Non-alignment was part of Nyerere's strategy to maximise the amount of aid that the country could expect. It was justified in terms of securing the 'independence of the republic' (Smith 1966: 368). Multilateral donors were sought where possible, along with relations with small European states as bilateral partners in development (Yeager 1982: 107). 'We shall be particularly anxious', wrote Nyerere in his preface to the first Five Year Plan, 'to get help from the United Nations when we can' (in Smith 1966: 368). The appraisal conducted on behalf of the World Bank that provided the background analysis for the priorities that were the basis of the Plan acknowledged the ongoing reliance on external support in the form of grants from the ex-colonial power and the wider international community, as well as the requirement for soft loans, which they recognised would impose a heavy burden on the frail economy. 'A development plan financed largely by foreign grants and aid and by loan funds borrowed at a low rate of interest would obviously present a more manageable burden for Tanganyika than a plan financed mainly by borrowing at high rates of interest' (in Smith 1966: 354).

## Community development

The new state's economic frailty, accentuated by its dependence on an underdeveloped agricultural sector, poor communications and low numbers of personnel with the kinds of skills necessary for a modernising economy, prompted the World Bank team to make another recommendation that has proved remarkably durable: that independent Tanganyika adopt what it called a 'community development approach' in which local communities contribute labour and cash towards the provision of public infrastructures. 'There are many valuable projects of construction and improvement which could be carried out in Tanganyika by voluntary effort, without the need for financing from scarce public funds' (in IBRD 1961: 109). Further, projects and other 'useful activities ... could be undertaken with great benefit on the basis of locally organised contributions of labour, materials or money' (ibid.: 492).

The community development approach advocated by the World Bank team was not a technical innovation associated with up-to-the-minute development expertise specially designed for newly independent nation states. It was an artefact of late colonial policy intended as a means of securing the engagement of rural populations in state projects supposedly for their own benefit.[8] Engagement was to imply a degree of committed

---

[8] The Bank's approach is worth quoting at length. 'The Mission also advocates the adoption of a community development approach to agricultural improvement and other aspects of economic and social development. In places it will be desirable to continue the present policy of concentrating extension effort on the few progressive African farmers who appear particularly willing to adopt new methods. However, in many areas it seems likely that more can be achieved by directing effort to the whole community in an attempt to convert the traditional African conformity from an obstacle to progress into a force for development ... At the stage of development reached in much of Tanganyika, agricultural improvement is often not merely a matter of changing techniques, but necessitates a revolutionary change in customs and way of life, requiring a process of education and guided social change. Secondly, community development aims at receiving the full approval and support of the

involvement. Community development was to be strongly differentiated from compulsory labour in development schemes and penalty-based systems, such as by laws and fines, through which compliance was often sought. It was conceptualised as a cultural endeavour. In order to break down perceived resistance to progress through commitment to old ways, an 'attack on the minds' was called for.[9] The weapons were education, information campaigns, including community cinema, and self-help projects in which communities could derive development benefits if they shared the costs with government. Although community development in practice made use of many of the same instruments of community mobilisation as had German colonialism, and the first phase of the British version which replaced it, for securing labour for local infrastructure and in lieu of tax, it conveyed a wider set of ideological commitments about local responsibility for development and the means of fostering this commitment.

Community development was adopted as colonial policy in Tanganyika from the late 1940s. The approach was informed by an influential Colonial Office report about the basis of social transformation in African colonies. 'Mass Education in African Society' (Colonial Office 1944; Holford 1988) argued for the importance of cultural change through education as the precondition for economic and social modernisation as well as, in the absence of social welfare systems and state investment in local infrastructures, the necessity of retaining strong community structures that would render self-help possible. While the principle of working through community was well established in the system of native authority governance, the rationale of community development was explicitly oriented towards co-operation rather than command. Its premise was intentionally distinct from the previous logic of social welfare as a paternalistic developmental responsibility of districts for the poor and indigent, which one colonial official likened to the giving of charity. The aim of community development in contrast was to achieve the co-opting of the population as collaborators within the ideological project of development, not only as labour or as beneficiaries. 'Community betterment' mattered because

(cont) people for the measures which it is desired to promote. The essence of community development approach is to win the confidence of the people and to stimulate and organise their energies to work for the improvement of their conditions of life. Community development may be regarded as "a method of giving back to African society the sense of community self help which it used to have".' (IBRD 1961: 109, citing the UN Trusteeship Council, Rural Economic Development of the Trust territories, report submitted by the Food and Agriculture Organization Concerning Land Tenure and Land Use Problems in the Trust Territories of Tanganyika and Ruanda-Urundi, United Nations, T/1438, 19 February 1959.)

[9] 'At present adult education is undertaken by means of *barazas* [small, participatory public meetings] only but estimates have been submitted for the purchase of a Mobile Cinema Unit with which it is intended to intensify the "attack" on the minds of adult Masai.' District Commissioner Masai, Monduli to Hon Member for Local Government, 12 August 1932, Comments on Sociological Implications of Masai Development by H.A. Fosbrooke, Senior Sociologist, Item 179 in File 40518/2 Local Government; Government Anthropologist programme of Work – Senior Sociologist.

large sums are being spent on economic development which will not bring their anticipated results unless the facilities provided are accepted and fully exploited by the whole population. The whole success of the development schemes and the future prosperity of this country depends on the willing acceptance and cooperation of the African producers in the schemes. At present the backward adult community is imposing its values, customs and low living standards on the rising generation, and existing primitive culture and custom is persisting in counter-acting [sic] the work of schools and other educational agencies making their efforts futile. (Tanzania National Archives 1949)

The practice of community development was conceptualised as interstitial, between the modern forces of state development and 'backward' rural populations. It was presented as scientific and highly skilled:

The department would be the handmaid of the provincial and district teams, to explain and gain support for local schemes and to stimulate people to make efforts to put them into effects. The community development staff comes into the picture as specialists using modern methods and apparatus to put over the policy and development plans of the administration. (ibid.)

Modern methods of communication were to be used, including mass education through community cinema. Importantly, community development staff were not foreign colonial officers. They were to be Tanganyikan subjects who would mediate developmental efforts in a locality. These efforts could include such activities as 'mass literacy movements, soil conservation campaigns, tree planting, health campaigns and other such measures'. Money was made available for locally initiated projects through the community development policy, with a view to using volunteer labour to undertake them. In language which anticipates virtually word for word that of the World Bank experts nearly a decade later,

The main idea behind the scheme is that there are a great many highly desirable minor development projects which could be undertaken without great difficulty or delay provided a) the local community concerned had the necessary keenness and enthusiasm to provide voluntarily and free of cost most of the labour and supervision required and b) Government was able to find the comparatively small sums of money needed in each case ... In the existing development schemes large and small the greatest problem is to secure the active co-operation of the people. (Tanzania National Archives 1951)

Community development as professional interstitiality between state and beneficiary, and which is charged with facilitating beneficiary responsibility for development, continues to play a central role in Tanzania's development order, anticipating the mediating positionality of contemporary social technologies of development in the form of participatory development and the creation of local civil society. (These issues are further addressed in Chapters 2 to 7.)

Community development entailed participation in what were deemed to be developmental activities for communities or villages. It also implied changed attitudes and a commitment to development on the part of community members as developmental actors who would come to want the developmental not only for community infrastructures but in their everyday lives. This kind of change was independent of government financing. Community members' adoption of modern farming practices, building improved housing and involvement in education campaigns were part of this strategy for developmental self-improvement.

## Decentralisation as development

Community development as a tactic for the developmental government of colonial subjects through their engagement in interstitial institutions was partially anticipated in the practice of indirect rule through native authorities implemented by Britain's colonial administration. Colonial government under the Covenant was to be concerned with the 'development' of subject peoples subject to the oversight of an international system. For Great Britain this could best be achieved through the system of indirect rule devised originally for Nigeria by Frederick Lugard, in which subject peoples were governed through what were represented as established structures of authority within the framework of the colonial state. For Lugard, indirect rule was more than a matter of using local institutions to effect rural compliance through the legitimation of 'traditional' authorities. It was about establishing the basis for modern government locally for the management of progress.[10] This in turn necessitated fiscal capacity. Taxation was the basic principle of this form of governance, not only because it was associated with colonial objectives of securing participation in labour markets, but as the fiscal foundation of development to be implemented locally. Taxation is, 'in a sense ... the basis of the whole system' (Lugard 1965: 201). This principle had been present in elementary form in the German commune system, abolished in 1908.[11] Collecting revenue was foundational rather than functional to the institution of the

---

[10] Lugard (1965: 200) describes the system as follows in his classic text on the dual mandate. 'The object in view is to make each "Emir" or paramount chief, assisted by his judicial council, an effective ruler over his own people. He presides over a "Native Administration" organised throughout as a unit of local government. The area over which he exercises jurisdiction is divided into districts under the control of "Headmen", who collect the taxes in the name of the ruler and pay them into the "Native Treasury", conducted by a native treasurer and staff under the supervision of the chief at his capital.'

[11] The commune system was abolished in response to pressure from settlers who opposed the fiscal autonomy it granted districts that were permitted to retain the hut tax they collected (Koponen 1994: 289).

Native Administrations, the smallest tax being, as the beginnings of a treasury, 'steps towards the fulfilment of the aim of the Government, to push each community further up the ladder of progress, by the realisation of the conception of individual and civic responsibility' (ibid. 113).

Locality mattered in this governance vision not so much because of claimed respect for local institutions, although this proved useful in bolstering the legitimacy of native authorities and the 'tribes' they administered, but because localised administration facilitated territorial control of dispersed regions and their inclusion within a single weak but centralised state. The village was imported from Indian models of colonial governance to the governance of African colonies. (The centrality of the village in Tanzanian development is discussed further in Chapter 5.)

The village in a context of scattered homesteads might have been difficult to define, Lugard acknowledged, but it was 'the administrative unit' on which the system was to be built (1965: 202). Across British colonies, local administration, with its emphasis on local obligations and responsibility, established the basis for local development strategies and ideas about community-driven development and the respective roles of central government and local authorities in the provision of developmental goods and services. Lugard wrote: 'It may be said that as Faith, Hope, and Charity are to the Christian creed, so are Decentralisation, Co-operation, and Continuity to African Administration' (1965: 113).

Lugard's articles of faith proved remarkably prescient. Decentralisation in various forms has remained the central organisational principle of government for development in Tanzania, throughout the twentieth century, as native administrations gradually transmuted into district authorities and as local government was successively reformed and adapted under socialism and the liberalising state. Community development principles and the rationalisation of development management in the 1950s saw the introduction of district development plans, normalising a set of practices around government in districts as being concerned with the implementation of development and establishing the principles that development depended on community participation and formalised processes of application to central government for funding. Planning had been introduced at national level across the colonies to meet the new long-term requirements of the Colonial Development and Welfare Act. District plans offered an opportunity to conceptualise districts in terms of their development potential, adopting a pro forma that enumerated natural and human resources, and to 'accent the tasks and ends which will form part of an integrated development'. District officers were instructed to 'to make district teams give priority to the maximum use of EXISTING resources and to distinguish between that and a second phase of their plans dependent on the resources for which application to the Government has to be made ...' (Tanzania National Archives 1954 – original emphasis). A range of formal structures were consolidated to facilitate local-level planning. After independence, local governance was reorganised. Native authorities were abolished along with the institution of the chiefship. What had been scattered homesteads under the authority of a headman were categorised as villages, which were to become 'the normal developmental unit at the lowest level. … It is the intention that when the community development approach begins that these village councils should become the village development committees' (Tanzania National Archives 1962a).

Ideas of community responsibility for development as the purpose of village government and the obligation of local-government staff were strengthened through socialist policy. Such understandings have been reinvigorated through local-government reform, with its emphasis on villages as lower local government, and modified through interventions intended to engage civil society as enablers of development. Despite successive iterations of local-government reform, which have formally shifted the balance of responsibility between central and local government,[12] the village remains the core organisational form through which developmental governance is supposed to take place. Villages are bodies corporate with their own autonomous governments within a vertical system of district and national governance. Village government as 'lower local government' in the Tanzanian governance system is not regarded as a tier of district government but as a distinct government at the lower level. Strengthening lower local government has been the focus of the final phase of the latest decade-long programme of donor-financed local-government reform: 'D by D' – decentralisation by devolution. Irrespective of divergences in the source of local-authority power and its separation from central government, local authorities have always relied on the centre for finance and have always struggled to extract contributions from residents, just as they have struggled to engage those residents through a range of instruments in the activities deemed necessary to the implementation of successive local development plans. Compulsory labour as a means to support local development programmes was by no means confined to the colonial or socialist forms of governance, just as the apparently new structures of development participation are in fact transformations of village-organising committees under socialism.[13]

If the basic building-blocks of Tanzania's integration into today's system of international development and national development structure, comprising the community as development agent within a vertical system of village and district, were put in place during under British trusteeship, there was one final innovation in colonial governance for development that was to have lasting consequences, not only for Tanzania, but for the evolution of the international development system. The 1940 Colonial

---

[12] There is no recent single volume history of local government in Tanzania. For accounts of different phases of local-government development in Tanzania, see Max 1991; Samoff 1979; Fjeldstad & Semboja 2000; Boex 2006; Boex & Martinez-Vazquez 2006; Lange 2008.
[13] For an account of the continuities in planning and participation throughout this period, see also Jennings 2003. Participation in development became compulsory from 1969 (ibid.: 181).

Development and Welfare Act (amended in 1945) was a radical departure from the previous Colonial Development Act of 1929. It 'modernized imperialism' (Cooper 2005: 37), reframing development as a long-term engagement that was oriented towards improving the social and economic conditions of the colonies. The new Act made provision for predictable development financing over decade-long cycles on the basis of ten-year plans. It encouraged investment in social as well as productive sectors through a system of grants, in addition to making loans available at preferential rates of interest. Recurrent costs were now permitted under the new system in the case of social expenditure on health or education, which had not been previously possible, and the principle was established that the tax payer in Britain had a moral responsibility for the improvement of the conditions of populations in the colonies. However, even with the new approach to development, the belief that development should ultimately not prove financially unsustainable along with the commitment to ensure that people financially contributed toward projects from which they were to derive benefit, ensured that the distinction between recurrent and capital expenditure remained fundamental to the design of developmental interventions. This insistence was as much moral as economic. Responsibility for development had to be shared. It was essential, wrote the Secretary of State for the Colonies in 1945, to 'arouse the interest of the inhabitants of the colony in the work of development' so that it would not be viewed as just as an 'activity of government ...'. Further, 'those persons who obtain direct benefit from [a] scheme should be made to pay at least part of the costs' (in Morgan 1964: 35).

The system established by the Colonial Development and Welfare Act, with its grants and loans, long-term approach and distinction between recurrent and capital expenditure, provides an enduring template for development planning into the present. Successive iterations of the Act over the remaining two decades of colonial rule did not amend its principles, but consolidated them, enhancing the durability of development forms and practices. Villages as the lowest developmental tier were situated within the vertical political topography of the state, through the intermediary institutional structures of districts and regions. British colonial thinking prioritised self-sufficiency as a principle of colonial social policy. Public actions and state responsibilities were to be limited, not only because colonial revenues were weak, particularly in countries like Tanganyika, but because citizenship and hence social entitlements were strictly differentiated between home and colonial territories (Lewis 2000). Once again, what were represented as apparently local social forms were invoked as the basis of development policy, this time not solely for political organisation – and hence the continuity that Lugard sought – but to justify a lack of investment in social support that was to be found instead within the 'traditional' extended family.

Independence under TANU in 1962 did not bring substantive changes in these principles. Nyerere's approach to development planning reconstituted community responsibility for development initially through local-government structures and eventually through villagisation (Maghimbi 1995; Caplan 1992). Development for Nyerere, as indeed for the working party of the International Bank for Reconstruction and Development that formulated the Development Plan, was primarily a technical project for which government was responsible, implemented through communities under the guidance of experts:

> It is essential that we consider further the use of our own national resources by placing the greatest emphasis on what we can do for ourselves, by the participation of the people in each district and village in the development of their own areas. Each village area should now be called upon to work out details of its own participation in development, not only in relation to the three year plan, but also in relation to the many things which can be done without national finance ... the district programme will be made up of all the villages in the district (Tanzania National Archives 1962a).

The kinds of activities that constituted participation in development and that could be done

> without government finance are those self help plans by the way of cooperative effort of the people themselves, for example roads, improved houses, drainage channels for water and so on. Every village will make its plan and all the plans of all the villages will be brought together by the council for development of the district (Tanzania National Archives 1962b).[14]

## Development as the project of government

Nyerere sought to depoliticise the content of development programming through a realignment of the role of government as administering development rather than formulating policy (Eriksen 1997; Finucane 1974; Costello 1996; Saul 2012). The move to a single-party state was central to this endeavour. After liberalisation, the proliferation of political parties has failed to politicise development as the practice of government not only because they are weak and disorganised but because of the hegemonic understanding that national development, conceptualised as the implementation of programmes, is the responsibility of government (Lange 2008). National plans and strategies, including the Development Vision, itself a standard instrument of donor-supported country programmes, are represented as route maps to national development rather than the products of

[14] In Kiswahili: '*Kitu cha pili ambacho kinaweza kufanywa bila fedha ya serikali ni ile mipango na kujisaidia kwa njia ya juhudi ya ushirika wa watu wenyewe, kwa mfano mabarabara..., nyumba bora, mifereji ya maji na khadalika. Kila kijiji kitatengenesa mpango wake, na mipango yote ya vijiji vyote itaunganishwe na Halmashauri ya maendeleo ya Wilaya.*' (Tanzania National Archives 1962b).

political interests. The emphasis on inclusion and participation, promoted through donor discourses and Tanzanian political culture, strengthens the hold of the ruling party, which can claim ownership of development policy while consolidating a culture of incentivising engagement in development through attending workshops, seminars and training for which allowances (*posho*) are received.[15] Certainly during the height of socialist austerity and immediately after, the amounts of *posho* awarded daily vastly exceeded even the monthly salary rates for government workers, a proportion that has fallen somewhat in recent years as public-sector pay has increased. *Posho* and expectations about allowances remains an important part of development culture in Tanzania, as in Sub-Saharan Africa more broadly, extending to participation through 'volunteering' in what are categorised as civil-society organisations (Skage et al. 2013).

Donor-financed initiatives aimed at fostering the evolution of national civil society in a bid to enhance the accountability of state, and hence the effectiveness of development spending devolved to national budgets, reinforce existing political institutions and cultures of governance, projecting (Heydemann & Hammack 2009) forms of development relations across rural districts legitimated through notions of community and sustainability. Despite political transitions from colonialism to the post-colonial state, and from Cold War socialism to the contemporary ordering of the neoliberal political and economic marketplace, the institutions of governance in Tanzania, and their relationship to the internationally overseen project of development, are characterised by a continuity of forms and relationships in which decentralisation and the idea of the local as agent and object of development endeavours remain central, along with the construction of development as a project administered by government but which is resourced through the contributions of donors and local communities. Therefore, community as a political institution and the institutional means through which it can be configured developmentally so as to make contributions comes to be foundational to development initiatives in Tanzania for both government and donor organisations. These drives towards community development as configured projects of administration that is depoliticised contrast with individuals' own aspirations for improvement as their personal projects of development, which some hope that relations with persons connected to development institutions, and hence potential donors (*wafadhili*), can enable.

---

[15] Posho refers to allowances or daily rations. In the contemporary context it refers to *per diems*, the daily allowance paid to staff on official business to cover their additional costs. Paying *posho* (lit. maize meal) has origins in established labour practices in the colonies where hired workers received daily food, and sometimes clothing and personal necessities, in addition to their wage, which was often paid at the end of the work. In development settings allowances are often paid for attendance at meetings and if work involves overnight travel a fixed amount is paid. Because allowances generally far exceed the actual costs of subsistence and accommodation and because they are high in relation to wages, especially for higher paid officials, attempts by development agencies to phase them out have had limited success.

# 2

**Participating in Development** | Projects & Agency in Tanzania

This chapter explores competing constructions of 'development' in a rural district in southern Tanzania in the late 1990s, shortly after it became involved in a large-scale donor-funded poverty-reduction programme. The programme was interesting for several reasons. As a district development programme concerned with improving local governance in order to deliver better public services, it was at the vanguard of the changes in development policy and donor relationships that anticipated the governance and accountability orientation of the aid regime in Tanzania and elsewhere during the subsequent decade (Craig & Porter 2006). The programme introduced novel forms of participatory development and community engagement at the same time as establishing the foundations of a pervasive aid economy that was, and is, simultaneously material and cultural. Finally, the imaginaries of development disseminated by the programme that emphasised collective involvement in forms of community inclusion promoted by development agents provided a contrast with indigenous aspirations for development as a personal project of transformation.

Distinctions between development as a personal achievement[1] through an individual's own projects (*miradi*) and community development initiatives remain important in contemporary Tanzania. State policies, supported by donor finance, have in effect 'scaled up' community development approaches through national strategies of local-government reform that feature village projects and what have become the standardised approaches to improving rural infrastructure, which are designed around participatory planning. Participatory planning and associated discourses of community empowerment thus inform everyday politics and local-government practices in Tanzanian villages. Frequently incentivised through the payment of allowances (*posho*) and the promise of

[1] Giblin describes a similar ideological construction of personal achievement through ideas about 'building a life' in Njombe, Tanzania in terms of ideas pertaining to what he defines as a 'the private sphere' in opposition to the state (2005: 8).

public goods, they have become the taken-for-granted way in which rural development is practised throughout the country.

Participatory planning as the institutional form through which village projects are organised continues to operate much as it did in the early 1990s. Its integration into the organisation of development has altered along with the transitions in the organisation of aid, as bilateral donors directed a greater proportion of funding to national budgets through the basket mechanism of direct budgetary support and, formally at least, moved away from localised project approaches. These changes have had little impact on the ways in which development is operationalised in villages as units of local government. Localised projects have simply been devolved to 'lower' tiers, to what are categorised as civil-society organisations (CSOs) and local governments, which are the main disseminators of participatory practice.

The project I describe here was an integrated rural development programme similar in scope to the kind of project described by Ferguson for Lesotho in southern Africa (1990). The Ulanga District Support Programme was implemented in the rural district of that name in southern Tanzania, commencing in 1996. Designed on the basis of extant policy paradigms and trends in development research, rather than on context-specific analysis, the programme approach was essentially to improve the services delivered by local government in order to meet the assumed priorities and needs of rural citizens. During its life cycle of slightly more than a decade the programme evolved from a standard district support programme that focused on local services into a more complex hybrid incorporating orientations towards public-sector reform, participatory development and good governance that would be incorporated into the national multi-donor donor-funded programme of local-government reform. The Ulanga District Support Programme was funded by the Republic of Ireland, which implemented similar programmes in the neighbouring districts of Kilosa and Kilombero.

The Ulanga District Support Programme, like all development interventions, was organised around a particular policy-determined understanding of what 'development' was. For the programme designers, working in the years immediately preceding the explicit poverty-reduction focus of the Millennium Development Goals (MDGs), 'development' encompassed a range of qualitative objectives, including enhanced popular participation, better local democracy, improvements in health and welfare, and the consolidation of community commitment to development so-defined.[2] The core objectives of the programme were 'growth with equity' and 'improving the quality of life of all the residents in the district'. These were to be achieved via the implementation of specific

---

[2] The MDGs were agreed in 2000. Prior to this, international development, for some donors, was structured by the very similar International Development Targets of the OECD countries. For an account of the evolution of the MDGs and their impact on the organisation of aid, see Hulme 2007.

interventions across a range of sectors, using a combination of 'top down' and participatory approaches. A concept of 'participatory development' was central to the project narrative as both a means and an end of development interventions. This was not limited to this particular organisation or development programme. The discourse of participatory development was fast becoming the new orthodoxy in development circles, from NGOs to the World Bank (Li 2007a), and was in the process being transformed from a once radical opportunity for engagement with the dispossessed into an authorised instrument in the development tool kit (Craig & Porter 1997; Cornwall 2004; Robins et al. 2008).

Although, at its most obvious, a commitment to participation simply entails ensuring some degree of beneficiary involvement in project planning and implementation, participatory development as articulated within development discourses implies something far less straightforward. Much of the literature on participation in development, and the kinds of programmes it legitimates, rests on a particular philosophical construction of participation as leading to the emancipatory empowerment of communities of poor people as participants in the development process. This construction of a causal relationship between participation and empowerment ultimately relies on the establishment of an assumed relation between knowledge and agency, in which individual agents are *empowered* at the level of consciousness, in a vacuum divorced from actual social and political action. Such approaches prioritise participation in terms of knowledge production, rather than programme management, and, in so doing, construct the target communities of development interventions as passive agents awaiting the emancipatory intervention of development organisations (Cleaver 1999; Kesby 2005; Mosse 1994, 2005a). Despite the claims of the empowerment rhetoric, poor people lacking the capacity to bring about social transformation by themselves can only participate in development through development agency institutional structures for participation (Chatterjee 2004). In premising the achievement of 'development' on community participation in a locally implemented programme context, the new development orthodoxy contributes to the perpetuation of the very problems it seeks to resolve by failing to acknowledge the broader economic and institutional constraints that ensure the continued impoverishment of rural communities in Africa, Asia and Latin America.

Spatialisation and localisation of poverty, and responsibility for addressing it, are profoundly problematic as political strategies (Amin 2005), at the same time as their promise of empowering the politically excluded has significant appeal. These constraints are recognised by rural southern Tanzanians, along with the changed opportunities for economic development afforded by liberalisation, in their struggle for *maendeleo ya mtu binafsi*, 'the development of a person by themselves' or 'privately' in the sense of opposition to the development practices and institutions of development organisations and the state (Giblin

2005). The goals of personal development encompass a range of lifestyle aspirations, including being more 'modern' (*kisasa*), access to higher levels of education for one's immediate family, increased access to off-farm income and, in the context of the inadequate-although-improving provision of state services and periodic food insecurity, enough money to provide for a person's family. A more long-term goal was, and continues to be, the construction of a 'modern' house, with iron roof and brick walls in contrast to 'local' style houses with earth walls and roofed with thatch. Modern houses are a sign of status, an object of inheritable wealth, a potential source of rental income and a more comfortable living environment for a person's family. Unlike state-sponsored development interventions, or the community development initiatives of foreign NGOs and donors, southern Tanzanians' understandings of personal development are premised on a recognition of the potentiality of individual agency in bringing about social transformation. A person's failure to achieve development, as they define it, is not conceptualised in terms of a failure of community resources potentially amenable to localised project interventions, but recognised as being due to a combination of economic, political and institutional constraints not confined to a local area of impact. These constraints render individual agency insufficient to achieve development, as it is locally defined, at the same time as people come to depend on access to the kinds of development goods associated with localised interventions as an essential means of bypassing extra local constraints.

## Empowerment through participation

Since the mid-1980s the notion of 'participation' has become virtually synonymous with 'development' in the discourse of development organisations and their personnel. Even quite conservative multilateral and bilateral agencies routinely invoke the concept as a basic requirement to be incorporated into project frameworks and evaluation procedures (Oakley et al 1991; Narayan & Srinivasan 1994). What 'participation' actually implies differs greatly between different agencies and organisations (Rahnema 1992). For some, participation simply entails involving project beneficiaries in the planning and implementation process, often through fairly brief and selective consultation procedures. For others, aligned with a more activist perspective, a positionality often claimed by representatives of CSOs, participation is a moral imperative that, as a precondition for empowerment, facilitates development itself (Bornstein 2005; Edwards 1994: 282; Friedman 1992; Booth 1994: 24; Chambers 1983, 1994). This notion of empowerment seems, at first sight, relatively unproblematic. The poor, divorced from centres of decision-making dominated by elites with different interests, must be *empowered* to participate in the decisions that affect them. This can be achieved through enhanced participation and structures of accountability in local organisations and political institutions at all levels. Empowerment, from this perspective, does not necessarily entail participation in broad-based political movements that seek to bring about radical social change, nor even in established political institutions. It can also occur in a local context, among 'the poor', through the formation of their critical consciousness via participatory techniques of knowledge generation and reflection (Friedman 1992; Chambers 1983). 'Development' is not then simply a process of directed change leading to certain kinds of economic and social transformation, but depends on the accomplishment of a series of corresponding moral transformations in the consciousness of people participating, as change agents and changed, in the development process. Consequently, the proper task of development organisations and their personnel is to facilitate the necessary transformations in consciousness that can *empower* the poor as social actors to embark on locally managed change. (There are many similarities of course between this understanding of development as empowerment interpreted in relation to knowledge, and colonial community development as described in Chapter 1.)

Participatory methodologies have now been used in a diverse range of projects and programmes, by NGOs, international agencies and multilateral organisations. While the long-term impacts of participatory approaches on development outcomes are uncertain, a powerful consensus exists within development organisations that such approaches are worthwhile. They provide a useful vehicle for 'stakeholder' engagement and can increase local 'ownership' of project objectives, especially where development interventions in local areas entail some level of community co-financing (e.g. Oakley et al 1991: 16–18; Eyben & Ladbury 1995).[3] The impacts on popular empowerment are less clear (Rahnema 1992: 122; Richards 1995).[4] More fundamentally, the assumptions underlying the concept of participatory development in the moral imperative tradition, concerning the implicit causality of the relation between participation and empowerment, have met with limited critical engagement (Pottier 1993a; Richards 1995, 16; De Koning 1995: 35; Cooke & Kothari 2001). This is largely because participation is morally appealing and politically acceptable to development workers and social scientists wishing for a fairer world (Henkel & Stirrat 2001: 178). Moreover, a critical unpacking of the concept, and the assumptions on which it is founded, raises uncomfortable questions for the existence of development as a profession and as a process of technosocial interventions (cf. Cornwall & Fleming 1995: 9). Either the poor are capable by themselves of transforming their own consciousness and empowering themselves to achieve development, as the ideology of participation implies, or they are not, and must rely on the intervention of professional 'change agents' as external facilitators of this process (Curtis 1995: 116; Goulet 1989: 166). This paradox at the heart of

[3] For contrasting perspectives see Cooke & Kothari 2001; Mosse 2004.
[4] But for an opposing view see Kesby 2005.

the participation rhetoric amounts to a denial of the poor's capacity for agency to bring about social change by themselves, on their own terms (cf. Rahnema 1992: 122; Hussein 1995: 173). As genuine 'development' refers only to certain types of transformation, usually the kinds mediated by development organisations working within the moral imperative tradition, agency can only be accomplished through imported structures for participation.

## Local knowledge and collective action

That 'the poor' must ultimately depend on external agents in their struggle for empowerment rests on a particular tautological construction of the relation between knowledge and agency pervasive in policy fields that assumes a linearity between knowledge and practice. As agents are thought to act on the basis of what they know, changed knowledge can bring about changed behaviours, hence the emphasis in behaviour-change interventions on education and sensitisation. The colonial community development approach, and its post-colonial successor, took this kind of assumption as its starting point, with cinema vans and the use of media among its initial instruments (Smyth 2004). Whereas development models derived from neoclassical economic paradigms ascribe agency to the individual as a rational actor, for example the maximising entrepreneur or rural producer, the community development model of development thinking from which the discourse of participatory development has arisen ascribes agency to collectivities of poor people whom, it is nostalgically assumed, live enmeshed in totalising kinship networks and the mechanical solidarity of 'traditional' peasant societies. Despite divergent political positions, the two approaches share a remarkably similar understanding of agency (cf. Booth 1994, 13). Active agents are knowledgeable agents, empowered through their rationality to become effective social actors (Arce et al 1993: 156). As collective agency is critical to community development, participatory interventions are primarily concerned with the construction of the right sort of knowledge as a precondition of its attainment. From the perspective of participatory development, because 'the poor' who are project beneficiaries occupy a local area in which a project is active, this is assumed to be 'local knowledge'. Paradoxically, 'the poor' need change agents to achieve 'development' because they are constrained by the very form of knowledge which contains the seeds of their empowerment.

Initially conceived as a corrective to the technical, expert-managed interventions that privileged Western scientific discourse on the basis of assumed local ignorance, the concept of local knowledge first came into prominence in the field of agricultural development, which had, through extension services, been closely tied to the conceptualisation of community development, which advocated a holistic approach. During the 1970s and 1980s, agricultural researchers associated with what became known as Indigenous Agricultural/Technical Knowledge paradigms (IAK/ITK) working on reasons why rural communities so often appeared reluctant to adopt new crops and methods, argued that poor farmers were not ignorant about their crops and production systems. On the contrary, their agricultural strategies were informed by years of experience and an in-depth understanding of their particular ecological and economic environments. The concept of local knowledge was gradually expanded to encompass other kinds of knowledge that were thought could form the basis for community empowerment (Scoones & Thompson 1994: 18; Marsden 1994: 46). 'Indigenous knowledge ... the local knowledge that is unique to a given culture or society' was held to constitute a 'critical resource' for development, because it 'forms the information base for a society which facilitates communication and decision making' (Warren et al 1995: xiv). Just as indigenous agricultural knowledge could be extracted through specialised techniques such as Rapid Rural Appraisal (RRA), local knowledge in general could be accessed through participatory methodologies, forming the basis for the design and delivery of projects that, it was claimed, would be both locally appropriate and sustainable (Chambers 1983, 1994). Since the 1980s a complex hybrid of approaches, derived from the Rapid Rural Appraisal techniques of development agronomists on the one hand, and the Action Research of Freirean social activists on the other, has evolved, initially into Participatory Rural Appraisal (PRA) and, more recently, into Participatory Learning and Action (PLA).

The rapid expansion of participatory development has resulted in the establishment of a range of authorised practices for its implementation, together with a cadre of technical professionals who promote them (Cornwall & Fleming 1995: 11; Richards 1995). Starting from the assumption that 'the poor' already know what their problems are and have better knowledge than the outside 'expert', participatory techniques strive to access and consolidate a domain of 'local' knowledge as the basis for the kind of critical reflection that can lead to social action. Within this discursive frame, research is no longer conceived of as involving a distance between subject and object, but as a process of mutual learning and interaction (Nelson & Wright 1995: 58). Project-related research is conducted by facilitators in collaboration with 'the poor' themselves. PLA techniques target villages or groups of people in the same administrative area who are thus constituted as communities, and work to construct a representation of their immediate problems, economy and social organisation. Transect walks, seasonal calendars and wealth-ranking all assume that significant social constraints and agricultural systems operate in a restricted area, that communities are local in orientation, and overlook diversity in livelihood strategies that are not simple reflections of differential wealth (cf. Mosse 1994). The routinisation of participatory development may actually work against the genuine participation of programme beneficiaries who find that the only avenues through which engagement is possible are those defined as legitimate participatory techniques (Richards 1995; Mosse 1994; 2005a; Cooke & Kothari 2001). These centre on the role of facilitators, the construction of restricted domains of local knowledge thought relevant for project implementation, and the perpetuation of project-centred, localised rural development strategies with bounded target populations.

Although the radical political framework of Paulo Freire and action research provided the initial legitimation for participatory methodologies, in practice participatory development is generally depoliticised as a technical intervention, a forum for restricted stakeholder engagement according to predetermined parameters of what is deemed pertinent to a project. Links with empowerment, even vaguely defined, are uncertain. Paul Richards' 'quick and dirty critique' remains valid in relation to many of the grand claims made for the transformative potential of participatory methods in the design and implementation of development projects, a critique that, as we shall see in Chapter 4, is equally applicable at scale (see, for example, Chatterjee 2004; Robins et al. 2008). According to Richards, not only are the theoretical assumptions that underlie the empowerment claims made for participatory methods implausible but, 'any confidence that PRA/RRA operates independently of local structures of political discourse, and is therefore effective in reaching goals of participative enfranchisement, is based on faith not science' (1995: 15–16). Like community development itself, confined to a localised project setting (Escobar 1995: 45–7), empowerment through participation is a fantasy divorced from political action beyond the local community, imagined as a homogenous mass of the poor and very poor, with an inherent tendency towards collective action (Cornwall & Fleming 1995; Eyben & Ladbury 1995: 194).

Even when freed from the burden of empowerment, the development concept of local knowledge as a distinct type of knowledge, potentially accessible via specialised techniques, remains problematic. It connotes a rigid, systematised version of knowledge, abstracted from individual agents, that is not historically determined and flexible (Agrawal 1995: 421), but fixed in the project present. In focusing on the 'local' as a bounded entity, the 'knowledge' of 'local' people is assumed to be not merely locally derived, but relevant to a particular locality. Development techniques for accessing 'local' knowledge emphasise and create rigid boundaries between what is 'local', and hence project-relevant, and what is assumed to be nonlocal and therefore not relevant to a project. A more generalised concept of local knowledge, derived from anthropology, is similarly narrow, constructing local or indigenous knowledge as a restricted kind of cultural knowledge, held by residents of specific localities who share a cultural affiliation. This knowledge is often held to be more relevant than Western technical knowledge, as well as being more authentic and 'traditional'. In what might be termed the anthropological view, projects fail because they do not take local knowledge and local values and priorities into account (Hobart 1993; Warren et al 1995: xv; Ferguson 1990).

Both development and anthropological constructions of 'local knowledge' rest on a conception of 'local' communities as homogenous and collectivist users and producers of 'knowledge'. In formulating an opposition between 'imported' and indigenous knowledge they conflate context-related project objectives and technical strategies with one type of 'knowledge', and some of what people living in an area 'know' with another. In actuality, what people living anywhere 'know' comprises a variety of different kinds of knowledge, some imported and 'scientific', some religiously derived, as well as more local strategies for dealing with their specific agricultural, economic and social environments (cf. Agrawal 1995; Massey 2005). Different kinds of knowledge are not separate and discrete, but form part of a person's total knowledge resources at any particular time. While certain kinds of knowledge may only be articulated in specific social contexts, this does not imply a rigid differentiation between them. Rather, it indicates the articulation of strategies of categorisation that classify practices in particular ways. As shown in Chapter 4, such strategies of differentiation, between developed and undeveloped, between implementer and beneficiary, and between community member and outsider, are foundational to the social organisation of development.

As with people in other countries subject to 'development' relations, Tanzanians make use of parallel dichotomies to articulate relations of difference between urban and rural, authentic and imported forms, and between specifically 'modern' practices, generally associated with foreign origins and scientific inputs, and certain kinds of practices oriented towards ritual and healing (see also Ferguson 1999; Wilk 1995; Pigg 1992, 1993). For example, although on certain occasions farmers in Ushambaa, Tanzania, discuss political legitimacy through the agricultural metaphors of healing the land, they readily adopt imported agricultural techniques for improving productivity on their individual holdings, and participate in the formal political institutions of state and party administration (Feierman 1990). The delineation between 'local' (*kienyeji*) as connoting 'traditional', and modern (*kisasa*) as conveying notions of foreign origins and specialised technical understanding, encompasses multiple domains of Tanzanian social experience. It is most marked in the domains of medical practice, a distinction consolidated through state regulation that has differentiated traditional medicine in an attempt to recognise and regulate it (Langwick 2011), and in agriculture, where generations of state initiatives aimed at improving traditional agriculture have normalised distinctions between 'local' and 'modern' livestock.[5] Throughout Sub-Saharan Africa farmers make use of agricultural chemicals where they can afford them, to the extent that imported techniques have become indigenised in 'local' farming

---

[5] The most common distinction is between 'local' chickens (*kuku wa kienyeji*) and 'modern' ones (*kuku wa kisasa*), which amounts to free-roaming 'village chickens' and imported breeds of birds that must be reared in cages and with special diets, and between 'local' breeds of cattle and *ng'ombe wa kisasa*, 'modern' cattle that are either Friesian or a mix of Friesian and 'local' breeds. Modern cattle require different management to local breeds, including stall-feeding. The input-heavy regimes of care that 'modern' livestock demand, and their increased productivity, provide a rich symbolic resource for thinking about development and difference.

systems, just as aspirin, antibiotics and the injection have an accepted place in diverse 'local' healing strategies (Green 2000). As we shall see in Chapter 7, practitioners defining themselves as 'traditional' healers make use of development-inspired narratives of public-service reform to modernise the delivery of their services, while insisting that their medical practice is strongly differentiated from allopathic medicine by the fact that its healing power derives from the spirits who possess them.

The eclectic nature of what people in an area actually 'know' implies that what development organisations seek to categorise as 'local knowledge' is neither inherently 'local' in its orientation and application, nor in its origins, which are not confined to a single self-generating source or range of practices. People living in rural areas listen to radios, attend schools and travel great distances to work and visit relatives, often for extended periods of time. They are increasingly connected to one another through cheap, accessible mobile-phone communications, which have recently become affordable for the rural majority. The 'local' person who lives in an area for much of their lives is likely to have social networks that extend across localities and regions, just as he or she is likely to have fields and income-generation strategies that are widely dispersed across different localities. In contrast to the representations of local knowledge 'systems' created through particitory methodologies, what people in an area know is neither specifically local, indigenous nor uniformly held. Similarly, the constraints people face that restrict their capacity to achieve development as they define it are not confined to the local areas of project interventions. This has serious implications for the effectiveness of development strategies that seek to use notions of community empowerment through local knowledge as the basis and justification of localised interventions. Given the 'capacity of an unfavourable macro or meso context to dissipate the gains from merely local efforts' (Booth 1994: 6), techniques that aim to access 'local' knowledge as the key to development problems and solutions in local areas may miss the point entirely. Macro policies and political variables exercise 'a critical influence on development processes, accounting for significantly different outcomes in broadly similar socio-economic settings' (Booth 1994: 8; see also Arce et al 1993: 155). The construction of local knowledge and local participation as key development strategies to empower local communities prioritises 'political ignorance' (Pottier 1993b: 31), localising development problems and solutions, which become conveniently amenable to the kinds of local project interventions (cf. Fairhead 1993, 197) that are easily controllable and politically expedient (cf Pottier 1993b: 17).

Political ignorance also makes possible the construction of an imagined community of participants who can, and will, act collectively. In Africa, while collective action is a possibility, it usually occurs at extra-village level, through organisations that transcend village boundaries while including only a proportion of villagers. These organisations include co-operative societies, political parties, kinship groupings and religious organisations. Moreover, collective action is most likely to occur where developmental returns can be claimed by participating individuals. Collective action took off in the Kenyan *harambee* movement (working together in self-help), Cowen and Shenton suggest, because it provided access to education that could transform people's chances of securing waged work and possible entry into the middle classes (1996: 311–27). Like the colonial policies of community development that assumed local populations were the major obstacle to achieving development in local areas, the prioritisation of the local and micro over the meso and macro effectively obscures and deems irrelevant the context in which people in rural areas find themselves, a context largely determined by the articulation of macro policies and meso institutional levels in which rural people are both actors and acted upon (cf. Caplan 1992: 105; Bebbington 1994; Booth 1994; van Ufford 1988). The local community of development studies, development practice and certain kinds of anthropology is in actuality an analytical category. The interaction of different institutional levels is neither bottom-up nor top-down, but can go either way depending on circumstances. That these are often stacked against the bottom tier is not due to an inherent causal priority of macro over micro, but to the interests and allegiances of specific social agents operating at what have come to be constituted as mediating levels within vertical structures of government.[6] Understanding the actual dynamics of the interaction between levels takes more than a simple notion of interface between micro and macro (Long & van der Ploeg 1994: 74), which continues to privilege the local and micro (Booth 1994: 18), at the same time as implying a rigid separation of what are in fact aspects of a single, highly complex and multifaceted reality.

## Development and going backwards in rural Tanzania

This complex intercausality of development problems is recognised by the rural population of Ulanga District, southern Tanzania, who seek to overcome constraints emanating from the interaction of macro policies with meso structures and local institutions in their struggle to achieve development as they define it. This is not dependent on community participation in externally initiated programmes, nor on the construction of a privileged domain of 'local' knowledge as a precondition for agency. Like rural people the world over, Ulanga's farmers strive to participate in development interventions on their own terms in a bid to bypass the very constraints that inhibit them (cf. Arce & Long 1993: 205). These centre on the restricted access to the capital, markets and credit that severely limits rural incomes and opportunities. Ulanga District is situated in the south-western part of Tanzania, occupying an area of mixed highlands and river valleys. Poorly served by road transport to the regional capital Morogoro, it is bounded on two sides by the Selous game reserve, restricting direct

---

[6] On the constitution of scale in relation to power, see Marston et al. (2005).

access to the coast. The District is generally recognised by outsiders as 'underdeveloped', according to criteria such as levels of income, life expectancy at birth and infant mortality rates. Poorly served by welfare infrastructures of schools and clinics, its dispersed population is made up of small-scale farmers and fishermen, in addition to immigrant agro-pastoralists seeking seasonal grazing on the plains, and periodic incursions by groups of artisanal miners. The District's permanent population comprises around six cultural and linguistic groups, who cultivate rice and maize staples, supplemented in suitable locations by a diverse range of crops and livelihood strategies, including fishing, hunting, wage labour and trade. The District is well integrated into the market and national economy. People depend on the sale of crops to earn cash, participate in local and national labour markets, and rely on the market to mediate seasonal food shortages. The District's farmers are not subsistence producers isolated from networks of trade and exchange, even though they may have appeared so in the 1980s as they withdrew from market transactions when terms of trade were unfavourable and transport difficult to come by (Green 2003; 1999). Liberalisation has achieved substantial transformations in the economy of opportunity in Tanzania, even for small farmers, especially for those near to transport routes and those who can take advantage of new agricultural technologies, such as cheap irrigation pumps, that are transforming smallholder production in many parts of the country. Farmers in Ulanga are not so fortunate. Their limited success in moving forwards is due not to their production practices or kinds of knowledge, but to the range of institutional constraints that continue to constitute barriers to their aspirations for 'development'.

These barriers have a long history in the District, albeit in changing forms. Constructions of development must be understood historically, along with the creation of underdevelopment as a social relation and economic reality. In Ulanga, as in much of East Africa, the generic term for 'development' is *maendeleo*, the Kiswahili word for 'progress', from *kuendelea*, 'to go forward'. This particular District has a negative experience of 'development', and of the kinds of state interventions so-justified, which have effectively consolidated the kinds of exclusion on which present-day economic and social marginality are founded. Beginning with the German administration, the district was denied the benefits of infrastructural investment in retaliation for some of its population's involvement in the *maji maji* war (see the section on 'Colonial developments' in Chapter 1). A scorched-earth policy depleted population and resources, while road networks were directed away from the district, effectively cutting it off from easy access to markets, to the railway and to the coast (Iliffe 1979: 454). This policy of exclusion was continued by default after the First World War by the British administration, which prioritised investment in other districts. British policy in what was then Mahenge District narrowly focused on enhancing food security through enforced agricultural practices, the planting of famine relief crops, and large-scale population resettlement, justified in terms of control over the tsetse fly. Rural development interventions in the 1940s and 1950s were founded on naive assumptions about the self-reliance of rural households in terms of food production as a goal to be achieved, together with the promotion of rice and cotton as crops to provide cash income, even though the District already had an established mixed economy based on the export of labour, as well as food crops, and cotton was only a preference crop in years when prices and input costs made it more profitable than rice (Larson 1976). Government agricultural directives were rarely adhered to without the imposition of penalties. Despite continued marginalisation, some benefits of economic growth and public investments in health and education filtered down to Ulanga. Though the bulk of the population remained poor in comparison with other parts of Tanganyika, in the decade immediately preceding independence the District was doing well agriculturally and economically, rural people had good access to shops, commodities and markets, and people with access to off-farm income could accumulate enough to make investments in housing, education and livestock. Although the 'development' interventions of the British administration had been a failure in terms of changing agricultural practices, a person could participate in what they felt to be the progress of the country and achieve an increase in living standards through a combination of luck and hard work.

The events of the following decade changed this situation dramatically. Nationalisation, collectivisation and villagisation policies were implemented with devastating effects. Forced villagisation entailed the destruction of houses that people had worked hard to build. Those with stock or plantations of coconuts found them collectivised as the common property of an artificially created village community. Production declined in all parts of the country. Producer prices dropped as national boards assumed responsibility for agricultural marketing, and control over co-operative societies was transferred to the state via the ruling party, Chama Cha Mapinduzi (CCM) (Maghimbi 1992). The quality of social services declined as the economy collapsed (Mapolu 1986; Lofchie 1993). Inadequate structures of accountability for village projects, combined with marketing collapse and a failure of input supply, including credit, meant that collective projects failed rapidly. Village shops, tractors and mills could get neither spare parts nor supplies. As people in many areas returned to pre-settlement homesteads to escape the localised land shortages that resettlement created (Maghimbi 1990), villages became semi-derelict shells, with no shops, no services and, as the co-operatives slithered further into bankruptcy, no way for farmers to earn money, even from farming. Interventions done in the name of 'development' had left people poorer and more bereft than they had been prior to villagisation, in a process that amounted to, in the words of one informant, the 'nationalisation of poverty'. He continued, 'If you have nothing and that is nationalised, then having nothing is nationalised. If your having nothing is taken from you, you are left with less than nothing.'

I began my research in Ulanga District in November 1989, and by the early 1990s people could say with accuracy that there was 'no development', referring both to the failure of state interventions and to the absence of any visible investments or improvements in their quality of life. What they consistently described was, in fact, 'going backwards' (*rudi nyuma*), as the opposite of development as *maendeleo*, 'going forwards'. For Tanzanians in the 1980s this implied a regression to a subsistence-style economy and, until after the import reforms of 1986 (White 1995: 47), the impossibility of obtaining even the most basic goods that had been available to rural dwellers for much of the British colonial period. It is not then surprising that during this period in many districts 'development' was defined and experienced in terms not merely of absence, but of negative progress (Caplan 1992). The absence of 'development', however, did not amount to an absence of change, merely to the absence of certain sorts of changes. Changes (*mabadaliko*) had occurred, some of which were held to be the direct cause of the District's problems. People did not see themselves as being in any way tied into a kind of 'traditional' time warp that an absence of development implied. Nor did they view the absence of 'development' as a persistence of things 'traditional', in contrast to the 'modern'. In this District, as in much of East Africa, 'tradition' (*mila/jadi*) refers to a kind of status, often invoked on ritual occasions for addressing the dead or spirits, rather than to a particular kind of life or range of practices (cf. Boyer 1990; Green 2003). Being modern or *kisasa* (literally 'now-ish') is also a status, articulated through participation in what are classified as Western, imported practices and styles, rather than referring to radically different production strategies or ways of living (cf. Moore & Vaughan 1994: 116). As statuses, being *kisasa* and 'traditional' are context-dependent, not incompatible. This is articulated in terms of living 'here and now' (*palahapa*), participating in *kisasa* practices and 'traditional' obligations, as situations demand, in world that is ever changing.

## Participation, projects and the politics of progress

In Tanzania today *maendeleo* is a generic term for the kinds of 'development' implemented by external agencies, through projects and programmes, with an emphasis on the physical infrastructure of roads and buildings and the kinds of facilities associated with urban areas. Not all 'development' comes from the state or other agencies. Private investments can also bring about 'development' on a smaller scale, in the form of shops, bars, electric lighting and transport. In Ulanga, what characterises development are its external origins and its absence from the District. *Maendeleo* is what is lacking, in comparison with other districts, urban areas and other countries. It is always wanting. This makes demands for *maendeleo* a salient political rhetoric in an ongoing and conflictual debate between ruling elites and rural populations, and among rural populations themselves, about the country's future. While the Government may promise *maendeleo*, it never appears, but wanting it becomes a catch-all critique of those assumed to have a responsibility for its provision. Whereas rural populations consider responsibility for development to lie with the state and external agencies, successive governments have long tried to shift responsibility for development back to rural communities, through ideologies of self-help and invocations to contribute (*changia*) in terms of financial contributions and labour for local projects.[7] That development does not happen is blamed on rural disinterest, laziness or cultural factors, which contradict the state's ambitions for progress (Caplan 1992).

The more recently introduced ideologies of participatory development deriving from international donor organisations and NGOs are similarly ambivalent concerning the issue of responsibility (cf. Marsden 1994: 39). Just as the localised community of programme beneficiaries can be potentially empowered to achieve development through project facilitation, the failure to achieve it ultimately lies with local populations, local knowledge and local constraints. Caught up in the logical frameworks of participatory development trajectories, the foreign staff responsible for the design and management of the Ulanga District Support Programme (poverty reduction) believed that community participation held the keys to achieving 'development' in the most rural parts of the District, even though the most significant constraints on achieving either the idealised, community 'quality of life' kind of development envisaged by the programme, or the more personal development as Ulanga's population aspires to it, lay well outside the local area of project interventions. Although participatory development and localised empowerment could not begin to address these factors, localised interventions did provide a way for a minority of people to bypass extra-local constraints and achieve 'development' for themselves. It is not then surprising in this situation that people throughout Tanzania welcome projects financed by foreign donors as a means to access the kind of *maendeleo* that seems to be associated with better living standards and personal wealth. This association is reinforced by perceptions of how people live elsewhere where 'development' is in evidence, for example in urban centres, capital cities and *Ulaya*, a category often translated as 'Europe' but which encompasses anywhere thought to have attributes associated with modern first-world infrastructures and their populations.

Alongside state departments and local government, a range of agencies now have a high profile in the distribution and delivery of development goods and services in Tanzania as a whole. These include the agencies of foreign governments, multilateral organisations and numerous international NGOs, as well as the long-established and more recently arrived Christian churches and Islamic organisations. While only a few are active in the District itself, the ostentatious branding of 'development' as a product

---

[7] Often described by local-government officers as 'volunteering', which has been in the past, and in some districts is still, compulsory through local by-laws that require citizens to provide labour for certain local projects, usually as part of a donor requirement for 'community contribution' or co-financing.

tied to specific agencies means that people are aware of development organisations through vehicle logos, project personnel and the labelling of donor products, like medical kits and food supplies, all of which are highly visible throughout the country. The District-wide PRAs conducted as part of the poverty-reduction programme had also sensitised people to the presence of a major new donor operating in the locality, even if they had only a hazy awareness of its intentions. The kinds of development activities associated with NGOs and donor organisations were clearly differentiated from state initiatives, which were generally less visible or are, in any case, implemented in collaboration with donors. Where this occurs, it is donor involvement that is recognised, transforming the activity into what is popularly regarded as a legitimate 'project' (*miradi*). Projects are associated with the provision and distribution of assistance or aid (*msaada*, literally 'help'), and with external – that is, donor (*wafadhili*) – funding. The concept of the project has also come to apply to a person's own ambitions to establish an enterprise or endeavour that they believe has the potential to lead to enhanced development for themselves. People thus speak about their projects as something they have embarked on or something they plan to do in the future. As with larger scale interventions implemented by development agencies, projects on a small scale can be catalysed to success by additional investment. Relations with potential donors, actual or potential, who might offer assistance are thus enormously important. The persona of the benefactor or sponsor is long-standing in Tanzania, as is the tradition of seeking support for specific developmental investments such as starting a small business or paying school fees. As idioms derived from the cultural economy of aid become nationally pervasive, the categorisation of donor can now be applied to any potential patron who is approached for assistance by individuals. As we see in Chapter 6, it is not unusual for such requests for support to take the form of letters of sponsorship carefully crafted in the language of development project proposals. A specialist niche has been created that provides proposal-writing services to those seeking donors for their projects. These range from attempts to establish the small scale civil society organisations which could attract donor funding to the request I received to support the extension of a restaurant at the bus stand in Mahenge town, justified in terms of enhancing district food security.

## The development of a person by themselves

According to the popular classification, a fairly limited range of goods associated with projects and donors constitutes *msaada*. The category is restricted to material items, access to transport, medical assistance and money. Other more intangible benefits, defined by development organisations as development 'goods', such as project objectives regarding social development, equity concerns or enhanced participation, are not viewed as belonging to the realm of 'development' or as constituting project benefits.

Although *maendeleo* continues to be associated with the state and external agencies, its goals differ from those espoused by the socialist policies of collective self-reliance. These resulted in going backwards. Going forwards depends on real *maendeleo*, as both a cause and consequence of development. From the perspective of rural people, this cannot be achieved collectively, but through an individual's struggle to bring about *maendeleo ya mtu binafsi*. The goals and aspirations of what might be glossed as 'private development' are anticollectivist and, while they encompass 'quality of life' issues, do not encompass enhanced participation, equity concerns or the kinds of changes in consciousness that underlie the assumptions of some development organisation interventions. Nevertheless, development projects are desired in rural areas because access to *msaada* via engagement with a project either as worker, beneficiary or, more indirectly, through personal networks with those closely connected to it, can be an essential stepping-stone to achieving one's own projects and hence one's personal development.

The urgency of demands for development in rural Tanzania, in terms of what people perceive to be a low standard of living and the lack of basic services, means that the desire for development emerges not only as a dominant theme in the accounts people give of their situations and of the problems they face, but as a goal to aspire to. While the achievement of the kind of large-scale infrastructural investments associated with state-led development is obviously beyond the reach of the rural population by themselves, development on a more individual basis is attainable in terms of aspirations to achieve a better life for a person and their family. This is defined in terms of the increased income security that enables a person to access the kinds of goods and services to which they aspire and which differentiates those on the knife-edge of subsistence insecurity from those with sufficient money and other resources to get by. Increased levels of education are important here, as is access to waged non-agricultural employment. Just as evidence of infrastructure symbolises the kinds of environment where development seems possible, irrespective of how people in such areas actually live their lives, the occupation of a brick and iron roofed house has come to symbolise a person's achievement of development for themselves, even if their economic circumstances and lifestyle are much the same as those of their 'undeveloped' neighbours.

Building a house is the ultimate goal of adult men and women, who strive to accumulate sufficient capital to invest in construction and roofing materials. The construction of a house is a slow process, completed in stages as the necessary inputs are acquired, often over a period of years. The core of the house is the walls, made from burnt bricks that are either homemade or, alternatively, purchased from local craftsmen (*fundis*), who earn their living through brickmaking and construction. Unlike so-called 'local' (*kienyeji*) dwellings, which can be built without hired-in expertise, the proper construction of brick houses requires the skills of a *fundi* to align the bricks and put in door and window frames. As cement was prohibitively expensive in the 1990s, floors were usually made of earth, with the option of cementing left open as a dream or possibility. What completes a house is the roof, ideally made of corrugated iron (*bati*), purchased progressively sheet by sheet. The expense of *bati* is considerable in relation to wage levels and producer prices.

Very few people manage to complete houses to their satisfaction. Richer people who try to build larger houses are often less successful in finishing them than those with less cash who aim to construct smaller, more manageable dwellings. As economic opportunities have proliferated for some people, particularly those with access to wage employment, ideas about what constitutes a 'modern' house in rural districts have changed, as new materials and building styles become signifiers of differentiation. At its most basic a modern house is one that is made of burnt bricks and has a concrete floor and corrugated iron roof, in contrast to 'local' houses made from earth and thatch or, if brick, not finished with concrete and thatched with grasses. Basic brick housing was first introduced to the region through British colonial initiatives directed at improving the lives and outlook of the rural population.[8] Desirable houses for the middle classes are now much larger and model urban forms associated with the city, including glass windows, interior toilets and externally plastered walls. Despite substantial changes in the district and national economies since the 1990s, building a modern house remains very important as a personal aspiration for adults of both sexes, and one that for many is unfulfilled. Village areas, and the district capital itself, are littered with unfinished, uninhabited dwellings and overgrown piles of bricks. In the late 1990s, investing in housebuilding took precedence over investments in agricultural production as a private development endeavour. Residents of five villages widely dispersed throughout the District who were visited as part of a study commissioned by the project implementer all stated that wanting to build a house was the most important reason for asking the poverty-reduction programme to supply credit, rather than a desire to invest in agriculture or micro-enterprise. (Changes in housing as they relate to social differentiation are described in Chapter 8.)

This emphasis on personal development and on house-building is not unique to Ulanga District. It is prevalent throughout much of Tanzania. It contradicts the ideological assumptions of the participatory development strategies of NGOs and donors, as well as the assumptions held by the Tanzanian state and external observers about the strongly collectivist values of rural African communities. It also contradicts the concerns with distribution and the consolidation of followership that are widely held to characterise rural societies in Africa (Gatter 1993: 179; Bayart 1993).

---

[8] See 'Inexpensive Burnt Brick Houses for Natives', Dar es Salaam, Tanganyika Territory Medical Department Pamphlet 23, by A.T. Culwick. Culwick was a former district office for Mahenge and a skilled ethnographer. He was the author, together with his wife, of *Ubena of the Rivers* (1935). The house design set out in this pamphlet is still in evidence today in the style of what have come to be considered 'local' housing, or burnt brick with thatched roofing.

Surely rural dwellers would be better served investing in the production or businesses ventures that could help sustain off farm incomes or, better still from the perspective of participatory development, pooling investments in community resources? There are sound reasons why they choose not to do so. In the absence of viable alternatives, house-building is a better investment strategy than investing either in agricultural production or public goods. Given the legacy of failed community interventions that levied significant costs on individuals for little or no returns, personal investments appear more secure and can lead to experienced improvements in a person's quality of life as they define it. Houses are less prone to failure or appropriation than either agriculture or livestock. Investments in construction also make sense when considered in the context of alternative off-farm investment opportunities. Banking facilities are unavailable outside the district capital and, in any case, inflation far exceeds the kinds of interest rates available to small savers. Unlike investments in savings, which can be eaten up by relatives or inflation, *bati* holds value well, as its price systematically rises. Hoarded sheet by sheet it can always be resold. If a person moves, they can simply take their sheets of *bati* with them, or alternatively sell them to others. For some people living near to schools and centres of administration, 'modern' houses provide an income opportunity through renting to teachers and government workers. The progressive nature of housing investments through gradual building means that it is always possible to stop and restart as resources permit. House-building also offers a way of being seen to invest in kinship, without having to redistribute everything for kin to consume. Relatives have latent rights to hospitality and residence. They can share in the investment without diminishing it. A person who opens their house to kin avoids the accusations of meanness that denying other kinds of assistance would entail, and can invest in their immediate family with less risk of being implicated in the practice of witchcraft (Green 1994, 1997). Even if the house is never completed, the builder feels that they have at least tried to achieve development. If it is finished, a person can potentially free up capital or future earnings to invest in better opportunities should the economic situation in Tanzania improve. In the aftermath of what is widely perceived as the failure of both state-led and community development, house-building in the quest for personal development amounts to a statement of optimism in the capacity of rural people to achieve development for themselves.

While house-building over an extended period of time seems to be a logical investment strategy, the fact is that current economic and institutional constraints render accumulating even small amounts of cash extremely difficult for all but the minority with access to investment capital. While public-sector pay has increased considerably, mostly for those in senior roles, the majority of people in formal-sector employment cannot generate sufficient savings from their salaries, which they have to supplement with agricultural and other income. In this situation, those with access to *msaada* have a considerable advantage as a means of bypassing extra local constraints on accumulation. During the decade the poverty-reduction programme was active in the District it provided unprecedented opportunities for public-sector staff and others in key positions, such as local councillors, to access additional resources, either through supplements to pay and allowances for engaging in project activities, or through unofficial channels in the form of expropriation of construction materials, fuel and transport. Other individuals secured resources as 'help' through personal relations with project staff, as colleagues, friends and employees.

Access to development goods assists individuals to achieve personal development goals in a number of ways. In terms of cash inputs, gifts and loans from benefactors and patrons, usually associated with the Catholic Church and external programmes, enabled recipients to invest in more profitable business ventures, such as grinding mills or the food trade, or alternatively, purchase *bati* directly in a job lot, escaping the ravages of inflation. Access to transport allowed project workers and their associates to transport food crops outside the District for better prices and to import commodities for sale within the District at a time when manufactured items were not routinely available there. Project workers, local-government staff and others with access to vehicles could also supplement salaries with fares from paying passengers, as well as profiting from the substantial allowances for overnight travel that cumulatively exceeded salary totals even after a few nights away. Other goods associated with development projects, such as fuel, drugs and concrete, could be sold to raise additional income, either as part of cost recovery for distributing institutions, or as a more private means of supplementing salaries for those charged with their allocation. Although only a minority of people had access to such sources of assistance, they constitute visible examples of the kinds of development a person with 'help' can achieve, especially in the parts of the District that have a long legacy of missionary influence (Green 2003). The result was a pervasive desire for assistance through development projects, rather than the evolution of a 'community development' ideology.

In Ulanga, although development in the generic sense implied by *maendeleo* continues to be experienced in the negative terms that ascribe agency to the extra-local institutions thought to be responsible for its provision, the aspiration for *maendeleo ya mtu binafsi* recognises the potentiality of individual agency in achieving development on one's own terms. These terms are premised on a rejection of collective ventures, based on historical experience, as entailing low rates of return for the very poor people who are expected to sustain them. In a situation where the operation of extra-local economic and institutional barriers renders individual agency insufficient in itself to achieve 'development', localised project interventions and access to the material assistance with which they are associated become the critical means of overcoming extra-local constraints and the essential shortcut to achieving development, as it is locally defined, contributing to the myth that localised interventions can provide localised solutions and effecting the appropriation of agency by development organisations. Despite the fact that localised interventions fail to address the broader context of underdevelopment, they do provide an opportunity for a minority to achieve personal development on their own terms. The result is the perpetuation of dependency and the consolidation of inequality, a selective material empowerment of the few rather than a genuine empowerment of the many. This situation is not inevitable. Participatory development and the empowerment of rural communities is a possibility, but its realisation depends on the recognition that empowerment can only occur through participation in structures of decision-making in a wider political context, as well in markets and trade. Assumed empowerment at the level of consciousness and the fetishisation of local knowledge consign rural communities to the client status of passive dependency on development interventions. As long as development as a practice ignores macro-economic environments and the politics that creates them, the poor in many countries will continue to depend on localised development assistance.

# 3

# Globalising Development through Participatory Project Management

Why are development projects so similar in so many places? Why, despite the rhetoric of participation in which the poor apparently contribute to the design of strategies to 'lift them out' of poverty, is the current incarnation of development so uniform wherever it appears? Can it really be the case that the intended beneficiaries of the international development effort are universally committed to the managerial models currently presented as solutions to the problem of poverty and to the neoliberal policy prescriptions they entail? This chapter offers some provisional answers to these questions through an examination of the planning practices through which 'development', defined in practical terms as what development agencies do, actually takes place. I argue that while the standardisation of development globally is partly a function of the standardisation of development problems and solutions (Arce 2000; Ferguson 1990), it is also a consequence of the kinds of practices used to plan and implement development as a process of transforming policy visions into *manageable* realities through the social constitution 'projects' subject to specific techniques of audit, organisation and control (Strathern 2000: 2). Development does not produce unanticipated effects in the sense proposed by Ferguson (1990). Although the long-term impacts rhetorically claimed by development are unlikely to be achieved, for reasons touched on below, those involved in planning development are well aware of the limitations of what they are trying to achieve, and their short-term objectives are realistic in relation to the particularities of development management.

## Development and its side-effects

International development is perpetually being reformulated. In the 2000s, assumptions about economic growth and modernisation theory were temporarily superseded by paradigms emphasising the multifaceted nature of poverty and the importance of human rights. The Millennium

56

Development Goals informed the policies of the whole hierarchy of institutions involved in development implementation, from the lowest-tier community-based organisations to the multilateral and bilateral agencies that provide the bulk of development funding. Consensus is not absolute. Critiques of the contemporary development agenda, and of the globalisation with which it is evidently aligned, take place on the margins of the formal development sector. For all their radical posturing, many of those talking against development remain committed to something of a 'developmentalist'[1] perspective in relation to the global South, and their positions are increasingly incorporated within the development mainstream via international civil-society organisations (CSOs).[2] While development represents itself in terms of the beneficial intentions of policy content, it is viewed in a less positive light by those who choose to position themselves outside its institutional structure. Development as an institution is seen by writers such as Shrestha (1995), Escobar (1995) and Ferguson (1990), among others (see for example Chatterjee 2004; Roy 2010; Gabay 2012), as a bureaucratic force with global reach and an explicitly pro-capitalist agenda, operating as a tool of regimes that seek to perpetuate relations of inequality and dependence between 'the West and the rest' and, through their representation, to perpetuate the construction of others as post-colonial subjects. Recent writings on globalisation have attempted to reconceptualise the geographical basis of this relation, in the process acknowledging the resituating of dependency in which the transnational person simply relocates their subjugation through economic migration (cf. Arce & Long 1993: 15; Massey 2005). The Mexican migrant worker cleaning in the rich households of California may be a 'post-peasant' in the new categories of post-modernity, but he or she remains poor. Moreover, this persistent poverty is a direct consequence of what 'development' has achieved. In the words of Michael Kearney, development projects implemented by state agencies and CSOs alike, in Mexico and elsewhere, 'actually function to reproduce rather than improve existing social, political, and economic problems' (1996: 143).

Perceptions such as Kearney's are not unusual in anthropology, which has viewed itself as a discipline to an extent outside of, hence untainted by, close engagement with a development sector that has dirty hands. In reality this claim to non-involvement is unsupportable. Even if most anthropologists do not engage in development in the 'hands-on' sense of 'applied' practitioners, anthropology has long been complicit in constituting development, through contributing to the kinds of representations of underdeveloped otherness which make development thinkable, as

---

[1] After Said's notion of 'orientalist', which entails representing the other and constituting them as a project in need of intervention (1995: 73–93, but much of the book has resonance with the argument here).

[2] This incorporation has been deliberately sought on the part of the multilaterals. The World Bank in particular has sought to include representatives of protest movements since the 2000s.

well as through the pursuit of intellectual agendas that have directly or indirectly served 'development' interests (Thomas 1994; Ferguson 1997; Mitchell 2002).[3] Anthropologists' claimed capacity to interpret local situations and grasp the underlying significance of discourses of power have now informed numerous accounts by anthropologists of development as failure, either because programmes failed to achieve what they set out to do or because they accentuated existing inequalities.[4] In these writings, which predominantly explore an apparent disjunction between development objectives and local realities in the context of fairly small-scale projects rather than national programmes, 'development' generally fails for the same few reasons: lack of 'local' knowledge on the part of the implementing agency, inadequate participation of beneficiaries in project design, or because the representation of the problem that a project set out to address had little basis in local realities (Hobart 1993; Crewe & Harrison 1998: 16). The more recent contribution by David Mosse stands out for its analysis, which shows how project failure and success are conceived within political narratives about development and aid. When these change, what was previously considered a success is no longer successful and faces either a negative evaluation or reframing (2005a).

According to James Ferguson, in what remains perhaps the best-known account read by anthropologists of development as failure (1990), the 'discourse of development' functions as a machine that obviates political understandings of local situations and ensures that 'development', whatever its intentions, always serves primarily to further the power of the state. While development might 'fail', in the sense of not achieving its stated objectives, Ferguson argues that it impacts on other areas through side-effects. In the project he describes, which worked with local government in Lesotho, these were, not surprisingly, to strengthen the institutions of governance in the interests of the state and state officials. According to Ferguson these side-effects were unanticipated and unintended by the people involved with the project as implementers and planners. 'The project ... may be said to have *unintentionally* played what can only be called an instrumental role' in strengthening state presence (1990, 253–4).

In Ferguson's analysis, which relies on a Foucaultian understanding of the relation between discourse and power, the good intentions of development implementers are subverted by the overriding discourse in which they find themselves. Even those regarded as potentially capable of presenting realistic information, such as anthropologists, are sucked into the system, producing reports, analyses and solutions that conform to the expectations of development discourse. Ferguson concludes:

[3] The same argument applies of course to colonialism. Considered thus the question becomes not whether anthropology was a 'handmaiden' of colonialism, but the extent to which the interests of the siblings diverged or converged during and after the colonial period.
[4] There are exceptions, such as McMillan's excellent (1995) account of the campaign against river blindness in the Sahel, and Crewe & Harrison (1998).

the development apparatus in Lesotho is ... a machine for reinforcing and expanding the exercise of bureaucratic state power, which incidentally takes 'poverty' as its point of entry – launching an intervention that may have no effect on the poverty but does in fact have other concrete effects. *Such a result may be no part of the planners' intentions – indeed it almost never is* – but resultant systems have an intelligibility of their own (1990, 255–6: emphasis added).

In an equally influential book exploring the significance of 'development' in general for the making of the 'Third World', Arturo Escobar (1995) makes a similar argument about how 'development' achieves its effects. These effects are not of course the stated objectives of development policy, but the reproduction of the relations of inequality on which global capitalism and United States dominance depend. In an account based on ethnographic research among civil servants in the Colombian Ministry of Planning, Escobar presents an image of development institutions as bureaucratic monoliths in which planners and technicians uncritically impose a hegemonic order on the global South through the manipulation of development discourse and planning certainties, and in so doing seek to reduce its people to objects of intervention and control.

## How anthropologists think 'development' works

Both Ferguson and Escobar set out to deconstruct the assumptions that they think liberal Westerners might hold about 'development', for example that its institutions work to eradicate poverty, through what are represented as examinations of what 'development' actually does. 'Development' in these accounts is not presented as a collective representation in the sense of the thoughts that development institutions think (Douglas 1986) in relation to the policy objectives shared by a range of social actors, including those of local political and civil-society organisations, as well as more obviously national governments and citizens. Nor does it appear as an analytical category pertaining to certain kinds of outcomes and effects. Rather, development both as discourse and the institutions it produces are presented as if they were discrete entities whose influence can be considered in isolation from the other factors that contribute to their emergence. Development appears as an agent in its own right, a thing with a life of its own. Development from this perspective concerns the domain of 'intentional' development (Cowen & Shenton 1996) or what Gillian Hart (2001) has called Big D development, confined to planning ministries charged with development programmes and to the multilateral, bilateral and non-government agencies explicitly oriented towards its implementation. Development failure *and* development power become the achievement *and* responsibility solely of development institutions and discourse, endowing 'development' with an influence that is quite remarkable considering its propensity to failure. In reality, of course, the 'side-effects' of development only appear as such when development is viewed as an institutional structure external to the states and structures of governance with which it works. The strengthening of state power in Lesotho, which Ferguson regards as an instrumental effect of development, was arguably an *intended* effect, a necessary precondition for strengthening the local-authority services that the project set out to support. Its appropriation by a repressive regime was more a consequence of the political situation in Lesotho than an automatic effect of 'development'.

Both Ferguson and Escobar present an alienated view of development as a reification of institutional practice in which human agency has a limited role to play. This stems in part from the anthropological perception of administration and governance as externally determined fields, whose content is reducible to the play of bureaucrats concerned with 'passing the buck' and preserving their own positions in what Herzfeld has characterised as 'secular theodicy', resulting in the 'social production of indifference' (1992: 7–10). This reification of development as a bureaucratic machine that overrides the agency of the individuals engaged in it permits the construction of an anthropological caricature of development as monolith, denying the capacities of social actors within and outside it to influence development outcomes.[5] More fundamentally, although planning is central to the operation of development in both accounts, this process is never explored ethnographically, merely attributed to the routine of 'bureaucrats' and the production of documents that reinforce the hegemonic representation. *Why* development bureaucrats should seek to reproduce development in the interests of global capitalism or state power is not questioned, but merely assumed as an effect of being caught up in the development machine.

What development bureaucrats are actually doing, or believe they are doing, in their everyday professional practice is less frequently the focus of anthropological attention. Significantly, the best accounts of this kind of work have been produced by anthropologists who are 'observant participants' in the development system (Mosse 2011, 2001). A critical site for investigation is how development practitioners work with designing interventions that they believe will have developmental outcomes, that is, will achieve some of the objectives that constitute 'development' as a policy-determined field at any particular time. Central to this key strand of development work is the purported relation between cause and effect on which much programming is premised. To return to the Lesotho example, while the 'planners' and the senior staff at the Canadian agency

[5] Gardner & Lewis challenge this representation when they point to the contested nature of development discourse, even within development agencies (2000). Similarly, Phillips & Edwards (2000) show how development is negotiated at project level through the strategies of evaluators, and evaluated at reviews and appraisals. Similar arguments are made by Mosse (2005a) and Li (2007b).

for international development and in the Government of Lesotho were doubtless committed to strengthening the capacity of different tiers of government to deliver various kinds of services, they may have been less critical of the cause and effect proposition that suggested that the range of interventions planned by the project would contribute to the reduction of poverty because of the short-term orientation of development planning and because of what development is really concerned with managing.

*Development planning*
Metaphors derived from stereotypical images of industrial production notwithstanding, development 'technicians' (Escobar 1995: 88) are not mere operatives mechanistically perpetuating the rituals of bureaucratic practice. Nor does development planning occur in an instant under the sole control of 'planners' in thrall to a development vision. Development planning involves representatives and professional specialists from donor and recipient organisations, as well as personnel recruited to manage implementation and representatives of the local institutions with which a project is to work. Increasingly, representatives of the so-called beneficiary groups are invited to participate at various stages in public design and management processes, for example the users of public services or members of farmer groups who are the intended targets of development assistance. Invited participation of this sort often occurs after an initial design has been agreed by an agency and recipient government and finance set aside.

Despite unequal relations of power between development agencies and the recipients of development assistance those at the receiving end of development have some capacity to influence programming and, on occasion, to reject it altogether. Even in the work of the International Monetary Fund (IMF), perhaps the most powerful development exemplar of them all, acceptance of the shared reality that will form a 'common ground' for policy development and planning is the outcome of a negotiated process between the multilateral agency and recipient government (Harper 2000: 30). Bearing in mind the fact that such programmes are often claimed as the initiative of recipient governments, particularly at national level, and that the planning process only starts in earnest once governments have agreed in principle, outright rejection almost never happens. Too much is at stake in the proposed transfer of resources to jeopardise the process, and vested interests on the part of donor representatives, as well as recipients, ensure that dialogue continues over an extended time frame. Agency staff have their own objectives to achieve in the contracts and performance plans derived from country and sector strategies that depend on securing the right kinds of agreements. However, other strategies are frequently adopted by 'stakeholders', including those within development agencies themselves, to alter or nullify proposed and ongoing programmes.[6] These

[6] For an excellent account of how development engages with stakeholders in project design and evaluation, see Mosse (2004).

include delaying tactics, insisting that a programme is redesigned from scratch, and the initiation of changes in direction as a consequence of review missions.

Planning in development – that is, in agencies that manage resource transfers to support policy objectives – really concerns the shorter-term 'purpose' of specific funded activities that are intended to produce measurable 'outputs' at the end of a finite three- to five-year period. It is less concerned with the goal, the higher-tier objective, towards which the purpose is intended to contribute. In the logic of the planning techniques used in development (output-oriented programming, or project cycle management, for example), outputs are distinct from impacts. Impacts are in fact inferred from the outputs having been achieved through what are known as 'output to purpose' reviews, that is, when, at the end of a specified time period, assessors try to determine the extent to which the achievement of the outputs stated in the original plan has contributed to the 'purpose' of a project.[7] Despite recent trends towards larger-scale and more flexible programmes, the aggregation of smaller-scale projects and public services into overarching national-level 'sector programmes', and the stated emphasis on 'process projects' in which some activities are determined on an ongoing basis rather than specified in advance, the package of activities and funding oriented towards the achievement of specified outputs and purpose constitutes a 'project', irrespective of scale, and are subject to the same techniques of representation and management. The project as a matrix of inputs and outputs subject to time and cost is conceptualised as an entity to be controlled in standard management terms.

Development management is concerned with the relation between investments and outputs over a specific time frame. Like other audit techniques, it relies on the production and manipulation of texts through which these relations can be quantified and controlled (Rose 1996, 1999; Miller & Rose 1990). The production of documentation at various points in the project cycle is the outcome of specific institutional practices that have become part of the recognised 'tool kit' for development planning and management. Project documents use current policy discourse to constitute particular representations of development problems as amenable to particular interventions. Project documentation is not intended to present an objective account of a social and economic situation, or a discursive assessment of how best to address the kinds of issues that might come under the ambit of current policy concerns, but to support financial transfers with a view to achieving carefully costed outcomes. Such documents support particular positions and courses of action within funding agencies where different sectors compete for limited amounts of cash, stating why and how what amount of money should be spent by whom to contribute toward what policy objective.

---

[7] Newer techniques in development evaluation, such as outcome-mapping, supplement rather than supersede this kind of concern with outputs.

Consequently such documents have more in common with marketing texts than with social and economic analysis. Given the virtual impossibility of determining with any certainty the actual relation between what a project does and other social processes, project documentation is vital in constituting the project as a slice of manageable reality where project inputs can be seen to relate to outputs and, largely by inference, to effects on the ground. Projects do not exist only at the level of documentation, although this is the only place where a pure development project, divorced from other institutions, can be represented. The pure project is also periodically brought into being as a social institution through the creation of project space via the techniques of participatory project management.

*Participatory project management*
I have been involved in around fifteen development projects in Tanzania between 1996 and the present, in various capacities: as an outside observer carrying out anthropological fieldwork, as a low-level development manager responsible for 'signing off' on projects within a particular sector in a bilateral agency, and as a social development consultant hired by various agencies to work as part of a team to redesign and evaluate projects and prepare project documentation (Green 2009). The following account is based on experience as a consultant working on the evaluation of a project, funded by the Government of the United Kingdom, that was intended to support the development of local-government capacity in Tanzania. Although this chapter describes a governance programme, many of the processes and practices involved recur across programmes in other sectors and at different scales. The recent channelling of external assistance to Tanzania, along with the tendency for international development agencies to adopt similar strategies and techniques, has contributed to the institutionalisation of development practices across a range of personnel, in development agencies as well as in central and local government, and, to a lesser extent, private individuals living in communities that have been at the receiving end of development interventions. In Tanzanian popular culture, 'development' (*maendeleo)* is no longer the prerogative of institutions associated with the state, but has come to refer more narrowly to the projects (*miradi*), paraphernalia and practices associated with international development assistance. As well as being associated with institutional presence in the form of offices, personnel and vehicles, which continue to be heavily branded indicators of donor presence in the country, the category 'development' conveys the performance of certain practices in particular institutional forms. These centre on the 'stakeholder' workshop as a site for the production of project reality through what have become recognised as specialist techniques of participatory project management. These techniques, promoted by practitioners who have their own professional accreditations and global networks, derive from the general project-management strategies used in Western industry

and commerce, combined with the participatory methods associated with rural development planning, but informed by the assumptions of the 'New Public Management' (Minogue et al. 1998) that the quantification of inputs and outputs can apply to the domain of the social.

Participatory project management explicitly makes the process of constituting the project a social process through the creation of institutional spaces in which different people can contribute to its construction and, to a lesser extent, control. The documented products of participatory processes feed into the documentation used to chart and direct the project through its funding cycle, from design to appraisal (when the design is assessed by interested parties) and implementation, which is monitored through a series of reviews. Mid-term and end-of-project reviews are the most important, the former for ensuring that a project can continue and allowing for some redesign, the latter for allowing funding agencies to determine whether or not a project has succeeded in achieving its purpose. Different agencies have different conventions about what can be altered once a project is underway. In the agency with which I worked the rule of thumb was that the goal and purpose of a project should remain for the life of a project, but that the outputs could be redrawn if necessary.

Major reviews and appraisals involve an assessment of the routine documentation of spending and progress that project managers generate, together with field visits by project teams. Such teams typically comprise agency staff, government partners and external consultants specialising in a particular sector that a project addresses, as well as the field staff responsible for day-to-day operational management. Given the centrality of 'managing the spend' to the constitution of a project, and the emphasis on 'bangs for bucks', it is not surprising that the methodology of review is very similar to that of IMF audit missions (Harper 2000). Quantification of inputs and outputs is critical to assessment of performance, hence the concern, both at the design stage and throughout implementation, with 'objectively verifiable indicators' (OVIs) as proxies for assessing impact and performance. The core team works intensely over several days to collect documentation, and holds discussions with a wide range of institutional representatives who have an interest in the project. These discussions provide reviewers with an indication of the possible basis for agreement about the future of a project, and highlight issues that may need to be addressed for a project to 'succeed' in the quite limited but realistic terms of achieving its *purpose*.

In addition to project teams, reviews and appraisals involve groups of people from a project area in what are known as 'stakeholder workshops'. Stakeholders in development parlance are the individuals and institutions deemed to have a stake in a project and who have the potential to impact either positively or negatively on project outcomes. Agency literature acknowledges the diversity of interests among stakeholder groups and that funding agencies often have the biggest stake in a project. In Tanzania such workshops (*warsha*) have become a routine part of the design of development interventions at all levels, from the senior officials and donor representatives involved in programming sector reforms, to the relatively small projects, perhaps financed by international agencies, but planned and implemented by national and local civil society organisations. Formally, such workshops provide an opportunity to clarify the purpose and outputs of a project. A more fundamental objective is to build credibility and legitimacy for the intervention among particular social constituencies recognised by the agency as having a 'stake' in the project. The stakeholder category includes representatives from donor and recipient organisations as well as carefully selected representatives of beneficiary communities. It is to an extent created through the selection of participants. In the context of projects that are increasingly invisible to outsiders in the form of spending largely allocated to 'capacity-building' (Phillips & Ilcan 2004) and training (Swidler & Watkins 2009), workshops serve two purposes. In constituting projects as social institutions they make projects tangible, and by creating a category of stakeholders (*wadau* or *washika dau)* they create a social group with a stake in perpetuating project space from which more immediate benefits of development derive. In Tanzania, at least, this visibility perpetuates stereotypical representations of development as material benefits and as particular techniques of project management.

## Workshopping in Tanzania's development culture

Stakeholder workshops in Tanzania's development culture assume a particular institutional form, and are conducted in fairly standard ways, in line with the professional expectations both of the development facilitators who specialise in their operation and of the category of what might be referred to as professional participants: those employed in professional capacities in public- and development-sector agencies and whose work in maintaining aid-dependent administrations involves participation in workshops. Participants from within donor agencies also have expectations about how workshops should be managed and what they are expected to produce. A shared expectation is that workshops are *professional*, that is, that they conform in their structure and sequence to the project management expectations of professional participants. Workshops, like projects, are units of management. As packages of inputs and outputs, they run to clear schedules and aim to deliver outcomes within a designated time period. The production of outputs, in the form of bullet-pointed assertions or project-logical frameworks, follows clearly determined sequences of facilitated group work in which each product is part of a sequentially managed process in the production of specific pieces of project documentation.

Professional participants also expect that the location and style of a workshop conforms to their own sense of being a professional involved in development, that is, as high-status persons engaged in high-status activities. Professionals expect to be valued and treated in a way that indicates their status in relation to other social categories, in this context the 'villagers' whom it is the responsibility of public servants to administer. In Tanzania, professional status, both within the wider public sector and outside it, is signified through reference to two parallel indices; notions about patronage and the power to command others derived from more regionally specific idioms of political relations (cf. Bayart 1993) and the material signifiers of global modernity. These include style of dress, access to the latest vehicles and electronic goods and, increasingly, a 'professional' style of accoutrements associated with management, symbolised by the ubiquitous business card exchanged between officials at all official meetings and gradually being superseded by the latest internet-enabled smartphone through which one's contact details and social media identities can be shared. The power to send juniors on errands and to exert control, even if symbolic, over other's time or labour by making people wait are key indices of an official's status, indices shared by the expatriate staff of development agencies, whose own status is marked out *vis-à-vis* their Tanzanian counterparts through better offices, luxurious housing, uniformed guards, private vehicles, extra benefits and higher pay. Being driven also indicates professional status, combining the power to control other's labour with the car as a key signifier of managerial status. Officials participating in project events expect to be driven in project vehicles, even for short distances, as an index of their recognition as professionals in a project setting, and expect to be able to 'send' project drivers on personal errands, even to purchase something from a shop next to which the vehicle is parked.

The association of externally funded development with signifiers of modernity and wealth as apparent characteristics of donor countries informs the ways in which development projects are instituted in Tanzania and the ways in which development professionals behave. Development professionals expect to stay at 'international' hotels, and are expected by their counterparts to do so, because such hotels are the most expensive and conform to expectations about internationality, in the sense of being outposts of world cities represented by Euro-American-Asian metropolises, with international media, including sports channels, high-speed internet, dollar currency and 'international' food. Similarly, international development projects are expected to have the latest in vehicles and electronic office equipment. The development workshops in which professionals participate tend to be held in explicitly 'modern'-style halls attached to ex-mission churches or to former parastatal training institutes in regional towns, and in 'international' hotels in larger cities. The expectation that workshops must be held in the 'right kind' of space, with 'modern' facilities, mitigates against the utilisation of other kinds of available public space, for example primary schools in rural areas, for the production of development and reinforces the contemporary association of participation in development with professional urban status. It also desituates projects and stakeholders from the geographical settings in which project impacts are expected to occur.

Professionals attending workshops do so as part of their professional vocation, but low levels of public-sector pay necessitate compensation for the demands on their professional time that participation entails. Daily allowances (*posho*) are paid to workshop participants, often with differential rates for government employees and 'beneficiaries'.[8] Rates for participation generally exceed rates of daily pay for public servants who have significant incentive to attend workshops and seminars wherever possible. The centrality of the workshop to the constitution of the project now means that attracting participants is essential for development managers, who need participants to constitute their project to be managed. Development agencies in Tanzania, as elsewhere (Crewe & Harrison 1998; Skage et al. 2013), pay attendance allowances even to salaried persons serving in the same vicinity of the workshop because they know that without pay attendance will tail off and the credibility of a participatory project will decline. In some instances different agencies compete by offering higher rates to attract participants involved in several projects simultaneously. Significant proportions of project budgets are spent on achieving this kind of professional participation, at the same time as the 'participation' of beneficiaries in projects through what are euphemistically referred to as 'contributions' (*michango*) of labour or time are taken for granted by the professionals and elite called to speak on their behalf. Stakeholder workshops have become so essential to the constitution of development that workshops have become proxies for project outputs, particularly in relation to intangibles like capacity enhancement and training. The Local Government Reform Programme, financed by multilateral and bilateral donors and designed by an international audit consultancy, essentially comprised a series of workshops through which local authorities were expected not merely to reform themselves but to attain appropriate levels of competency as 'capacity' for programme implementation.

As well as allowances, participants are issued with notebooks and pens and, as befits professionals, are served with elaborate meals featuring choice combinations of high-status foods, including fish, meat, chicken and rice, in contrast to the average daily diet of maize and vegetables that a rural person would usually eat. Styles of clothing and self-presentation are also indicators of the professional and international status associated with development both as project and as progress. Project workshops are occasions for participants to dress in professional style and for representatives of 'local' communities to dress in prestigious clothing to mark what have become prestigious occasions for participants, often reported in the national media where 'development' events are news. Professional

---

[8] Per diem culture also extends to staff of donor agencies who receive allowances for overnight stays and out-of-office work, some of which are substantial.

photographers often attend such workshops in order to take pictures of participants to be sold to them as they leave as mementoes of what has been a very special occasion. A beneficiary attending a stakeholder workshop may not receive the same amount of cash stuffed into their brown envelope as the district engineer received in his, but they are likely to have more cash than when they entered the workshop and will have eaten luxuriously in pleasant surroundings for several days in succession.

The professionalisation of participation in workshop settings, and the association of workshops with status, means that participants, even in smaller NGO projects, are overwhelmingly drawn from among the local elites who come to the attention of project staff and of public servants and whose levels of education and familiarity with the group work required of the workshop make them ideal participants. The relativity of poverty and of developed versus developee as categories of beneficiary and recipient (cf. Pigg 1992) means that these representatives of local communities are perceived by largely elite project staff and expatriates alike as 'poor', while communities themselves will perceive them as lower-tier officials and patrons, who are at the same time clients of those with higher-tier positions in the public administration and wider social networks beyond the immediate area (cf. Haugerud 1995). 'The real poor are invisible, they don't come to meetings', a project manager from Dar es Salaam told me, an invisibility reinforced by the exclusivity the professionalisation of such workshops creates.

Although stakeholder workshops are concerned with participation, they are not necessarily participatory (cf. Pottier 1997). The structure of development planning in which workshops take place after the basic design is in place, and the ways in which the workshops are organised, preclude the kind of input from 'stakeholders' that would significantly alter the conception of a project once the workshop has been convened. This is not to suggest that participants *cannot* influence workshop outcomes, but to point out that in order to do so they would need to be in positions from where they have the authority to influence, and to be conversant with the skills of manipulating discussion and its representation on which the role of facilitator depends. Even where representatives of beneficiary groups are present in a workshop setting, they are likely to be fewer in number than the professional groups and, given the etiquette of hierarchy and power in Tanzania, will be less likely to speak critically before those representing themselves as government. The tight organisational structure of facilitation and the construction workshops as a site for the *management* of outputs ensures that workshops produce highly limited visions.

## Project propositions and the practice of management

Workshops derived from management practices reproduce the kind of text-based approach to the production of social outcomes on which project documentation is based. Facilitators, generally self-employed consultants with backgrounds in development management (that is, with the production and manipulation of project texts), adopt standardised approaches to workshop structure based either on the requirements of the project cycle, or derived from their own experience of similar workshops. The detachment of facilitators from specific projects and the professionalisation of facilitation doubtless contribute to the standardisation of workshop products and of participants' expectations. Facilitators are usually hired specifically to do workshops and possibly to prepare key components of project documentation, usually positioned around a logical framework that it is the objective of a workshop to either refine or produce. A facilitator charged with the preparation of project documents knows that she, or more usually he, has to get the workshop to produce the kinds of material they need to make an acceptable project, that is, to produce the kind of analysis which will be accepted by the agency as presenting the 'right kinds' of relationships between different inputs and outputs, and which is supported by the 'right kinds' of indicators that are realistic enough to be convincing and are consistent with agency policy priorities. Facilitators must also create apparent consensus among participants, who should feel as if they have all contributed to the design of the project through what is represented as a discursive analysis of key problems and solutions.

Facilitation in such settings is a highly skilled activity. As workshops may take several days to work through a sequence of problem identification and analysis that will lead into project solutions, a facilitator must be able to retain the interest of the people in the room. He or she has to be able to remain the centre of attention while encouraging participants to share ideas publicly and to contribute to writing these on flip charts and post-it notes that can be displayed for public discussion. The facilitator also requires a sound understanding of the logic of project management. The latter is graphically represented through what continues to be the basic project management tool in international development: the logframe, or logical framework. The logframe is in essence a matrix representing chains of causality in such a way that certain inputs, cash and activities, produce certain outputs that achieve a specific purpose that contributes towards a higher-order goal. The creation of its different components through group work is what allows a facilitator to structure a workshop. Conversely a representation of the hierarchy of causes contributing to a particular problem, such as local poverty due to poor farmer prices due to lack of access to markets due to poor roads, can be reversed by visually uprooting the 'problem tree' to produce a 'project' once priorities for intervention have been agreed. These priorities are not primarily determined through research or analysis but through the pragmatic requirements of sector budgets and policy objectives.

Once timetables have been agreed for a particular workshop, with essential breaks for tea, snacks and meals, participants are taken through sequences of plenary discussions and group work around the management stages determined by the logic of the framework. Groups may be asked to produce lists of key problems using marker pens and flip charts, or state reasons why certain things occur. These are then reported back to the wider group and stuck on the wall for people to look at, literally enveloping participants inside the project text. Reporting back provides an opportunity for the facilitator, standing in front of the seated participants, to verbally edit the suggestions and analytical contributions from groups, and to obtain support for his or her editorial decision. This is achieved through rhetorical questioning of the point that he wishes to reject and through seeking the support of professionals in the audience, who may also need to be edited out where their own interests would threaten the policy objectives of a project (such as working with the poor). The facilitator writes up the new points on flip charts. These will form the basis of the written-up account of a workshop circulated to participants and kept in project files, and inform the production of project management documentation. The debates around why certain points are rejected or retained are not recorded.

The analytical constraints of the logical framework and the 'problem tree' in demanding simplistic causal hierarchies produce simplistic strategies to address complex multifaceted realities. This limitation is not perceived as a problem in the workshop setting because what matters, to facilitators and participants alike, is what is made to matter by the constitution of projects as outputs to be managed. Achieving the outputs that constitute project success does not depend on an analysis of causality, but on the production of a hierarchy of causality. Effort is expended to produce quality documents and logframes, rather than quality understanding or analyses (cf. Stirrat 2000). Perhaps the most significant aspect of kind of analysis and the planning it informs is that the problem analysis contains the possible solutions likely to be accepted by project teams and participants alike. These solutions, like the analysis itself, are apparently straightforward inputs that will impact in a management sense on the problems they are intended to address. The selection of solutions – that is, inputs and activities – creates the project as a manageable entity subject to audit and assessment. Activities *can* be performed, funded and evaluated, and inputs measured as related to outputs. A structure for success is in place.

I have suggested that the social constraints on workshop formats and the rules of participatory engagement and facilitation serve to reproduce the pure project as a particular kind of social institution that conforms to the representations contained in project texts through which select aspects of social reality become manageable. In collaborating to make reality manageable, stakeholders contribute to project management, although this participation has little impact on the ways in which a project is conceptualised. This is partly due to the project politics around the selection of stakeholders and the various professional interests in the perpetuation of development as this kind of management process, but also partly due to the constraints on thinking and on argument imposed by the dual frameworks of development and management.[9] Some of these assumptions concern the necessity of continuing to practice development and its administration in their current forms. Others centre on the apparent truisms of managing within neoliberal paradigms concerning the means through which efficiency and effectiveness can be achieved in public services and the idea that better government or female participation in education will lead to poverty reduction. In such contexts where truths about development are not negotiated but axiomatic, and where expertise seems to be on hand to make development work, certain things become simply unthinkable, or if thought, are soon discarded as untenable (Douglas 1986: 76), while others are 'thought without thinking'. The management paradigm that underpinned the Local Government Reform Programme, for example, emphasised privatisation as the key to efficient public services. In the neoliberal logic of 'New Public Management', efficient public services meant reduced public spending, which it was assumed would lead inevitably to increased services for the public, and hence reduced poverty. The restructuring manual, prepared by an international audit consultancy, around which local authorities were expected to implement the reform process, encouraged local authorities to privatise public toilets in order to achieve a 'quick win' for reform. The provision of public toilets, certainly in small and medium-sized district centres, was not a core activity of local government in Tanzania and it is unlikely that this course of action yielded much additional revenue. In districts I visited where public toilets had either been privatised or charges imposed, town centre workers, often market traders, complained that costs were prohibitive. Despite these obvious shortcomings in the design of the programme, not one of the local-government officers or development professionals participating in workshops around public services challenged the proposition that the privatisation of public toilets might be a useful activity.

The propositions put forward in project settings acquire a degree of plausibility that participants appear to accept, at least for the duration of the workshop, where the diagrammatic representations of cause and effect can represent a social reality detached from both macro-politics and the micro-universes of individual decision-making. The conviction of the management models and the facilitators, the assent of experts and professionals, gives the projected project credibility. Logical frameworks seem logical, analytical. Projects *do* produce anticipated outputs, at least in the short term. What is less certain is the extent to which the outputs will inform the purpose of a project, or whether the purpose of a project will inform the goal. However, for the purposes of development management, a project exists as a time-bound grid of relations between

---

[9] Ferguson makes a similar point in relation to the limitations of development thinking, but he does not connect this to the construction of development as management (1990: 260).

inputs and outputs subject to assessment and control, and has been brought into being through the matrix of workshops and documentation through which this control is exerted.

## Making manageable realities

Project documentation and, to an extent, project workshops create the project as a kind of entity separated off from other kinds of social realities in order to make it manageable. This separation is achieved through specific styles of documentation and analysis, as well as through the dynamics of workshopping, where management logic ensures that participants produce standard project documentation as the outputs of a restricted style of 'logical' reasoning that is diagrammatically represented. Project workshops bring together different representatives of those deemed by development agencies to have a stake in the project, dramatising a particular representation of development as a matter of professional style and the performance of management practices. The agency staff, project managers and professional facilitators who meet in project spaces come from a wide variety of countries and backgrounds, but all subscribe to the conventions of development as the performance of management practices with which they have expertise. This expertise is not viewed as location- or country-specific but as generic to development. In terms of the production of projects in the sense described in this chapter, it is.[10] Location and local knowledge are simply not relevant to the construction of chains of causality and indicators of assessment that development-constituted-as-project entails.

The social reality of project space as detached from wider social processes and where the usual conventions of political engagement, and opposition, do not apply, and where different stakeholders have may completely different understandings of what the issues are and why they matter, brings to mind the image of the non-places proposed by Marc Augé (1995, 1998). Non-places are, for Augé, sites constituted by contemporary social relations and detached from the territorial place and social contexts that comprise what he calls 'anthropological place' (1995: 101). Paradigmatic non-places are places through which people pass in their capacity as individuals detached from social networks and obligations. Such places include the airports and freeways of contemporary travel, constituted through text instructing the user how the space should be used. The idea of non-places is similar to the notion of hyperspace proposed by Jamieson (cited in Kearney 1996: 118), premised on the deterritorialisation of place where particular kinds of places as sites for the constitution of particular kinds of relations are freed from geographic

---

[10] This assertion is based on personal experience. The only time when knowledge of Tanzania mattered to my job as a development manager was when I could produce the documents that would have otherwise been contracted out to consultants.

location. Both non-places and hyperspace are real places in that they are territorially situated. Their existence as such is relationally determined whether one is working there or passing through. As non-places are constituted through social relations, not location, the constitution of others as representations and as strangers eliminates the possibility of dialogue or debate.

While some of Augé's wider theoretical claims about non-places as characteristics of what he calls 'supermodernity' are unconvincing, the notion of non-place can provide insights for thinking about development spaces such as projects and workshops. Development spaces are similar to Augé's non-places in that they are constituted through social relations, texts and deterritorialisation in two senses. First, global templates are imposed on local realities in a kind of franchise of social and economic policies, creating a kind of 'hyperpolicy' for the global non-places that recipients of development transfers become. Second, those coming together for a project only do so through the project itself, and represent not themselves but a professional position for an agency that is explicitly operating not only outside its place of origin but to agenda determined in the national and multilateral policy spaces where the content of international development is negotiated.

Agency staff do not often engage with location outside the non-places of the projects they are hired to implement, living their lives not as 'cosmopolitans' partaking of hybrid cultures but as 'metropolitan locals' seeking 'home plus' (Hannerz 1996: 107) in the shopping malls, gyms and cappuccino bars that international development assistance produces as a side-effect of massive spending in the capital cities of poor countries. The true scale and socio-economic consequences of this are unknown, but some indication of the enormity of development's side-effects on national economies is provided by the example of Kenya. Of the US $350 million that the UN alone brought into the Kenyan economy in 1998 'less than half comes from direct programme assistance. The rest accrues from myriad spin-offs from transport, salaries, international conferences and secondary employment' (Turner 2000:5).[11] Up-to-date estimates are unfortunately not available for any country or for the development sector as a whole.[12]

The detachment of agency staff is shared to an extent by all workshop participants in the deterritorialised setting of workshops as project space,

---

[11] The figures given in the *Financial Times* of 16 January 2000 state: 'The UN employs 1,291 national and 922 international staff – excluding short term contracts – at a salary cost of more than $130m. Almost $6m of that is distributed via secondary employment of UN house staff, including servants, gardeners, guards, and drivers' (Turner 2000: 5).

[12] The economist Oliver Morrissey informs me (personal communication) that there is no study that looks into consumption spending by donors in recipient economies. It would be possible to estimate some of the side-effects on the economy by assessing spending in the tourism sector, as much development spending supports this through workshops, accommodation for consultants and conferences, but the scale of spending on salaries, including those of national staff, paid at 'international' rates, on housing and on services are also significant.

held in locations detached from everyday social processes, involving strangers and divorced from local political processes. Being in a non-place serves to make the manageable realities of projects seem plausible and amenable to control through the global tools of the development profession in policy hyperspace. Development management entails the social constitution of projects as slices of manageable reality in which, in the short term, outputs can be achieved. Development technicians are not mere bureaucrats perpetuating hegemonic representations of the Third World through projects that perpetuate poverty. Stereotypical representations of the targets of development assistance are invoked in project documentation as a justification for, rather than as a consequence of, development spending. Designing development interventions is a contested process involving groups of people representing different social positions at different points in a project cycle. The fact that participation has little impact on development outcomes, and that outputs have a weak relationship with impacts, is partly explained by the limitations of the management paradigm for dealing with the social, where the relationships between development spending and social outcomes are not well understood. As long as development is conceived primarily in terms of managing finance, rather than supporting change, vast sums of public money will continue to be wasted, and development spending will continue to finance management and its associated spin-offs.

# 4

**Making Development Agents** | Nationalising Participation in Tanzania

In the 2000's, Tanzania introduced participatory planning into its reforming local-government system.[1] Enshrined in the 2002 national framework on participatory planning and budgeting, O&OD, an acronym for Opportunities and Obstacles to Development, is now the required methodology for the production of the village plans that feed into the district planning cycle. The institutionalisation of participatory approaches in Tanzania is not simply a product of donor interventions. Commitment to participation is part of a long-standing discourse of national development that anticipates more recent technologies of participatory development (Samoff 1979; Jennings 2003, 2007; Moore 1977) by more than a decade. Not only were some of the core approaches now associated with participatory development first devised in Tanzania (Hall 1992, 2005; Swantz & Green 2009),[2] they continue to perform important work within a state originally constituted as an object of development under a League of Nations mandate and for whom development, now encompassed within the reduction of poverty, remains the primary objective of the national Development Vision.[3]

Participation was defined as a developmental good in Tanzania in the 1960s. It has consistently occupied a central place within the Tanzanian political imaginary as action that, as instrument and outcome of development, is the embodiment of nation-building (Samoff 1979: 33; Marsland 2006; Jennings 2007). Commitment to participation through a range of institutional forms as a core attribute of the developmental state is enshrined in current national frameworks (PORALG 2002; Chaligha 2008: 7). The adoption of participatory approaches to the planning and management of development interventions by government agencies and civil-society organisations is well established as a preferred means

---

[1] It was formally announced in 2002 but not actually implemented as the national approach until 2006 (Pallotti 2008, 227).

[2] Personal communications, Marjorie Mbilinyi and Marja Liisa Swantz.

[3] See the Tanzania Development Vision 2025 (URT n.d.).

through which communities can be brought practically and representationally into the development process. Despite efforts to engage citizens in development through participatory institutions and the use of more specialised development technologies of community inclusion over a thirty-year period, it is far from evident that this translates into increased commitment to the investment and maintenance of public infrastructure, let alone the reduction of poverty (see also Li 2007b; Lange 2008; Jennings 2007: 91). Legal instruments such as by-laws are routinely invoked to enforce compliance with government demands for participation in development in many districts. Yet despite the substantial transaction and financial costs associated with lengthy participatory planning and problem identification exercises, they not only continue to be advocated by government and donor organisations, but have become part of the normative expectations, especially among rural citizens, that 'development' and 'participation' are mutually constitutive. This chapter considers why this is the case.

I suggest that participatory methods have traction in Tanzania, and in places like it, not because they make development better but for other reasons. The hybrid of institutional forms and standard practices encompassed by the category of participatory methods and approaches has significant representational effects (Hart 2001: 655; Williams 2004; Craig & Porter 1997) encapsulating the hierarchical relationships between central and local governments, between ordinary citizens and the administrative elite, and between the poor and the national project of development.[4] These include creating an impression of community engagement in the form of reports, action plans and budgets that delineate the relation of local communities as villages to higher tiers of government; the association of communities with poverty and hence as constraints on national development; and their relation to time, which situates development in a future unattainable through communities' failure to act. Representational effects, however useful, do not fully account for the persistence of participatory forms. Examining aspects of three large-scale participatory exercises carried out in Tanzania over the past decade, I suggest that participatory forms here, as in international development more generally, come to operate as 'boundary objects' that, in effecting the possibilities of translation between disparate communities of meaning, and hence offering a means through which divergent interests can be enrolled in a common activity (Star & Griesemer 1989: 392), constitute tangible artefacts for the orientation of development practice.

---

[4] Samoff's (1979) insights on what he called the 'bureaucratic bourgeoisie' remain applicable here, although members of this category are increasingly likely to come from the expanding civil-society sector, some of whom are 'volunteers'; that is, they are paid only for projects implemented for as long as the organisations with which they are associated are in receipt of funding.

## Boundary objects in international development

According to Star and Griesemer, boundary objects are artefacts, practices, representations and technologies that are shared across two or more distinct epistemic communities (ibid.: 393). Boundary objects acquire status through recognition across distinct interpretive communities, enabling them to transcend core differences in interpretation and practice for the purpose of the alignments required to perform particular work. Methodological standardisation is a significant characteristic of boundary objects, which require a degree of stability about what particular objects connote (ibid.: 393–410; Bowker & Star 2000: 16). Examples of boundary objects pertinent, but not confined, to international development include budgets, time lines and targets (Yakura 2002); maps, reporting styles and visual representations (Star & Griesemer 1989: 405–7); concepts and categories, as in the 'village' (Pigg 1992: 504) or 'most vulnerable children' (MVC) (Green 2011); and the special practices devised for programme design and implementation (Sapsed & Salter 2004).

Participatory forms as boundary objects create the possibilities for groups with divergent perspectives and interests to enter into temporary collaborations around shared objects of management. These kinds of collaborations, initially theorised in studies of scientific working across dispersed communities (e.g. Star & Griesemer 1989; Bowker & Star 2000; Bowker 2005; Latour & Woolgar 1986), are fundamental to international development . Development's managed interventions as projects – that is, the costed bundles of relations intended to produce specific outcomes – are premised on a basic organisational division between developer and developee, that is, between those making an intervention and those who are supposed to benefit from it, reiterated at different scales, as well as that between representatives of diverse agencies, organisations and disciplinary perspectives within and outside the country of implementation (Pigg 1992; Craig & Porter 1997). Division is not merely built in, as Albert Hirschman realised in his classic study of development projects, to the very organisation of development – it is essential for its operation (1967: 46).

Boundary objects as artefacts through which alignments can be effected are not only representationally interesting. They have obvious political implications (Law & Mol 2008). Participation is made to work as a boundary object because stakeholders committed to international development require a common object that can be 'bought into', literally in the form of financial transfers, and conceptually in terms of the kinds of interventions that can be legitimately (that is, morally) supported. The fact that participation can operate within statist top-down or devolved neoliberal programming, as well as within emancipatory discourses of liberation and learning, makes it especially durable in this regard (Craig

& Porter 1997; Cornwall 2004). Participatory approaches in Tanzania operate as boundary objects between multiple categories simultaneously: between international donors and the national development community, between transnational civil society and its local forms, and between national government and those defined through it as local communities and thus as agents and subjects of development.

While status as boundary object can be ascribed to participation as an abstract concept, a moral good associated with positive democratic and sustainability effects, and as a value around which disparate institutions and individuals can cohere, there is a technical dimension to boundary objects that enhances their tangibility. This is the effect of standardisation and the centrality of methods that are shared across collaborating epistemic communities. Knowing *how* is more effective as a translation device than knowing *why*, because a number of different rationales can comfortably support the same technologies (Star & Griesemer 1989: 407). Technologies of participatory development around community-based research and mobilisation are highly standardised, not only in Tanzania but internationally. This standardisation and the increasing formalisation of participation within a restricted set of practices affects the opportunities participatory institutions could potentially present for innovative approaches to problem-solving or for political debate (Klodawsky 2007) and, by extension, for the broader project of development. In closing down the discursive frame through tightly controlled facilitation and problem specification rather than the open-ended iteration of the action research from which these methods originated (Hall 1992), the routinisation of participatory methods may inhibit innovative approaches to problem-solving through dealing with the unanticipated; what Albert Hirschmann called the 'hidden hand' of development creativity (1967: 35). In relation to local-government planning, not only is participation restricted by the constrictive framing between 'problem-making and policy-solving' – to invert Hirschman's phrase (1967: 4) – but financial shortfalls combined with the doctrines of sustainability and self-reliance (cf. Swidler & Watkins 2009) mean that what is planned is rarely implemented, rendering participation in planning both the end and the core activity of village-level local government.[5]

## Participation in development

What are categorised within academic and practitioner literatures as participatory 'methods' and 'approaches' are now commonplace within

---

[5] Planning has always been a core activity of all levels of government in Tanzania, although participation prior to the reform process was associated with the Village Development Committee meeting as the primary institutional form. For accounts of village-level planning in the 1970s, see Schneider (2007), Rigby (1977) and Moore (1977, 1988), and for the 1980s Eriksen (1997).

international development practice (Brett 2003; Cleaver 1999; Cornwall 2006). Used as a means of incorporating a wider representation of stakeholders into project organisational forms, and for the production of local knowledge through the collection of data involving perceptions of informants that can be aggregated within a spatially circumscribed social situation (Amin 2005, 618), their routinisation has led to, and been fostered by, a burgeoning global community of participatory practice comprising individuals from universities, research institutes, civil-society and development organisations. A vast practitioner literature now exists, along with an expanding warehouse of techniques and 'tools' for a plethora of participatory activities. These encompass appraisal, research and evaluation, and more recent introductions such as participatory expenditure tracking (PETS).

The labels 'participatory methods or approach' apply to a variety of different practices and ways of organising those included as participants (Cornwall & Jewkes 1995; Campbell 2002, 2001; Cleaver 1999). It is helpful to distinguish between what might be termed their instrumental orientation – what the participatory dimension is claimed *for* – and the specific practices that comprise it. The former is what characterises participatory approaches in the sense that interventions claimed as participatory are claimed as such because of the assumed effects of their utilisation (Robins et al. 2008: 1069–70). These normative claims are not unitary, ranging from a liberatory perspective that views participation as a potentially transformative strategy affecting the subjectivities of those engaged in it through learning and reflection (Hall 2005; Chambers 1983, 1994) to the more pragmatic mobilising aspirations of participatory instruments as a means of achieving the inclusion of target groups within project managerial frames.

Those working within an activist orientation are likely to insist on a meaningful distinction between participatory *approaches* as potentially transformative, and participatory *methods* as simply instrumental (Pain & Francis 2003: 46). Actual practice defies clear categorisation. It is recognised by activists and practitioners that the practices subsumed under either label may look identical and make use of the same sets of organisational tools. What matters, they argue, is the intention underlying the endeavour (Cornwall & Jewkes 1995). Therefore, participatory research methods can be claimed as either enabling local ownership of a research agenda that, because it reflects community interests, can be presented as less extractive, or they may be perceived more instrumentally as a 'quick and dirty' means of getting 'good enough' information about an issue or area fairly rapidly (Richards 1995). What matters here, as in social research more generally, is not then actual differences in terms of what is done or of the 'methods' themselves, which are neither technical nor disinterested, but how certain practices and interventions are presented and interpreted by implementers and participants (Law 2004).

Participatory methods and approaches within development such as Participatory Rural Appraisal (PRA) and Participatory Learning and Action (PLA) have much in common with counterpart technologies now standardised in management sciences, adult education and community research internationally (Bartunek 1993; Cooke & Cox 2005). Sharing common origins in the social inquiry of Paulo Freire and a commitment to participant ownership of interventions directed towards change, knowledge is conceptualised as generated by participants and as transformative of a situation that is rendered comprehensible through participatory action. At its most basic this can simply involve a group of people engaging in discussion around perceived problems and constraints with a view to altering either their situation or response to it (Hall 2005). Participatory outcomes in development as the anticipated result of these kinds of discursive process have come to be associated with the particular institutional forms designed to facilitate them. These tend to be extremely formalised as a package of techniques and organisational templates intended to generate certain outputs over a period of time. Facilitators, assistant facilitators and key informants work through a sequence of analytical and data-gathering stages in collaboration with representatives from beneficiary groups. The aim is the production of information about people and place that can be accorded the status of local knowledge (Mohan & Stokke 2000: 252) and hence as generative of local ownership and implied sustainability of an investment perceived to be based on local realities. Where local knowledge is deemed too general to be immediately useful, these techniques are used to narrow knowledge down so as to be amenable to incorporation into the programmatical interventions of project forms.

Participatory methods and approaches in development occupy an ambiguous position as institutional forms that can operate as management technologies, and hence as modalities for governance, *and* as potentially transformative institutions through which participants could confront and challenge existing systems of knowledge and organisation (Cornwall 2004). The fact that they can be either, depending on how they are appropriated and by whom – that is, the ideological context of their implementation (Craig & Porter 1997) – has contributed to the chasm of interpretation within and beyond the practitioner community, a division articulated in the claims that there are essential differences between participatory *approaches*, which are intrinsically liberatory, and participatory *methods*, which are inherently instrumental, even though both may use identical tools and modalities of organising participants (Cornwall 2004; Pain & Francis 2003). In actuality, as is clearly the case in Tanzania, the discourse of transformation persists even where participatory systems are extremely bureaucratic and offer little scope for devolved direction. O&OD is justified on the lead ministry website in terms of community empowerment.[6] To some extent these

---

[6] www.pmoralg.go.tz/menu-data/programmes/O-OD, accessed June 14 2014.

moral attributes are artefacts of participation as an abstract value. From this perspective, which views participation as a moral good, the fact that its assumed transformative effects are perceived to inhere within a restricted range of accepted institutional forms (van der Riet 2008) explains the kind of criticism to which apparently 'failed' participation is subjected when its sought-after effects are not brought into being (see for example Hickey & Mohan 2005; Cooke & Kothari 2001; Leal 2007). This is to be expected. As Robins et al. make plain, neither proponents nor critics of participation have paid adequate attention to what actually happens when so-called participatory approaches are carried out by real people in real places. In working within the dominant conceptual frames of governance, rights and accountability associated with the 'democracy industry', they have thus prioritised the normative over the empirical (Robins et al. 2008: 1069; see also Pain & Francis 2003; Fraser 1992).

The interpretative chasm between proponents of participation as liberatory and those who believe that at best it fails to achieve its potential is articulated not so much as a critique of the claims made *for* participation, which are shared in some form or other by many of those critiquing it, but of actually existing participatory forms (Robins et al. 2008).[7] Far fewer studies interrogate the epistemologies of participatory approaches, the kinds of methods used and the representational effects of its trademark 'epistemic forms' (Osborne 2004: 436–7; Campbell 2001, 2002; Kapoor 2002). Accounts of participatory practice tend to focus on shortfalls in the inclusivity of participatory forms and the extent to which emancipatory potentialities are lost through the power imbalances inherent in elite-dominated implementation or through depoliticisation (Leal 2007). Some of these criticisms are valid. But so are claims made by advocates and practitioners (Williams 2004). While participatory forms can doubtless provide a forum for the elite hijacking of local agendas (e.g. Mosse 1994; 2005; Cooke & Kothari 2001), they can equally constitute a space and time for critical reflection on practice that is genuinely transformative of social subjectivities (Kesby 2005; Cahill 2007; Hall 1992). Open-ended iterative action research that is driven forward by participants has quite different potentialities than the Rapid Rural Appraisal (RRA) type of undertaking that aims to confirm planners' expectations about core livelihood and land use strategies in a small area (Klodawsky 2007: 2849).

As combinations of organisational form and specialised practices deemed to generate participatory effects, participatory approaches in development are neither method nor organisation but mobile institutions, travelling technologies of the social, that can be instantiated in any place at any time to produce their anticipated outputs. These take the form of the reports and prioritisations that can be translated into project plans and budgets to be enacted at different scales. Examination of three iterations of this institutional form in Tanzania provides an opportunity to

---

[7] See for example Cooke & Kothari (2001); Hickey & Mohan (2005); Brett (2003).

explore some other aspects of participatory practices of which, arguably, participation is the least significant. It also sheds light on the recurrent limitations of participatory approaches against the grand claims made for them. It is far from certain that expectations about transformation as an inevitable outcome of participation abstractly conceived can ever be realised in practice.[8] There are two reasons for this: first, as I have shown, the ultimately philosophical assertion about normative outcomes of participative deliberation that derives from democratic theory, and second, the content of participatory practices within participatory forms, especially where these are rigidly organised to preclude participative deliberation and iterative open-ended dialogue around the politics of problem solving.

## Participatory forms in Tanzania

Participatory institutions are not a fast track to an on-demand 'public sphere' of the kind imagined as an ideal type by Habermas (Fraser 1992). Their effects depend on the extent to which their institutional form permits deliberative discourse and, of course, on their situation within structures of politics and power (Cleaver 2007; Corbridge et al. 2005; Kesby 2005). In Tanzania, participatory approaches to rural development are popularly perceived as a means of project implementation. They are, in the words of an informant familiar with 'Green Revolution' terminology, a 'hybrid of method (*mbinu*) and project (*miradi*)' intended to sensitise beneficiaries to their responsibility within the sustainability paradigm, rather than a means of fostering innovation through new thinking. Participatory forms in Tanzania have become highly formalised over the past twenty years, at the same time as they have become ever more ubiquitous in practices promoted by government, development partners and civil-society organisations (CSOs). Large-scale donor engagement in Tanzania has contributed to their embedding in recognisable packages of form and practice that can be promoted as a value-added component of supported interventions. The accompanying proliferation of training, seminars, workshops and materials means that many government staff, including representatives of village-level government, have some familiarity with what are termed *mbinu shirikishi*, literally translated as 'participatory methods'. So do many rural residents as participants, either as representatives of communities and villages or as people with some kind of involvement in the proliferating number of district-based CSOs.

'Participatory' (*shirikishi*) and 'participation' (*ushirikiano*) have long been politicised terms in Tanzania, connoting popular inclusivity without specification of institutional form. Participation has been associated with meetings, electoral representation and with the financial or labour

---

[8] But see Kesby (2005) and Cahill (2007) for a contrasting perspective.

contributions (*michango*) to state-facilitated public goods (Marsland 2006; Samoff 1979; Moore 1977, 1988). The participatory methods now associated with development projects that combine the populist inclusivity of prior forms of participation with innovative ways of engaging in group discussion, something halfway between a seminar and a meeting, appear truly at home in the national development consciousness. The seemingly natural affinity between Tanzanian governmentality and participatory methods is strengthened by their shared history. Indeed, the continued claim to national ownership of participation as a characteristically Tanzanian way of doing development, as developmental in itself (Samoff 1989), has legitimated their widespread acceptance in the country. This has been considerably enhanced in Tanzania, as in other poor countries, by the culture of incentivisation surrounding participation in development through the payment of allowances (*posho*), although this is not the only factor.[9]

The kinds of participatory methods first developed in Tanzania in the late 1960s and the early 1970s were very different from the standardised packages now being implemented. The former were exploratory endeavours that aimed to involve local people in defining their own concerns and agendas for research and action (Hall 1992, 2001, 2005; Swantz et al 2001; Swantz & Green 2009).[10] These were often in conflict with top-down development initiatives. Originally conceptualised within an animation paradigm associated with adult education and social pedagogy, these emphasised popular leadership in taking issues forward analytically and in terms of practical action. Researchers influenced by Paulo Freire, who was invited to Tanzania in 1971 (Hall 1992: 18), sought to establish a collaboration between themselves and other citizens in a shared commitment to socialist nation building.[11] Nyerere's commitment to inclusive approaches that transformed the knowledge of the poor, the influence of radical academics working at the University of Dar es Salaam and the emergent professional developments sector enabled a space in which research-driven experimentation could flourish and be influential.[12] This proved to be short-lived. The action research community in Tanzania became increasingly drawn in to development projects initiated by the state and donor organisations. Participatory approaches were

---

[9] Participation here must be differentiated from what is also called participation by government but which refers to communities making contributions for development. For an account of these differences, see Marsland 2006.

[10] Interview with Marja Liisa Swantz, June 2009.

[11] Personal communication, Marjorie Mbilinyi.

[12] Budd Hall, who worked in Tanzania at the time, confirms the personal influence of Julius Nyerere on the emergence of participatory approaches. According to Hall, Nyerere 'used to say that "poor people do not use money for a weapon ... they use ideas and leadership"'. Hall continues: 'When Paulo Freire and Mwalimu Nyerere met for the first time (facilitated by Paul Mkaiki with me [Hall] as a 'fly on the wall'), he acknowledged that Mwalimu Nyerere's thoughts on development, on education, on participatory planning were the most extensive applications of the kinds of ideas that he himself experienced in the "*movomiento de base*" in north-east Brazil that he had seen'. Budd Hall, personal communication.

incorporated into donor funded initiatives undertaken by the ministries of planning and culture during the 1970s and were increasingly routinised, formulaic and bureaucratised. At the same time participatory approaches were being globalised through networks seeking to share practice (Hall 2005), a movement that was overtaken by the increasing standardisation and professionalisation of participatory methodologies (Chambers 1994).[13]

Participatory forms in international development have become domains of specialist expertise associated with specific templates of techniques for participatory working (Cornwall 2006). These approaches are largely modelled on a set of accepted tools associated with Participatory Learning and Action and a means of organisation that entails a division between facilitators and facilitated, locals and outsiders, working through a fairly set sequence of activities intended to generate a representation of consensus. This template informs the design of three participatory processes implemented in Tanzania between 2003 and 2008 that can be taken to be paradigmatic examples of participatory forms. These are a national Participatory Poverty Assessment (PPA), undertaken as part of the Government's poverty-monitoring system between 2002 and 2003 (Green & Waterhouse 2006); a multi-district initiative supporting CSOs to undertake participatory action research in communities between 2003 and 2008; and, finally, the ongoing local-government planning system, O&OD.

## The Participatory Poverty Assessment

The national PPA was initiated at the height of the mainstream donor conversion to participatory approaches following on from the World Bank 'Voices of the Poor' study, which had included Tanzania (Narayan 1998; Narayan et al. 2000). Promoted vigorously by international donors keen to see a replication of the Uganda PPA in a country with broad commitment to a poverty reduction strategy (PRS), the PPA was intended to provide methodological legitimacy to the new national project of poverty-monitoring as part of the institutional architecture of the PRS (Green & Waterhouse 2006). It essentially replicated PRAs at multiple sites to create a national social portrait of poverty. Implemented by a cohort of specially trained personnel, many drawn from among CSOs, under the direction of the same technical expert who had previously overseen the exercise in Uganda, the initiative was designed to contribute to a policy consensus among development partners and government representatives about the priorities for the second iteration of the PRS. It was also intended to contribute to national capacity-building in partic-

---

[13] Also by the decreasing time scales in which it was conducted. The shift from participatory appraisal to *rapid* appraisal has consequences for the open-endedness of these approaches (interview with Marja Liisa Swantz, June 2009).

ipatory approaches. While the national PPA process was innovative in its explicit utilisation of the politics of knowledge, implicating demand within the research paradigm as the future users of policy findings were intentionally contracted to carry out the research, it adhered to a limited portfolio of methods associated with participatory appraisal. These centred on a particular local area, a concept of community as participants, and included focus groups, wealth-ranking, transect walks, seasonal calendars and preference-ranking. The process associated with participation is time-consuming. Teams spent around one week in each of the 30 study villages.

The problem to be investigated did not emerge from participants' concerns but from a prior policy orientation that had a clear commitment to the identification of 'vulnerable groups' in order to inform the second PRS, the National Strategy for Growth and the Reduction of Poverty. The concern with vulnerability was influenced by the World Bank's theorisation of the distinction between poverty, which people can escape through economic opportunity, and 'vulnerability', which is recognised as determined by structural constraints. Vulnerable categories and persons thus require additional support either until they can become self-sufficient, or long-term if they fall into the category of legitimate dependency, for example older persons and young children. The objective of the PPA was therefore data collection rather than analysis. There was little scope for either participants or facilitators to influence the orientation of the exercise or contribute to the analysis. Tools captured static information, descriptions of places and situations. They did not access why such situations existed or how certain individuals came to be affected by them. The final report, oriented solely towards the question of vulnerability, imposed a livelihoods analysis on this description to present a picture of individuals within certain social categories as vulnerable to shocks and trends without which they would be more resilient and hence experience less poverty.

## Community action research with civil society organisations

The programme of action research into community problems conducted by district-based CSOs was financed by a leading national research centre, itself in receipt of development partner basket-funding. Over a period of five years from 2003 some 70 district-based CSOs carried out research on community issues in some 40 villages across seven districts in the country. Representatives of these organisations, usually senior staff or 'volunteers',[14] took part in a two-week training programme where they were

---

[14] Members of local organisations and 'civil society' refer to themselves as volunteers when they are working for a project even if the project is funded because volunteering signifies the fact that they do not have a permanent contract or source of funds. When there are no funds

taught basic participatory methods by trainers with considerable professional experience of major participatory initiatives in Tanzania. Additional guidance was provided by a 'technical committee' comprising individuals who had gained experience of participatory programming in the country. Once they had been trained, organisations sought villages in which they could conceptualise and implement a participatory research project with a beneficiary community, not necessarily within the same sector in which their organisation was active. Projects were selected based on the submission of proposals and funded through the research organisation. An initial proposal, itself generated through participatory techniques of problem-ranking, became the basis of a two-week village project of action research oriented towards understanding the problem prioritised, and producing an action plan for the interventions to address it.

The training programme emphasised a standardised approach to problem identification and solving using a sequenced set of tools aimed at prioritising community problems and demonstrating solutions likely to be effected through defined inputs. The programme rapidly lost its initial research focus and evolved into an exercise in participatory planning as the basis for producing a request for funding, something with which villagers and local government felt extremely comfortable. The research in communities focused on a problem identified through the participatory exercises of group discussion, voting and ranking. Trained in PRA methodology to feed into project design, the village studies became the basis of action plans as outputs justified by the research. Rigid adherence to the methods template ensured that there was little scope for the emergence of new issues or understanding. Reports produced through the process frequently reiterated issues that were already part of pre-existing village plans.

## Opportunities and obstacles to development

Opportunities and obstacles to development (O&OD) originates in the same kinds of processes that have informed these other initiatives, and through the intellectual and financial inputs of many of the same individuals and organisations.[15] Adopted as the methodology for local-

(cont.) these people do indeed 'volunteer' because work has to be put into securing the next tranche of funding. When there is funding related to a specific project or activity they take an allowance that may be equivalent to a salary, but continue to think of themselves as volunteers. This is also the case in Malawi (Swidler & Watkins 2009). This situation is described in more detail in Chapter 6.

15 UNICEF is claimed as being influential in the dissemination of the O&OD method and in persuading the government to adopt it. Individuals who have experience of such methods within the UNICEF programme, not necessarily inside UNICEF, had also been involved with other major projects in Tanzania, including the *Jipemoyo* initiative implemented by the Ministry of Culture in the 1980s and the Finnish-funded RIPS project that ran for around 20 years from the 1980s in the south of the country. Interview with Marja Liisa Swantz June 2009.

level planning in 2001, before it had been fully piloted, the intention was to reduce the high transaction costs of having multiple, often donor-funded systems for stakeholder inclusion in problem identification by having a single standard of practice (Cooksey & Kikula 2005). Its adoption was also clearly influenced by pressure from donors, including UNICEF, which had been a strong advocate of participatory approaches over many years in Tanzania, and the various co-funders of the Local Government Reform Programme. A number of these had previously contributed to participatory interventions, including: the United Kingdom, which, along with other donors, had supported the PPA; Finland, which had a long-term history of participatory development through its RIPS project in Mtwara; and Ireland, which, as we saw in Chapter 2, had promoted participatory approaches in its district development programmes. The lead ministry responsible for local government has worked to achieve a degree of standardisation together with technical inputs from various donors through the production of field guides and manuals, training courses and the dissemination of a coherent rationale for participatory planning. It is not clear how far this standardisation is actually achieved. In any event, financial constraints mean that not all local government authorities can afford to implement full-blown O&OD exercises that take at least seven days for each village, every three to five years. Some districts, Magu for example, simply build on pre-existing plans through village meetings.[16] Others, for example Mbulu in the north of the country, have adapted the standard methodology to enable the exercise to be completed more rapidly.

Like the other participatory exercises, O&OD is centred on the residents of a village as participants in a facilitated process that aims to produce an understanding of priorities and commitments as the basis of village plans. The policy rationale is the identification of the resources that exist in a local area and hence opportunities that can be mobilised for development through the creation of local ownership, which contributes to sustainability. Like other participatory approaches in Tanzania, O&OD relies on a package of sequenced activities intended to generate the information required for the development of a suitable local plan. These are derived from the PRA library and include the use of focus groups selected on the basis of social category, village meetings, annual calendars, seasonal activity charts, gender resource maps, wealth-ranking, transect walks, and institutional mapping.[17] Voting and ranking feature prominently through such techniques as 'pairwise-ranking' as a means of transitioning descriptions towards preferences and preferences to choices that can be transformed into actions and budgets (Campbell 2001, 2002). Claimed local prioritisation is less evident from the plans produced and the

[16] Interview with planning officer, Magu District, April 2009.
[17] See the list of tools provided at the website of the Prime Minister's Office Regional Affairs and Local Government in a document titled 'Historical Perspective on Participatory Planning in Tanzania', http://pv01.pmoralg.go.tz/documents_storage/2007-4-21-3-2-22_historical.pdf, accessed 28 June 2014.

sectoral investments at village level that appear in district budgets. The O&OD process situates village prioritisation within the sectoral frame of the National Development Vision 2025 in which health and education take pride of place, and which firmly situates village aspirations within national and district budgetary processes augmented by new sources of infrastructural support.[18] Local plans then focus on village contributions to these investments (Lange 2008; Harrison 2008). In this, as in other aspects of its practice, O&OD reiterates antecedent forms of local-level planning (Eriksen 1997; Rigby 1977).

## Commonalities

The three participatory processes described here were designed independently, but there is substantial overlap between them. This is not only due to the similarity in methods and approach and their situation within the national discourse of participative development. They have a shared ancestry in terms of the personnel and institutions involved in their implementation. The poverty think-tank that commissioned the action research with CSOs had been involved in oversight of the PPA process through its role as the secretariat of the research and analysis working group of the poverty-monitoring system. Training for the community organisations was provided by staff at the University of Dar es Salaam and other contracted individuals, some of whom had worked with well-known participatory programmes including the Finnish-supported RIPS project in Mtwara and Lindi. The RIPS approach to participatory planning in villages was informed by the work of Robert Chambers, who provided some consultancy inputs to the programme. Experience from RIPS through core personnel in the relevant ministry informed the design and approach of O&OD.[19]

Each of the three processes took the village as a local area and unit of engagement from which individuals could be selected as representative of specific social categories to participate through meetings and focus groups. All were organised through a basic division between external facilitators and informants, and all made use of a standard portfolio of participatory techniques for the collection, presentation and organisation of informants and information. The overlap between what are in fact discrete participatory exercises is experienced by participants. Villagers in Moshi rural, interviewed as part of an evaluation of the action research conducted by CSOs, spontaneously formed themselves into a participatory-style focus

---

[18] Health and education are currently prioritised because of the availability of sectoral funding for infrastructure through successive education development projects and the Tanzania Social Action Fund (TASAF). These investments require joint funding, with a specified proportion as a community contribution. Participatory planning here facilitates the legitimation of this contribution, and incorporates these objectives within district plans and community priorities.

[19] Personal communication, Marja Liisa Swantz.

group, but could not differentiate between that exercise and the village government O&OD exercise that had preceded it.

Facilitators in all three processes were usually local-government or development organisation personnel with a very basic level of training in participatory methods. This training was often delivered as part of the participatory exercise. Facilitators did not have backgrounds in social research or analysis. Many were familiar with proposal-writing and community planning. The training that facilitators received focused on the transfer of a basic set of techniques that could be easily replicated for the collection of information. How to analyse what was collected was not addressed. This was partly because of the ideology of participatory approaches, which emphasised that the priority of local knowing could be invalidated by external analysis, and partly because the tools used were expected to produce an analysis through their insertion into a narrative structure working through descriptions of social organisation, economy, inequality and so on within the village community (see below).[20]

Participatory approaches in all three processes were conceived as technical interventions, literally as 'tools', that would produce certain results systematically. Knowing how to use the tools was considered to be sufficient to undertake the process, hence the brief training with an emphasis on replicable techniques as adequate for equipping personnel with the necessary skills to engage with research participants. The civil-society programme was overseen by a 'technical committee', the PPA by a 'technical adviser'. The technical orientation of participatory approaches here is related to the discourse of the technical in development planning and policy work more generally, which is pronounced in Tanzania (e.g., Eriksen 1997). It is also a feature of regimes of development knowledge that seek to occlude the politics of the social through what Li has termed 'rendering technical' (2007a: 7). In recent development technologies the social is effectively reconstituted as a set of standard places, problems and solutions through such evaluative frameworks as CWIQs (Core Welfare Indicators Questionnaires), PRAs and PSIAs (Poverty and Social Impact Assessments) which, for all their asserted simplicity, demand specialised expertise and ways of seeing.[21]

With the exception of the district departmental staff trained as part of O&OD facilitation teams, who were likely to have some kind of future involvement in the villages where the process was conducted, facilitators were involved in these participatory exercises on a one-off basis. Where the exercises had explicit capacity-building dimensions, this was oriented towards the capacities of interstitial personnel to facilitate participatory exercises in villages, rather than the capacities of villagers. Facilitators

[20] Chambers, for example, in his overview of participatory approaches and methods does not differentiate between analysis and the participatory exercise. The methods he describes are presented as *inherently* analytical because they involve the participation of local people (1994).

[21] CWIQs and PSIAs are used extensively by World Bank country programmes.

saw themselves as persons newly skilled in techniques that could benefit villagers through helping them to understand their problems and make plans to address them. They did not see themselves as learning from villagers, or participation as an exercise in mutual transformation. In the areas where the exercises were undertaken, these individuals were not actually structurally powerful. They were technical staff for whom acquisition of competencies in the application of participatory tools was another technical accomplishment that could help them move further along in the development sector. Their learning and reflection, if it occurred, would be taken elsewhere and applied generally. It would not inform local power dynamics or ways of working. Training in participatory methods was a step in their anticipated professionalisation as development personnel. For the representatives of district CSOs, vulnerably interstitial between unpaid volunteering and paid project staff and between the rural and urban middle classes, this was extremely attractive (Swidler & Watkins 2009).

Participatory processes focus on a spatial understanding of the local as territorially located, not as situated within a broader nexus of influences that impact on livelihoods and choices (for example Cornwall & Jewkes 1995; Hart 2001). Villages as the lowest tier in the vertical hierarchy of governance are not only targets of development and government interventions. Villages as communities in the Tanzanian system are responsible for enacting development through levies and contributions. Villages as places where communities live are both agents and objects of development. The identification of issues affecting communities is politically salient as an act of responsibilisation here, as identifying those for which communities can be held responsible, or which they can potentially address with inputs (Rose 1999: 172, 2000: 1400; Amin 2005: 619; Harrison 2008). The process seeks to establish constraints and opportunities for development, determining the possibilities for local inputs to address community deficits, and outlining where deficiencies require investments of a different order. Issues are then presented in standardised ways in reports that present them as community issues. Reports generated through such activities present very simple problem analyses based on vertical causal chains, a 'pollarded' problem tree that presents problems and solutions as directly related. Low income in one village is an outcome of poor education linked in turn to the absence of a village secondary school. In another, poverty is associated with lack of available domestic water and the drain this causes to the potential agricultural productivity of women. In these reports and analyses public goods are equated with public services – health with dispensaries, education with school buildings, transport with roads within a specific place. Issues of value, pricing, access, the ways in which residents use facilities across locations and how actual economies work are not brought into the frame.

With group work oriented towards reduction through prioritisations, and hence the elimination of complexity, there was little scope for the kind of deliberation that could lead to different kinds of understanding. These findings and priorities are reflected in the written reports that form the basis of village plans and budgets submitted upwards to the next level of the government system. The end points are simple things that can be related to other things, cause and effect, programming possibilities, inputs and outcomes. The simple lines of cause and effect in these analyses are partly a consequence of participatory tools that seek to convert problems into solutions, and hence into outputs for project management. They are accentuated by the need to have easy-to-administer techniques that will produce the same effects in village after village within a specified time. Finally, certain effects require certain causes because government policy is poised to recognise them through sector programmes. The policy integration of O&OD in which the goal and purpose of the village plans are derived from the Tanzania Development Vision 2025 ensures that village priorities are national priorities and hence that the plans made by village governments contributes to the project of national development.

## Simplification through certainty

Participatory approaches derived from Freirian action-learning prioritise critical reflection (e.g., Chambers 1983). The self is transformed through a political engagement that constitutes a changed subjectivity with an enhanced capacity to act. Once participatory transformation is assumed to take place outside the subjectivity of individual consciousness, it has to be situated within actionable events. There needs to be the illusion of potential agency. Simple cause and effect relations that can be addressed with accessible actions and inputs existing in the real world are the foundation of plans that could be realised subject to resources being allocated. The straightforward transformation of social issues into costed action plans belies the apparent complexity of social realities in Tanzania and the drawn-out process through which the material is generated. Indeed, what characterises reports of participatory processes and the plans that follow is their simplicity (Campbell 2001, 2002; Eriksen 1997): the presentation of simplified relations of cause and effect. The banality of what such approaches produce is notable (Li 2007b: 283). There are good reasons for this. The first is to do with what these approaches are oriented towards, which is the production of knowledge that can be represented as consensual and thus is that to which everybody can agree. It is the kind of knowledge that almost goes without saying because it is what everybody knows. Facilitation aims to articulate this knowledge through the elimination of what cannot be claimed as shared. This is why participatory methods emphasise voting and ranking as methods of elimination, excluding that which is not deemed relevant because it cannot be claimed for community. Second, and related to this, these tools are designed to *reduce* not enhance complexity. These processes emphasise conclusions and consensus, the tangible 'take aways' that can be included in documentation (Campbell 2002, 2001; Cornwall & Jewkes 1995) and materialised in budgeted plans. The intention, explicable within the evolution of participatory approaches within technical paradigms about development knowledge and agricultural research, and within the aspiration to make investments address objective problems, is to generate a kind of para-scientific certainty (Star 1985).

Producing participatory knowledge takes time not because it is complex but because of the necessity for simplification (Cornwall & Jewkes 1995: 1673). This works through a process of formalisation as initially fuzzy knowledge is fixed and framed, a shift from open-ended debate to closure, from uncertainty to common knowledge, from contested possibilities to community priorities.[22] Processes that are worked through facilitated consensus and cumulative simplification progressively edit out complexity. Ambiguity is not tolerated by techniques that seek to eliminate 'blank spaces' (Campbell 2001: 25). The practice of participation entails organising successive groups and stages into processes of elimination, of simplification. Although what seems at first sight to characterise participatory process in general is the provision of spaces in which participants can engage in various forms of deliberation, acknowledging the conditions in which this deliberation can or cannot occur is critical (Kesby 2005). Spaces are not inherently open. Created spaces imply boundaries and closure of various sorts (Cornwall 2004). Bringing to a conclusion, prioritisation, preference-ranking and so on, are rendered visual through mapping and pictorial representation, performing consensus and community publicly and graphically (Brosius 2006), a performance often recorded in film and photography to enhance the claims made by community reporting.

This process of closing down the possible scope of interpretation is not only associated with the final stages of the participatory process.[23] Framing of the kinds of possibilities the process can be expected to generate occurs at the outset, not necessarily as explicitly as in the PPA, which identified vulnerability as the focus prior to embarking on community work, nor even through the delineation of the local and community orientation, but through the very contents of the participatory tool kit. These tools operate as a categorical construction kit for the production of the rural community as the object of development well beyond Tanzania (Craig & Porter 1997; Pigg 1993). These categories and their implications are not self-evident. This is why training is so prominent in participatory

---

[22] This can be seen as analogous to the transition from structure to anti-structure and re-formalisation characteristic of anthropological accounts of publicly legitimated, often highly ritualised knowledge processes (Douglas 1966).

[23] Accounts of how participants get to prioritisations and the factors that impact on selection are rarely included in reports produced through these processes. Neither are analytical rationales regarding the validity of the particular choices in relation to specific socio-economic condition, for example.

methods, for facilitators and participants. Village residents involved in the civil-society action research remarked on this aspect of participatory engagement.

Because the categorical grid imposed through participatory exercises was so different from ways in which they would ordinarily apprehend their society, they had to be taught to impose it. Participatory sessions were thus likened by participants to 'seminars', to occasions of formal learning. Seminars as the prime educational vehicle through which development is transmitted are an established part of Tanzanian's development infrastructure. Associated with formal training and capacity-building, often with certification for attendance and allowances, seminars became a way of distributing developmental training beyond the civil service in the 1960s when village leaders, executive offers and members of women's groups were suitable targets. This experience of being educated or instructed (*elimishwa*) is of a very different character to the conscientisation imagined within the empowerment discourse of PLA. Participatory sessions frequently take place in village classrooms. Facilitators address groups in styles similar to teaching/directing, in front of the group, asking questions, writing on the board and giving instructions (Marsland 2006: 71). Participants likened the experience of participation to attending a training session, to being instructed. A trainer explained, in relation to community research to be carried out by the civil-society facilitation teams: 'You start with telling them about the concept of development step by step. Understanding leads to planning and they are happy.'

Participants have to learn how to participate in a participatory process, that is, how to perform the specialised tasks associated with the exercise – from pairwise-ranking to transect walks and how to see the community as comprised of particular social categories responding to particular forces. The purpose of these exercises is not to generate new learning and hence produce the unanticipated, but to formalise a kind of knowledge in relation to community as a political category. Community knowledge produced through participatory processes is not new knowledge but a representation of what everybody knows. Reproducing knowledge in a setting associated with learning through the hierarchical enactment of a classroom situation confirms the status of common knowledge as legitimate knowledge, the kind of knowledge that can become officialised as the basis for action through incorporation into official plans. Useful knowledge here is not cumulative in the sense of layered understanding and greater complexity as this develops. Rather it is knowledge pared down to its core components, as each stage of the process renders what is agreed to be categorised as the known less and less contentious (Li 2007b: 283; Campbell 2001: 25: Cornwall & Jewkes 1995: 1673; Pain & Francis 2003: 50).

Designed to literally draw (out) key themes in an imagined agricultural community in which people have shared simple institutions – mosques and churches for example – a local focus and sustainable livelihoods, these select and demarcate what are predetermined as the salient social categories divided by lines of cleavage around gender and assets. Drawing out is often visual, partly due to the emphasis on technologies of inclusion that permit the illiterate to participate, and also because charting findings for public display (and later integration into reports) accords them a reality and status not merely as knowledge but as what knowledge produced through a set of methods and hence as certain kinds of facts. Focus groups therefore have to include those who can be categorised as the most vulnerable because they are defined within the model based on an assumed dependency on an able-bodied adult male farmer – children, orphans, widows, older persons. Transect walks delineate the boundaries of community and the kinds of crops grown by certain kind of people. Livelihoods, like local persons, are confined within strict locational parameters.

Standardisation here, of methods and of categorical frames, imposes a strict interpretive grid on what is collected as data. This in turn is produced according to standard forms, a standardised image of developing communities. The methodological copying of participation as development project produces 'true copies' (Hirschmann 1967: 21) of development's objects in the form of villages that are, subject to slight variation in details, identically arranged. Standardised reporting formats and presentation of findings as facts and checklists permits their easy translation into the numeric form of budgets required by district planning and donor proposals. If such reporting formats add little to understanding of local situations or the multifaceted complexities of rural life and politics, they produce an inscription (Latour 1990: 35) of the process of development, presenting a tangible, mobile impression of participation. Reports as artefacts of participatory processes present participatory process in material form. Findings and preferences can be 'brought to the table' as the perspectives of villagers who are not themselves enabled to engage. This representation of the villagers in maps and tables, and by extension the vulnerable, included through special groupings, in the form of 'voices of the poor' is of a radically different kind than a real representation of villagers at a real table. The disembodied homogenised voice is confined within the report produced through a one-sided dialogue in which powerful institutions do not engage.

## Boundary work

Reports and plans as the impressions of participation are perfect boundary objects, materialising the abstract moral qualities of participation as a development good, and demarcating, through distillation into budget lines representing future projects, the divisions through which development is organised – between international organisations and the national government, between central and local government and between donors and beneficiaries. The reports and priorities produced through participation have a legitimacy because they conform to moral expectations about participation as a method (Hart 2001) that valorises local knowledge, and because they conform to expectations about what this method comprises. The methodological standardisation that characterises participation in Tanzania has several boundary effects beyond recognisability. Standardisation of participation as an approach enables different people to engage in development through participation because the application of methods as template can be adapted quickly and instantiated in new sites with new participants. Not only do these forms give credibility to a project of intervention as appropriately developmental, they allow the enactment of development. This is particularly important where a large proportion of activity categorised as developmental is rather intangible for observers, the kinds of 'enabling' interventions that seek to develop capacity through training and network building, what an informant in a village in Lindi memorably referred to as *miradi ya maneno*, 'projects of words' (see Chapter 5).

Participatory approaches are visible and tangible forms of development in action. They provide a mobile institutional form through which diverse stakeholders can situate themselves within development categories as the right kind of social actors. The form has different meanings for different people and presents different opportunities. For intermediary organisations and civil-society groups who perceive themselves as situated between potential donors and a beneficiary community, engagement as facilitators enables the performance of this anticipated interstitiality. They are likely also to perceive participation here as a form of capacity-building toward the increasing professionalisation of their organisation. District staff members of facilitation teams have similar perspectives. They may also value the extended field visits entailed in exercises that generate allowances for overnight stays. Allowances for villagers are considerably less than for officials and facilitators, if they are paid at all. Some village residents value the opportunity to engage in discussions around development as the performance of responsible citizenship. They may value the learning opportunities presented by participatory exercises. Some enjoy the opportunities for formalised displays of leadership that mark out the beginning and end of the participatory process. Those with less time on their hands can find the demands arduous. Participation tailed off considerably after the first few days of the initial round of O&OD (IDCJ 2006: 43).

Participation remains popular among village residents, not necessarily because of the possibility of allowances, but because it is in some sense a 'trait-taking' (Hirschmann 1967: 128) institution in Tanzania. Based around oratory and the formality of public meeting styles that appear inclusive but within which very few people have the authority to speak and which are deliberative and time taking, participatory approaches as practised in Tanzania can easily conform to pre-existing expectations about political discourse (Moore 1977; Berry 1993). Participation here, as in other settings (Rose 1999, 2000; Amin 2005), assumes an empowerment function within a discourse of responsibilisation, practically and representationally situating villages within the frame of national development while offering the promise of autonomous development within it. Status as participants, as community and hence as potential beneficiaries of development is sought by citizens as villagers or as representative of CSOs as an indication of recognition of one's relation to the state and to the national project of development. While recognition is achieved through taking part in participatory institutions, responsibilisation frequently remains representational. Citizens participate in planning as an opportunity to perform development and their place in it. District governments achieve a devolution of responsibility onto communities through village plans within the organogram of vertical governance. Whether development is materialised or not in the form of planned projects and so on depends on whether other contributions are realised, the resources from central government and donors that communities claim are what prevents their engagement and those required by government from communities in the form of cash and labour, which if not forthcoming hinder the attainment of the Development Vision. For citizens and district governments, planning remains not so much a site where development is effected as a site for the enactment of their relations with each other and with the state (Schneider 2007: 24, 31).

Participatory institutions facilitate the performance of development in Tanzania as a certain kind of practice. They align diverse stakeholders around a set of activities deemed developmental that produce, in the form of plans and budgets, outputs for development activities. They generate representations of undevelopment in the form of village problems that can be addressed by villagers, and they produce in the form of documentation tangible impressions of participation.[24] These attributes of participation in Tanzania are not inevitable effects of participatory forms, which could potentially be put to work quite differently. They are arguably an effect of the ways in which very different interests require some kind of boundary device if they are to continue to collaborate, and of the difficulty of materialising the new development of intangibles with its emphasis on community responsibilities and capacity-building.

International development, perhaps more than other kinds of activities, is constituted through relations of collaboration premised on difference. The very project of development as a transfer of technology, resources and policies between unequal players implies that differentiation is intrinsic to its ordering – the distinction between donor and recipient, between technical expert and client, between countries requiring reform and the institutions regulating the reform endeavour. While the population of these categorical divisions is shifting, with multilateral agencies and new

---

[24] This is of course similar to the established role played by planning within Tanzanian local government (Schneider 2007: 24, 31; Eriksen 1997).

entrants such as the African Union acquiring increasing influence and power, differentiation between categories of actors is the basic premise of how development is organised. Institutions like participation are made to work here as political technologies (Law & Mol 2008), providing objects around which new coalitions across difference can operate at the same time as delineating the divisions and differentiation between them. As boundary objects generating new objects, these institutions allow new activities constitutive of the endeavour, in this case development itself, to come into being (Star & Griesemer 1989).

Participation in development works well as a boundary device because it has abstract dimensions around which various political positions can unite, and because it is organised into a set of fairly fixed practices that enable different players to make specific contributions. These practices in turn generate standardised representational forms and artefacts that are recognisable as impressions of participation. As Star and Griesemer anticipated, standardisation of methods contributes to the effectiveness of boundary objects because knowing *how* and *what* is more transferable across different interpretive communities than knowing *why*, which is likely to be differently epistemologically constituted across them (1989: 407). At first sight this seems to apply less to the situation of participatory forms in Tanzania, where the *why* is the moral good of participation as a normative project. However, some critical interrogation of the question of 'knowing' in participation prompts further reflection on this. As we have seen, knowing *why* in the sense of analytical knowledge is underplayed in participatory forms, designed out through endless simplification (Green & Hulme 2005). The process of generating apparent consensus, at least representationally, is a feature of boundary devices (Star & Griesemer 1989: 413). Where this is not generated through participants seeking a level of agreement about what they can consent to representationally, this can be achieved through other means. In the words of Star and Griesemer: 'The production of boundary objects is one means of satisfying these potentially conflicting sets of concerns. Other means include imperialist imposition of representations, coercion, silencing and fragmentation (1989: 413).'

Participatory knowledge production processes prioritise common knowledge as unitary, a singular knowledge that has been publicly verified in community fora (Chambers 1994). This kind of knowledge is not contested because it has been corrected, through presenting back, at the point of generation. It is then ring-fenced through presentation as local knowledge, and therefore as not only authoritative because produced by local people, but as relevant to a particular locality. Products of partici-patory process are protected from criticism, internally and through their lack of relations to other kinds of knowledge; either that generated within knowledge disciplines, and hence by outsiders, or the findings of other participatory processes that are not considered relevant beyond their local area. Because participatory analyses are neither critical nor comparative, they cannot be contested as divergent visions of the world, only evaluated as lists of facts as attributes – widows have less land in village y; planting seasons are short in village x. In this way participatory forms multiply depoliticising. As we have seen, they bring the voice (singular) rather than the (multiple) poor to the policy table. Second, they preclude political analysis in foreclosing the kinds of comparison that prompts consideration of other possible orders (Law and Mol 2008).[25] The non-standard village and its potentialities for positive differences cannot be visualised through this particular process. Finally, in constituting a unitary community in place of a political social they usurp the place and political potential of considered, and potentially unruly, social analysis.

The more that standard methods and sequences are adhered to organisationally, the less likely participatory approaches are to generate the unexpected. The copy of the community with its social cleavages and inadequate resource base is generated again and again, just as the methods used in each exercise described were copies of the other and of preceding PRAs. In generating iterations of the standard problems faced by the standard village to be solved by the standard villager, it produces templates of relations between cause and effect and between levels of government; that is, of governability. Closing down through standardisation of tools and forms of organisation restricts the kind of analysis that could emerge through an iterative open-ended politicised conversation. The opportunity to view things differently is precluded within this formal representation of governance, and with it Hirschmann's 'hidden hand' of development creativity (1967: 35). Creativity in local government is corralled outside the formal system, in the break between formal government systems and local networks, between formal development contributions and individual contributions to the development aspirations of kin and neighbours, between politics and government (cf. Guyer 2004; Chatterjee 2004: 73).

---

[25] Eriksen (1997) remarks on the similar separation of planning from politics in Tanzania – plans are presented as technical and hence as not subject to contestation.

**5**

**Localising** ▌ Civil Society
**Development** ▌ as Social Capital
▌ after Socialism

This chapter explores some dimensions of the transnational attempt to establish civil society as both category and organisational form in a post-socialist setting. An examination of the efforts of an international NGO to develop community groups shows how the normative representation of state society relations promoted through neoliberal policies is confronted in practice by a particular cultural representation of governance. In Tanzania, where developing the civil-society sector continues to be the focus of much donor activity, not only is there little indication of the assumed break between civil society and the state, but civil-society organisations (CSOs) readily emulate cultural styles associated with central and local government. Such continuities call into question the political science categorisations of 'state' and 'civil society' and 'before' and 'after' socialism. They also shed light on the ways in which culture matters in the constitution of power (cf. Verdery 1991: 431; Yang 1988). The significance of culture is pertinent in this post-liberalisation setting, where the erosion of the resources available for redistribution has transformed the content of political relations at the same time as it has resituated substantial resources outside government control. Models of governance adapted from the government sphere come to encompass relations between people involved in the emerging civil-society sector. In adopting the cultural practices associated with what is popularly defined as 'government', the civil-society sector has become part of governance processes in Tanzania, although not in quite the way policy makers intended.

## Civil society after socialism

Tanzania is among the countries in Africa known for its commitment to what was claimed as a uniquely 'African' socialism in the 1960s and 1970s. The country's eventual policy mix of a single-party regime and parastatals was not confined to socialism in the context of Africa at the time (Simon 1995; Fatton 1985; Ferguson 1995). Tanzania could be hailed as a genuine partner in socialism by China and East Germany, at the same time as its non-alignment ensured that it was able to maintain credible, if at times strained, relations with Western countries and multilateral institutions. These relationships sustained its socialist policies into the late 1980s (Mueller 1980; Freund 1981; Rugumamu 1997), and, after the Cold War, necessitated Tanzania's formal transition into the post-socialist era and the adoption of polices oriented towards political and economic liberalisation. Tanzania's first multi-party elections were held in 1995. Major public-sector reforms in health, local government and education followed soon after (Kelsall 2002). International development agencies have expanded their presence as international capital floods into the country. On the face of it, Tanzania's status as a post-socialist polity seems indisputable. The content of this transition is less certain. *Chama Cha Mapinduzi* (CCM), the Party of the Revolution, remains in power almost a quarter of a century after the formal transition to a multi-party system of government. Ongoing reform processes remain premised on a model of state-facilitated transformation that envisages its relation with rural communities, and their role in this transition, in ways that are identical in form to those of the socialist period, which were, in turn, profoundly influenced by colonial models of community development. Where concessions to post-socialist liberalisation have been made in relation to rural modes of social organisation is in the promotion by international organisations of CSOs. While the bulk of this effort, and the substantial resource transfer through which these new entities are brought into being (cf. Sampson 1996), has been concentrated in urban centres, attempts are being made to establish some semblance of a 'civil-society sector' in rural areas. The analysis of one such example reveals intriguing parallels with popular expectations and understandings of local governance, and shows how the practice of imported organisational forms adapts existing structures of governance.

The vignettes in this chapter are derived from my involvement in an NGO project that was trying to build local social capital during the early 2000s. The country manager, based in the capital city, earnestly believed in the mantra of strong local organisations and community development. He was committed to the emerging narrative about social capital and development that was gaining credence in donor circles. Aware that I was an anthropologist with some experience of the development sector he asked me to spend a month exploring reasons why the community in rural Lindi District, a somewhat marginal region in the south of the country, was finding the assertions linking groups to development unconvincing. Village groups were being formed enthusiastically by residents, allocated chairpersons and secretaries, and given inspiring names such as the 'Ten Commandos'. But the groups themselves were doing very little. In the district centre, a small town, around five small groups existed, the products of a recent national initiative introduced by the wife of the then president to promote the formation of local CSOs. The urban groups were equally limited in scope. Generally conceived around the agenda of a single individual keen to attract funding to create not merely an organisation, but one that would allow a central role for the founder, they had neither clarity of purpose nor a coherent programme of activities.[1]

Initiated as an attempt to grow the kinds of autonomous local organisations that would fill the assumed gap between the family and the state in the neoliberal discourse around the causative links between strong civil society and social capital,[2] the project aimed not only to contribute to the elimination of poverty[3] by helping people work together, but to enhance local participation, democratisation and responsive governance through creating the kind of civil society that could hold government to account. As such it was firmly embedded within the global 'good governance' agenda that for much of the past two decades has conveyed its core ideals of regulation, accountability and democratisation through the massive funding transfers that comprise the bulk of international development assistance. The project was by no means unusual in comparison with other rural community-based projects in other parts of East Africa at that particular time. Nor was it unusual when compared with other internationally driven civil-society support projects in other newly democratic countries after the Cold War (Sampson 1996, 2002; Mandel 1997). The main premise of the project was that local, community-based organisations would evolve naturally as part of the democratic transition if provided with the necessary support and guidance. The support available in this instance was conceived as 'technical', in that groups were to be provided with assistance in the mechanics of setting up and running 'groups' as membership organisations. This kind of support is referred to as 'capacity-building' in the development literature. Such support is explicitly ideological, containing explicit and implicit notions about what constitutes effective organisations and what kinds of activities are pro-developmental and thus justify capacity input (Phillips & Ilcan 2004). In the context of this project, as in other civil-society support projects internationally, the image of a 'good' organisation was based on a mirror image of the kind of Western voluntary-sector organisation that the international NGO had itself evolved from. Indicators of functionality as 'capacity' were couched in these same terms – the ability to maintain

---

[1] The emphasis on the founder is not confined to Tanzanian organisations. In Kenya, organisations formed for the interests of their founders are known as MONGOs, an acronym for 'My Own NGO'.

[2] Promoted in Tanzania at the time by the World Bank and the United Kingdom's Department for International Development after a study by Narayan et al. that seemed to 'prove' the link between civil society, social capital and development (Narayan 1998, 1999; Narayan & Pritchett 1999).

[3] The objective of all international development interventions shared by the multilateral and bilateral agencies that had signed up first to the International Development Targets (IDTs), superseded after 2000 by the Millennium Development Goals (MDGs).

records, whether a group had a chairperson and a bank account, and the number of meetings held.

The idea that 'capacity' as proper institutional form is the missing link in achieving development is also central to the ways in which governance as the function of different tiers of government is being reformed across Tanzania, and in other so-called developing countries. What is currently promoted as 'good governance' requires efficient management of public resources by accountable local or national governments. While civil society contributes to holding government to account in this policy vision, what constitutes *good* government should be able to manage its resources properly in order to deliver services to populations and to contribute to international development agendas (Minogue et al. 1998). Civil-society support projects complement a public-sector reform agenda that in Tanzania, as in other reforming countries, encompasses local-government reform. In 2001 the lowest tiers of local governance were as yet largely unaffected by the reform process, which in any case would seek to strengthen existing systems of village government rather than restructure them. This continuity of forms has implications for the continuity of content between socialist and post-socialist modalities of governance in Tanzania (cf. Mamdani 1996) and for shaping popular expectations about how rural communities are integrated into national society as dependants on the largesse of the centre and on the whims of *wafadhili* (donors) rather than as citizens with rights to a proportion of national resources. Such expectations, based on an acknowledgement of the hierarchical structuring of the national order in which rural areas, and the people who live there, are at the very bottom (*chini kabisa*), also inform rural people's expectations about their role in and the situation of the new rural civil-society sector, which donor models have based around similarly hierarchical models of funding.

In Tanzania this representation of governance as a vertical, as well as spatial, is not merely a 'metaphor' for the relationships through which different social groups are integrated into the state (Ferguson & Gupta 2002: 984). Verticality is effected through the myriad social interactions of governance through which inequality between levels is reiterated, along with relations of dependency on the upper levels' control over real and symbolic resources. Such interactions amount to a distinct culture of governance in many parts of rural Tanzania, characterised by a preoccupation with adherence to the forms and practices of governance rather than content, in the form of policies or plans, although the enactment of planning as the work of village government that we saw in the previous chapter becomes significant. This preoccupation with form is partly explained by the fact that lower tiers, whether they are community-based organisations or village governments, lack resources to implement any plans they might make, but they nevertheless know that conformity to processes set by higher tiers is the first step towards being 'recognised' (*tambulisha*), which is a precondition for potential eligibility for funding.

Being recognised is not only about potentially accessing development resources. It is fundamental to legitimation as being part of government. Where lower tiers stand in for government in the absence of higher tiers, this recognition is central to the constitution of certain forms of local power relations as governance.

## Snapshots of governance in Tanzania 1: government

In 2003, over a decade after the formal of the end of Tanzanian socialism, a person making an official visit to a government office would have found themselves in something like the following scenario. Approaching the building where the office of the official is located, the visitor reports to the gatekeeper and explains his or her request, perhaps adding their name to a book indicating whom they are to see and which institution they are representing. Directed to a waiting area near to the office they are visiting, they are instructed to report to the deputy or secretary of the official in question. There are usually others already waiting to see government officers, whom the visitor must politely walk past in order to make his or her request. This often entails waiting at a counter, or speaking through a small grilled opening in a wooden partition used to divide official offices into distinct zones: an outsider space for visitors and inquiries, an intermediate space or sub-office for clerical staff, and, finally, the inner sanctum of the official's official office. Secretaries and clerks occupy the middle space, mediating between public and officials, surrounded by old-fashioned telephones and colourful government calendars. Told to wait, the visitor takes a seat on a chair or bench lined up against a corridor wall, where the previous arrivals sit in silence under the stern gaze of the secretaries. After some time, depending on the visitor's perceived importance and the urgency of the visit, the visitor will be called in to the office of the official.

Official offices in Tanzania follow a fairly standard pattern in the utilisation of space. The offices of senior officials, that is, of senior staff in regional administrations and of senior civil servants in the capital, are laid out slightly differently from those of middle-ranking and local-government staff, with large rooms subdivided by an enormous desk behind which the official sits facing their visitors, and a separate area with comfortable sofas in ostentatious plush for more relaxed meetings. The office style of senior district officials is generally more subdued, utilitarian, with smaller rooms commonly arranged as follows. The official sits behind a desk, overlooking several clunky telephones now virtually unused, facing a table along which guests are seated in a T-shape with the official occupying the head of the table at the bar of the T. An official's desk may be covered with an embroidered cloth or a lace decorative mat. The desk is likely to have office artefacts – penholders, glass dishes full of paperclips, filing trays and the like – alongside the telephones. It is not likely to be covered in papers. Typing and paperwork are the responsibility of the secretaries and clerks, struggling with out-of-date computers and ancient typewriters in the adjoining offices. The clear desk of an important official conveys further evidence of the official's status and that of his office, namely that this is the office of a person who signs, rather than writes, papers; who heads the table at meetings; and who receives important calls from multiple telephones. If it is not already on the table, in anticipation of the visitors, the official quickly places before them a large bound and covered book, perhaps in simulated leather binding, on which the embossed words *Kitabu Cha Wageni* (visitors' book) feature prominently. The visitors' book is the quintessential artefact of official offices and spaces[4] in Tanzania where the names, addresses, institutional affiliations and perhaps even 'tribe' (*kabila*) of visitors are recorded, along with the date and possibly time of their arrival.

On the wall directly behind the official are framed photographs of the president of the United Republic of Tanzania. In 2003 this was President Benjamin Mkapa. Elsewhere in the room are photographs of Julius Nyerere, the first president, and very possibly a photograph of his successor.[5] Official calendars with photos of ministers, and posters promoting party events, are displayed on the walls. Organisational charts also feature strongly on the walls of government offices, diagrams representing the connections between different organs of government and between different tiers of governance, including the committees comprising district councils. The visitors enter the room, shaking hands with the official and, invited to sit, occupy the chairs arranged along the table in front of the big desk, along the base of the T. The official sits at the big desk surrounded by his telephones and his guests. He knows that the visitors know who he is, and waits for them to make their introductions in turn, proffering their business cards if they have them, as further evidence of a visitor's official status. The visitors' book is passed along the line of guests. Solemnly filled in by each silently in turn, the visitors respectfully explain the purpose of their visit as the official, framed by the president's gaze, looks on expectantly.

---

[4] Apart from obvious places such as hotels and guest houses, visitors' books are found in the offices of NGOs and, at least between 1998 and 1999, in the business-class lounge of Air Tanzania at Dar es Salaam International Airport. Indeed, being presented with a visitors' book for a formal signing in an office arranged in conformity to government style at Oxfam's Arusha headquarters in 1999 first alerted me to the continuities of style between the government and civil-society sectors in the country. Neither of these two incidences are surprising. NGOs striving for official recognition try to make themselves recognisable to officials through adapting to Tanzanian expectations and styles of governance, just as government adapts to the expectations and styles of the international organisations that provide the bulk of government funding. Air Tanzania was formerly a parastatal.

[5] Kelly Askew gives a good account of the significance of the presidential portraiture in relation to officials' offices, which she likens to Corrigan and Sayer's understanding of royal portraiture in the United Kingdom as the 'sanctification of secular power' (2002: 50).

## Structuring governance

For the one-off visitor, the forms of office space and decoration, the highly formalised rituals of waiting patiently (*subiri*) and the visitors' books may seem to be attributes of the particular places and offices of the officials with whom they interact. This is not the case. The forms and layout of official offices, and associated modes of official behaviour, including visitors' books, are in fact replicated across the numerous offices of lower, middle and higher-tier officials all around the country. The organisation of such offices is not simply a coincidence of styles, but is central to the constitution of governance and office as modalities of power in Tanzania, and to the imagination of both national order and national transformation founded on the village as the basic building block of planned development and hence as an object of governance.

How does this assertion relate to the description of official offices above? Officials, as holders of office, see themselves as intermediaries between the central government (*serikali kuu*) and the people, a position realised representationally through the structure of the official's office, in which the official sits facing his guests or staff with the president's picture behind him and the open channels of government communication to hand. District-level officials, whether working for central or local government, view their task as effecting governance (*utawala*) through the virtue of office. This necessitates implementing the government policies that cascade downwards through regional administrations to district level and below, and striving to amass local resources to plug the funding gaps for the delivery of local-tier services. Officials occupy distinct tiers within a hierarchical structure of government. This position gives senior officials at each tier the responsibility of representing the next level up to those below, as well as being the link with the tier above. Interstitial between different levels of power and powerlessness, such officials can thus legitimately demand respect from those seeking a response from 'government'. While the balance of responsibilities between regional officials and district administrations has changed under the Local Government Reform Programme, senior officials of the kind likely to receive official visitors quite literally *embody* government in the area for which they are responsible. Such officials represent government (*serikali*) in the dual sense of *standing in*[6] for and *standing for* government. In this context, working for/ as government implies representing the power of the centre relationally, whether that centre is central government in relation to regions, or district government in relation to villages and wards. Like the organi-

---

[6] Hence when the *Mkurugenzi* (District Executive Director, or DED), the senior district manager, is absent, heads of department will 'stand in' for him as 'Acting DED', representing the district authority and not themselves or their respective departments.

sational charts through which it is represented graphically, government in Tanzania is essentially about levels, about the staggered hierarchical intersections of governor and governed.[7] This is enacted through financial relationships in which the centre allocates cash to lower tiers, as well as through the dynamics of official relations in which officials strive to enact control over their level by claiming to control resources filtering downwards, whether this be cash or people.

Governance, from this perspective, is not concerned with the political economy of husbandry in service of the state as a national enterprise, as Foucault describes for the particular governmentality of the West that centres on the management of population as the main productive resource (2000: 219–20). In Tanzania, aid dependency and the absence of a developed infrastructure has meant that control over populations has failed to generate substantial resources for government. Governance in post-socialist Tanzania is concerned with managing the proper relation between higher and lower tiers. Therefore enacting mediation between tiers becomes a critically important act through which the verticality of governance is established. Consequently, access to officials at all levels is rigidly controlled. Even when officials are not occupied, the difficulty of access must be maintained, hence the formalisation and arbitrariness of the waiting process. The former objective, concerned with managing relations between government and governed, influences expectations and attitudes towards government shared by public servants and population alike. Visitors' books in such settings are not merely records of who has visited an office and the official who controls it, but in effect constitute policed entry posts to domains and territories of governance. These entry points are reiterated at all levels of the Tanzanian system of government, from the offices of numerous village governments (*serikali ya kijiji*) to those of Permanent Secretaries, the most senior civil servants working in ministries at the very heart of government.

## Local government

In Tanzania, government (*serikali*) as in the material offices of government, is differentiated from the process of governance (*utawala*), which is conceptually bound up with the administration of the geographical entities into which the country is divided.[8] As the responsibility of government is to manage the developmental state, the responsibility of officers of government is to involve the population in the current

[7] The importance of organisational form is not a recent phenomenon. The one-time personal assistant to the president remarked at a 1971 conference on administration that there is 'an exaggerated belief in the beneficial effects of formal organisational reforms, in a few cases, even to aversion of what might be called Chartomania' (Svendsen 1974: 23).

[8] Utawala is also translated as 'administration', which means that governance is essentially administration; hence good governance becomes *utawala bora*, 'excellent administration'.

incarnation of the Development Vision. This is achieved through local government as the mechanism through which popular involvement is made part of the system of governance. What is now presented by the state as a distinct system of 'local government' (*serikali ya mitaa*), associated with local authorities and district councils, continues to convey the local representation of central government. This association is to be expected. Successive local-government reforms since independence intentionally blurred the separation between elected local authorities and centrally appointed officials, a distinction that has only recently been reimposed.

The category of local government also conveys the whole swathe of administrative structures from district level downwards.[9] Under the present post-socialist system these are the divisions (*tarafa*) into which districts are divided and the wards (*kata*), villages and neighbourhoods that comprise them. In many places villages and neighbourhoods – *kitongoji* for rural, *mitaa* (streets) for urban – remained further divided into the old socialist *nyumba kumi kumi* (ten-house cells) for more than a decade after its abolition. Where the ruling party dominates there was a strong tendency, particularly in rural areas, not to differentiate between party (*chama*) and government (*serikali*), hence CCM positions continued until recently to be indistinguishable, at least for supporters of CCM, from positions of village government. In some sense, then, village government is considered as representative of government in the village, as well as being the agent of village governance. This merging of meanings and association should not surprise us when we consider that 'government' is essentially concerned with representing the next level up to the tier below and with implementing a Development Vision. Logically, village government becomes the vehicle through which the local is governed and, consequently, the locus of specific responsibilities in effecting development. Within the system of government at sub-district level, that is, local government that is at the same time the means through which the local is acted on by government, the significant institutional arrangements centre on the middle tier of ward committees and officials (*afisa mtendaji wa kata*/ ward executive officers), who, in standing between the village and the local outpost of government, comprise *de facto* local governance. The ward is important as the level that once more has elected representation on the local council.[10] Prior to this, wards were represented by state servants who were simultaneously party officials and agents of rural co-operative societies (Moore 1988).[11]

---

[9] Hence local government is more popularly talked about as *serikali ya wilaya*, i.e. the district government.
[10] 'Councillor' is *diwani*. Not all councillors are elected. In each council a number are nominated to ensure representation of minority groups and women.
[11] The Ward Secretary (*Katibu Kata*).

## Reforming rural society

This framework of village government through which the rural citizen could participate in national development as the project of governance was fundamental to the African socialism with which Tanzania under Nyerere was associated (Mueller 1980; Saul 2002; Leftwich 1992; Pratt 1999). 'Villages' were not a part of the colonial system of administration, which was constructed around ethnically based local administration through districts and the areas, across dispersed homesteads, associated with particular headmen (Mamdani 1996). Independence in 1961 brought gradual changes in the design of governance. Socialism in Tanzania could not follow foreign models but had to adapt itself to local social realities.[12] For Nyerere, this was not a matter of inventing the kind of socialism that would be suitable for Tanzania so much as rediscovering an apparently indigenous form of African socialism (Ferguson 1995: 134; Fatton 1985: 4–12).[13] Nyerere referred to this kind of 'socialism' as *ujamaa*, which he translated as 'familyhood' (Caplan 1992: 108).[14] By representing socialism in Tanzania as a pre-existing 'attitude of mind',[15] Nyerere could present socialism as a stance that could be realised through 'self-reliance' (*kujitegemea*), requiring little economic investment (cf. Blommaert 1997: 140). The absence of indigenous social forms that corresponded to this utopia of collaboration (Maghimbi 1995: 27–8; Kopytoff 1964: 52–62) meant that such apparently 'traditional' forms had to be created by the state through the category of the 'village' as naturally self-contained units of production, consumption and governance. Nyerere's villagisation policy was implemented between 1973 and 1978 in the majority of regions in Tanzania. Initially voluntary, the move into villages became compulsory after 1973, and by 1980 some 90 per cent of the population were living in villages.[16]

Nyerere's[17] view of the village as the engine of development was influenced by a synthetic mix of romanticism and orientalism, which

[12] Nyerere did not consider indigenous Tanzanian society to have classes.

[13] In his speech on 'Ujamaa – The Basis of African Socialism', Nyerere states: 'We in Africa have no more need of being converted to socialism than we have of being "taught" democracy. Both are rooted in our past – in the traditional society that produced us.' (Nyerere 1968: 9).

[14] In Kiswahili, *jamaa* refers to a person with whom one has social relations that are distinct from kinship. Ujamaa is not then 'familyhood', but an acknowledgement of sociality.

[15] '... the same socialist attitude of mind which in the tribal days gave to every individual the security that comes of belonging to a widely extended family must be preserved within the still wider society of the nation ... Our first step, therefore, must be to re-educate ourselves; to regain our former attitude of mind.' (Nyerere 1968: 8; see also Uzoigwe 1988: 126).

[16] Force was used to move people into villages. As the scale of the operation became unmanageable the rules were changed to simply reclassify any settlement of over 250 houses as a village and to insist that the population resided in them (Maghimbi 1995: 32).

[17] Nyerere said, in his 1962 inaugural address: 'If we do not start living in proper village communities then all our attempts to develop the country will be just so much wasted effort.' (Cited in McHenry 1979: 16).

owed much to colonial thinking about the social organisation of rural society in India and elsewhere (Ludden 1993: 226). But the British never applied this thinking about peasant society to East Africa, which was seen as essentially 'tribal' and thus by extension pre-peasant in the evolutionist thinking of the day. Moreover, while the British administration, like that of the Germans before them, had perceived the advantages of keeping people in the same areas and near to communications arteries (Shao 1986: 228; Chachage 1988), the idea of villages as functionally undifferentiated units of production, consumption and exchange which were simultaneously points of integration into the wider polity, was beyond the colonial imaginary. Colonial settlement policies merely aimed to move people to a central place for ease of administration, without altering the social relation through which governance was effected. Villagisation, in contrast, strove to remake national society through the creation of new units of governance.[18] Villagisation was not primarily about resettlement, although this was an important dimension. While much has been written of the failures of villagisation in Tanzania, its negative consequences for agricultural production and the heightened climate of political repression with which it was associated (Scott 1998: 223–8), villagisation was successful in its restructuring of governance and the modality through which rural communities were incorporated into the state. Indeed, the model was adopted by development organisations seeking to foster participatory village-based decision-making in other countries (Jennings 2002: 528–9). The village as a unit of administration survived and, like the *kolkhoz* in parts of the former Soviet Union, has widespread legitimacy in the country (Humphrey 2002: 169).

## Villagers, villages and the state: governance under socialism[19]

If villages as the locus of rural society were by definition objects of rural development (cf. Pigg 1992), villagers were the subjects charged with taking an active role in bringing it about. This role was predetermined by the minimalist orientation of Tanzanian socialism. 'Self-reliance' (*kujitegemea*), in practice a consequence of the failure to establish adequate revenue models for government to function, meant that lower tiers of administration had to provide their own resources for conforming to the project of national development. But as the agents and subjects

[18] This went hand-in-hand with the policy to stamp out the 'tribalism' created by the Native Authority system. In independent Tanzania until very recently government staff were posted to locations outside their home areas and constantly moved around to prevent building up ethnic power bases.

[19] After Ray Abrahams' (1985) edited volume of ethnographic accounts of precisely these relationships at the height of the village system in Tanzania.

of development, villages were also objects of governance, having, at the height of the socialist period, centrally appointed managers and offices of the ruling party, with associated officials, in each village centre. Villages also had their own governments, *serikali ya kijiji*, consisting of several sub-committees under the authority of a chairperson, an institution that continues to exist (albeit in modified form) and structure governance in rural Tanzania today. When villages were envisioned as collectivities responsible for communal production, village councils comprised 25 members, including representatives of the 'ten-house cells' and the chairs of the various subcommittees dealing with specific areas of activity, such as water or village assets (Abrahams 1985: 8). Annual general meetings of all adult villagers who were party members, were supposed to be held in order to make the council accountable. Not all adults in villages were party members. Village governments as laid down by statute met rarely and were not functional. As collectivism failed and village enterprises collapsed across the country, village government had less to concern itself with, although the positions of chairman and the *balozi*, the leaders of the 'ten-house cells', remained significant.

The role of village government in this system was essentially to channel party directives to rural areas and ensure that instructions from ward levels were implemented.[20] The village chairman was simultaneously party secretary, and villages functioned as party branches (Abrahams 1985: 8). By-laws and compulsory labour were used as means of ensuring compliance with government directives, for example building roads and schools (Hasset 1985: 19; Burke 1964: 217; Freund 1981: 191). Whereas opportunities for popular involvement in decision-making were claimed to exist by government, there was actually very little about which to make decisions. The key planning mechanism in rural areas, the ward development committee, which, after 1969, superseded the village development committee, consisted mainly of government staff from the departments operational in rural areas, party appointees, the district councillor (*diwani*) and the ward secretary, a party/government administrator (Samoff 1981: 303). Technical staff dominated local planning and budgeting processes.[21] The ability of these committees to plan anything was also limited by the fact that they were implementing top-down directives but lacked the resources to take any significant initiatives.[22] Planning in this system became a matter of form, of presenting requests and budgets to the next level up, with the ultimate objective of securing funding via the district from the regional development fund (Finucane 1974: 89). Even when bids were directed upwards to the appropriate

---

[20] For many villagers in the 1970s, '*Ujamaa* means to comply with government directives' (Uzoigwe 1988: 135).

[21] The majority of projects put forward for regional development funding originated from technicians (Collins 1974: 113).

[22] For accounts of the limitations of village planning see Caplan (1992), McHenry (1979: 103), Samoff (1981: 292) and Freund (1981: 490).

committees, very few were successful (Collins 1974: 107). Adherence to forms of governance in the absence of content was established. Content came down from higher tiers in the form of policy directives. The doctrine of 'self-reliance' meant that resources had to be locally generated, through labour and levies, which for rural villages usually meant no resources at all (cf. Caplan 1992: 111).[23] Popular disillusionment with resettlement and village governance contributed to low levels of involvement in village government. Titles, office holding, meetings and plans became the work and signifiers of 'government' and party as the party of government (Uzoigwe 1988).

## 'Government on paper'

The formal end of the one-party system in 1992 and the implementation of reforms have altered local government. The ruling party is no longer legally the party of village government, and some attempt has been made to separate local party offices from government offices and from local government. There have also been moves to enhance the powers of locally elected councils, and to devolve responsibilities and resources from central government to local authorities. Villages are no longer managed by government appointees working alongside chairmen, but by their own chairpersons together with unpaid executive officers (*afisa mtendaji*) who, while they have to be members of a party, are no longer tied to being members of CCM. The position of Ward Executive Officer (WEO) has replaced the state/party post of *katibu kata*, but as recently as 1999 the WEO in many districts reported to the District Commissioner, the political appointee representing the Regional Commissioner, also a political appointee, who represents central government and state security throughout the country.[24]

Village governments include the chairpersons of the subdivisions introduced post-1992 (*kitongoji*) and are now subdivided into between three and five committees, responsible for such areas as peace and security, collective works, education and water. Village offices, which in CCM areas are also CCM offices because CCM is the party of government, give an impression of a struggle to be organised amid extreme poverty. A dark room, perhaps with a rickety table half-consumed by termites, a couple of simple benches, and hand-drawn diagrams of organisational charts and committee structures on the earth-plastered walls are typical of village offices in rural areas. A village executive officer has extensive

[23] Tanzania underwent massive economic crisis and stagnation between 1963 and the early 1990s, during which period its dependency on international assistance increased (Rugumamu 1997). Ironically, even at the height of the period of 'self-reliance' in the late 1970s the country obtained 68 per cent of its non-recurrent budget from the international community (Freund 1981: 486). Even the apparently successful Ruvuma Development Association on which *ujamaa* was modelled was aid-dependent (McHenry 1979; Jennings 2002: 522).

[24] The village security police, *wanangambo*, reported to the WEO.

knowledge about his village. Collection of local tax is his responsibility, as is organising village contributions (*michango*) towards projects initiated by district and regional officials. As during the socialist period, these take the form of cash or labour, which is compulsory for those in the social categories deemed responsible for its provision. Refusal to participate can still result in the imposition of fines or even imprisonment. It is not unusual for people to describe relations with 'government' in terms of 'sucking blood' (*nyonya damu*) or 'sweat' (*jasho*), or as each level 'treading' on (*kanyaga*) the others all the way to the top in a ladder of exploitation.

Village governance may appear to be more democratic and more concerned with village matters than previously. In actuality there is little change. Village committees have different degrees of effectiveness, some meeting rarely, if at all, and meetings of village governments are few and far between in many districts. Village inputs to ward planning processes are constrained by the objectives of ward officials and the interests of councillors, who strive to ensure that their own village benefits from district spending. Even where village initiatives make it through ward committees to be put forward to district councils, the shortage of funds at district level means that the likelihood of receiving funding is minimal. Top-down directives continue to shape local policies as a response to the availability of donor development funds, as currently with the additional funds available for classroom building and rural secondary schools, and with the community development support for similar infrastructure projects associated with the World Bank-financed Tanzania Social Action Fund. Government officers continue to regard themselves as an educated elite with responsibility for telling peasants how to develop because they 'don't know anything', attitudes replicated throughout the civil service in the country (see also Costello 1996).

Meeting with representatives of village government in Lindi Region in 2001 to talk about public services, some fifteen male villagers and myself crammed along benches in the tiny CCM office. Seated facing the group I looked at the organisational charts on the walls behind them, the lists of committee members and the carefully drawn representation of which committees fed into which branches of governance. The men talked about problems in accessing resources, about the now failed water system built by the Finnish government in the 1980s, and of their difficulties in accessing education and markets. Glancing at the wall, I asked about the committees, about the role of village government. 'Aha,' said the Ward Executive Officer (Acting) – present for the meeting because he was 'government' and we were visitors on 'official business' – 'It hasn't any strength (*nguvu*). It is government on paper.'

Village government in Tanzania may not 'govern' in the sense of managing resources towards the achievement of a political vision, but it performs governance as the articulation of relationships between levels of the Tanzanian political system, representing the level down to the next level up, making contributions upwards and in adherence to form, anticipating (optimistically) the possibility of assistance from higher tiers. Village government in enacting governance thus makes use of titles, office, bureaucratic forms, charts and representations in dramatising governance as a matter of form of the relation between it and those governed below it and the upper tiers of local and central government. The visitors' book is replicated in the offices of village governments across the country.[25]

## Snapshots of governance 2: community-based organisations

Visiting eleven villages together with national staff of the international NGO project aimed at fostering strong local CSOs, I had the opportunity to talk at length with people involved in the 'community-based organisations' the project promoted. The groups, ranging in size from seven to twelve members, were not in fact community-generated, but had been brought into being as a result of the project that had set out to create them. Part of the reason groups had to be created for the project was that civil society did not appear to exist, at least in forms recognisable to the international models that drive the development agenda. As with villagisation under *ujamaa*,[26] a somewhat mechanistic understanding of the role of the social in bringing about change resulted in an orientation toward institutional form, rather than content. A limited number of groups had been encouraged to form in each village, under the direction of a ward-based project co-ordinator. Groups were organised according to the prescribed rules set down by the project. Membership was formal, and entailed paying a fee or making ongoing contributions to group funds. All the groups had names. As well as the 'Ten Commandos' there were *Umoja* ('Unity'), *Jiungeni* ('Join In') and *Nguvu Kazi* ('Strong Work').[27] A minority of groups were single sex. The majority of groups had formed around a specific planned project for income generation, although the proposals groups had for this varied from raising chickens, bee-keeping and carpentry to small-scale farming.

The organisation of groups around assets, combined with the project criteria for assessing capacity based on the audit criteria used in larger-scale international organisations, meant that even these very small groups had a number of formal office holders, including chairperson, treasurer and secretary. As with the holders of office in village government, titles are taken seriously and used formally to emphasise the official nature

[25] I have signed visitors' books in various capacities in numerous villages in Tanzania, including in Morogoro, Mwanza, Kilimanjaro, Singida, Mbeya, Mtwara and Lindi.
[26] Or after *ujamaa*. As commentators have pointed out, the more socialist ideology of *ujamaa* was soon superseded by the policy of villagisation. Collective cultivation was dropped, and villages became simply 'development' rather than '*ujamaa*' villages (see, e.g., Maghimbi 1992).
[27] *Nguvu kazi* also refers to 'voluntary' labour for community projects.

of the enterprise in which people are engaged, for example at meetings. As minute taking was defined as a criterion for assessing the assumed 'capacity' of the CSOs the project created, the groups formalised their meetings with minutes kept in worn-out exercise books. Groups also had bank accounts – another criterion of functionality – even though the costs of transport to the bank branch in the nearest town, in excess of 40 miles away, far exceeded the amounts members had saved and the minimum required deposit for opening an account.

Group members had tried a range of strategies for getting cash to continue their groups, including brewing, farming together and rearing chickens. These strategies were no different from those commonly pursued by individuals who were not group members to make ends meet, and the constraints were similar. It was not surprising therefore that group members questioned the rationale of joining groups and sought to query project staff about where the benefits would come from. Popular expectations, shaped by Tanzania's dependency culture in which *wafadhili* (donors) are assumed to provide for projects at all levels, had led members to believe that groups formation would lead to consideration for assistance (*msaada*) in the form of cash or the *utalaam* (expertise) that they saw as the missing element that had been holding back their access to development. This model of group formation was well known in the area as the basis for the women's micro-credit programmes being promoted at that time as part of the then president's wife's initiative. Indeed, members were disappointed when told that there were no definite *material* benefits from the project, but that the project would provide 'help' to strengthen groups organisationally. This was viewed with suspicion by group members. 'It is nothing but a project of words!' said a disappointed woman villager.[28] The implicit rationale of creating strong social networks through CSOs, promoted along the models of voluntary sectors in the West, in line with the donor assumptions about social capital derived from Robert Putnam's (1993) work on Italian local government, was not articulated to project beneficiaries. It remained obscure to project staff, who found themselves having to promote local groups with no clear reason why groups should be promoted. Members of groups had no clear ideas as to why working in a *group* would help them or bring about 'development'. 'That is what we thought you were here to tell us', they said in response to this question or, alternatively, 'we are awaiting sensitisation'.

Groups were not only forming themselves so as to be able to conform to project expectations, and thus be eligible for inclusion in the various capacity-building activities that they knew would be associated with the project, including workshops, seminars and exchange visits. Group members also believed that in order to get 'recognition' from the 'government' they had to conform to certain forms and practices. This is partly a throwback to the time when NGOs were proscribed at the height of the socialist government,

---

[28] As we have seen, the idea of the 'project' (*mradi*) is strongly associated with material resources.

but it also reflects current government policy at national level regarding NGOs, which have to be registered by 'government' in order to have the recognition that allows them to function. At village level, registration of such small groups was not in fact a legal requirement. Nevertheless, group members believed that it was necessary to register their group with village government (and possibly also the district office dealing with community groups) in order to become 'recognised'. With 'recognition' comes not only the opportunity to function but also, it was hoped, the possibility of accessing sources of funding from higher up, perhaps from the *wafadhili* (donors), a category about which not much is known for certain, apart from the fact that most development initiatives in Tanzania are funded by them, from repairs to a local school to support for the national budget, and that they are known to channel money downwards.

## Cultures of governance in Tanzania

In a prescient article written at the start of the post-socialist transition, Katherine Verdery remarked on the centrality of culture and what she referred to as 'symbolic-ideological control' in socialist systems. Marketisation and liberalisation might, she proposed, erode 'this special significance of culture' (1991: 434), as in post-socialist settings cultural power tends to shift towards practices that are 'not seen as imposed by power' (ibid.). In rural Tanzania, at least, such practices and the power they imply continue to be critical sites where the dramatisation of a particular kind of political relationship and the control over subordinates that this implies is articulated. Such practices situate the performer, whether person or institution, within a hierarchy of staggered subordination, from young villager to village chairman, from village chairman to district official, from district official to man from the ministry. Tanzanian socialism, unlike the former Soviet states (Verdery 1996: 25–6), never managed to successfully place redistribution at the centre of its configuration of power (Mueller 1980). Local governance in this system becomes as much about accessing entry to the sphere above as controlling the access of those below to the level that one controls, albeit often symbolically. Both the local manifestations of government and the organisations created in communities exhibit a preoccupation with bureaucratic forms as a performance of governing. In this, governance is constituted not so much as the marshalling of resources towards an object of government, but as the articulation of hierarchical relations between organisational levels through which lower tiers hope to access resources channelled through higher tiers. That so-called 'civil-society' organisations are adapting these modalities of governance is not surprising. As well as being part of the overarching system of governance – indeed, as central to the good governance agenda – these organisations find themselves enmeshed in the same kind of relationship with higher tiers for recognition and resources, at the same time as popular expectations about what constitutes development organisations and mechanisms for participation are shared between spheres of government and outside it.

In Tanzania, as in other post-socialist settings, the efforts of government to pervade virtually all social arenas through the extension of state responsibilities down through levels of cadres virtually into the household itself have contributed to the establishment of cultures of local governance as accepted modes of self-presentation across the country. Socialism and the party regime, dependent on an army of voluntary post-holders at sub-village levels, gave numerous ordinary people the opportunity to participate in governance, even if it reduced the opportunities for participation in policy making (Moore 1988; Yang 1988). Any Tanzanian knows how to make a formal entry to a village, how to wait to see a district official and what to do when presented with a visitors' book (which is to sign it even if they have already signed it on several previous occasions). Aid dependency and the perpetuation of the single party's rule means that government is still very much about requests upwards for resources, rather than policy in what is represented as the continued quest for development and governance as serving the interest of what could be termed an *apolitical* economy. In this neoliberal representation of governance as being about the rational management needed to support national strategies for poverty reduction, planning, accountability and civil society become part of the package of reformed practices and social forms that ensure governance is 'good'. However, the performance of planning as request for funding is little altered, likewise the relationship between tiers of government. The emphasis on accountability seems to have legitimated adherence to form in both government and non-governmental organisations. Governance is not necessarily *good* in the sense proposed by donors, whose reforms seem merely to accentuate existing cultures of governance in Tanzania. This may be intentional. Rural empowerment and effective government would threaten the vested interests that have skewed government focus towards urban areas and certain rural districts. Despite trajectories of modernisation, there is no universal 'governmentality'. The bureaucratic orientation of Tanzanian governance is not so much concerned with surveillance of populations as a resource as with policing access to what resource is in the hands of government. It is for this reason that everybody wants to be part of government and the culture of governance is so widespread. Under the post-socialist system what has changed is the kind of resources that government can access as the mechanism for development. A shift away from infrastructure and investment towards reform and capacity improvements has entailed a shift from tangibles to intangibles. Governance becomes ever more about practices, performance, words and paper.

# 6

**Anticipatory
Development** | Building
Civil Society
in Tanzania

Numerous small-scale non-government organisations (NGOs) are seeking to establish themselves as development actors across Sub-Saharan Africa. Often comprising serving or former public officials or staff of development projects, who consider themselves to be 'volunteers', such organisations aim to form partnerships with larger development agencies in order to attain a place within the social relations of international development. Tanzania as a state has been constituted through such relations: initially as Tanganyika, a development colony of Bismarck's Germany; then as a British-governed protectorate under a League of Nations mandate after the First World War; and then, following independence in 1961, as a non-aligned nation state embarking on a strongly ideological strategy of African development (Iliffe 1979). The move away from socialism since the 1990s and the Government's acceptance of new forms of economic adjustment have altered the direction of national policy and dramatically reconfigured the basis of the Tanzanian social order. The past fifteen years have been characterised by new forms of international influence and inclusion within transnational policy regimes associated with the hegemonic policy models of the World Bank and the IMF, promoted through multiple relations with a range of bilateral, multilateral and non-governmental donor organisations.

The extension of small-scale NGOs in Africa, which can count as what donor organisations consider a local civil-society sector, are in part an effect of these endeavours (Fisher 1997; Mitlin et al. 2007). Ascribing the mushrooming of local NGOs to the power of international development spending and the ideological appeal of the civil-society concept cannot fully account for the scale of this expansion (Robins et al. 2008; Heydemann & Hammack 2009). In Tanzania, perhaps the majority of these organisations are not engaged in development projects and have not obtained access to donor funds. The proliferation of local NGOs here is not best understood in terms of the practical extension of neoliberal governing in which civil-society organisations (CSOs) assume responsibilities of the state within relations of verticality and encompassment (Ferguson & Gupta 2002; Ferguson 2006). New local NGOs regard themselves as development agents in waiting, occupying a position of adjacency to development relations.[1] Consequently, much of their everyday practice is oriented towards enacting a state of readiness for inclusion in development. Although individuals associated with such organisations may not be active in development work, they are actively engaged in the work of organisational development. This work takes the form of engagement in what are termed in the sector 'capacity-building' activities, as well as the production of a range of representational devices that articulate the possibility of a future engagement in development. These include the forms of documentation associated with developmental civil society, mission statements, budgets and project proposals, as well as enacting readiness through institutional conformity to accepted civil-society forms. Anticipatory development as a set of practices through which a relation of adjacency is established characterises the kinds of work associated with local CSOs.[2]

This chapter explores the extension of the local NGO sector in Tanzania through an exploration of its core practices of anticipatory development. Local NGOs in Tanzania, as in some other aid-dependent settings, strive to convert their peripherality to development orders into an adjacency that will permit them to be recognised and hence included in funding streams (Dill 2009; Mercer & Green 2013). Such relations of adjacency to development are not particularly new in Tanzania, where national discourses of inclusion in development subject to citizen ownership and responsibility are long-standing, as are relations in which the national government relies on external assistance for a substantial proportion of public spending. Where aspirations routinely exceed the available financial capacities of national and local governments, processes of planning and budgeting assume disproportionate significance in the everyday practice of governance at national, district and village levels (Wildavsky 1986; Eriksen 1997; Schneider 2007: 31), as does trying to obtain funding through fostering relationships with *wafadhili* (donors). What is interesting about the contemporary situation is the ways in which these practices have shifted laterally to emergent organisations as these assume positions in the reordering of Tanzanian governance and development.

Neoliberal political orderings have brought about important changes, not so much in the way that the state is organised in practice, but in the division of labour between government and citizens and between village and district government. Local NGOs and the volunteers who comprise them compete for donor funds to undertake what has become a business of facilitating community development. Ambiguities in the constitution of civil society as a contractor in development partnerships are accentuated where discourses of sustainability and the idea of civil society as

---

[1] On waiting in development more generally see Chakrabarty (2000) and Jeffrey (2008).

[2] For a similar notion of anticipatory action in relation to risk, see Anderson (2010).

distinct from private enterprise are not only unrealistic, but also occlude the motivations of actors in attempting to become social entrepreneurs (Swidler & Watkins 2009). Despite almost two decades of liberalisation in Tanzania, enterprise models do not structure the organisation of state and public services, which remain dominated by government. Paradoxically, perhaps, market relations and enterprise models, through competitive tendering and the sale of services, structure the organisation of local and national civil society where organisations compete to become development contractors. The 'knowledge economy of capacity-building' (Phillips & Ilcan 2004: 393) is central to this process, as are the technologies of replicability and dissemination that enable the dispersal of civil-society forms. The extension of local NGOs in rural districts is explained in relation to the emerging market in development activity, the replicability of NGO practices and technologies of organisation and low barriers to entry.

## The privatisation of community development

In the past decade Tanzania has witnessed an unprecedented expansion in the number of small-scale organisations seeking registration as NGOs. Initially associated with the major cities long integrated into development relationships, ongoing decentralisation initiatives, combined with donor programmes of civil-society support, are pushing this extension into small rural towns. I have increasingly come across new kinds of smaller organisation at meetings in rural districts or assuming positions as 'stakeholders' in local-government consultations. In the course of everyday conversations I have been told about the NGO projects of numerous professional people, including university teachers, district officials and clergy. Offices of local NGOs specialising in *mazingira* (environment), WASH (Water Sanitation and Health) or, almost everywhere, HIV and AIDS, are now not unusual in administrative centres smaller than the district. In district centres such as Bagomoyo and Magu,[3] with populations of well under 40,000, brightly painted signboards at road junctions announce the presence of international *and* local NGOs.

This presence in district centres is more than visually striking. It presents a strident claim to reorganise social relations in Tanzania in relation to development. This reorganisation is not in practice of the kind envisaged in the donor policies influenced by World Bank conceptual frames, which equate civil-society expansion with enhancing accountability and creating social capital. In fostering the establishment of civil society as a distinct category of institutions, it enables the basis of differentiation between state and non-state and between market and non-market entities, forming a niche

[3] The research in Magu was carried out as part of the Department for International Development (DFID)-funded Religions and Development Research Programme, with supplementary research on social change supported by the NGOs Twaweza! and SNV.

in which organisations achieving categorisation as civil society can potentially flourish. Such flourishing is made possible because of the redesign of development relations in which what is classified as civil society is contracted to play a particular role. Under current institutional regimes of international development as enacted in Tanzania,[4] local NGOs assume a facilitation role in relation to communities as agents and subjects of development interventions, a role previously assumed by district officials and by representatives of village governments. What amounts, in effect, to the privatisation of development facilitation does not imply a wholesale transformation in the ways that development is imagined and implemented in rural districts, which continues to be based on the idea of the village as a unit of development action and responsibility. It does offer opportunities for third parties to become development entrepreneurs. Because many district NGOs are made up of staff or former staff of local-government authorities, and because such staff are frequently engaged by them as short-term consultants to provide technical expertise, this situation consolidates professional relations of inequality between districts and villages, between district staff and village residents, and between agents and subjects of development.

The privatisation of rural development through civil society is a significant transition in the political culture of Tanzania, which under socialism associated entrepreneurial activity with capitalism (*ubepare*) and self-interest (*ubinafsi*). Responsibility for mobilising populations to *maendeleo* (development), connoting a range of activities that supported national aspirations to progress, rested on government staff and members of village government (Maghimbi 1995; Caplan 1992). Government was structured hierarchically into national, regional, district and village tiers, in which policy comes down from the top and plans are submitted upwards from villages, through various committee structures. Villagers as socialist citizens bore ultimate responsibility for development as a national project made up of the development activities of the country's villages multiplied (Saul 2002; Leftwich 1992; Pratt 1999). Village government operated as the lowest tier of government aligned with national development objectives, village leaders as representatives of government and of the ruling party (Abrahams 1994).

Economic and political liberalisation have altered this system considerably in some respects, but not in others, resulting in a hybrid institutional architecture of governance comprising a mix of community development village-based structures and neoliberal forms. Systems of village governance, consisting of a council and committee structure, are in the process of being strengthened through the final phase of 'decentralisation by devolution' (D by D) as part of local-government reform. Whereas under socialism villages operated as a lowest tier of government within a vertical system in which villagers contributed labour and

---

[4] For accounts of these changes in the institutional and policy context of development through poverty reduction strategies , see Craig & Porter (2006) and for Africa, Harrison (2004).

revenue for local infrastructure projects that would contribute to district development plans, the village has regained more autonomous status as a unit whose primary function is no longer its integration into wider systems but its status as a unit and agent of development. Under D by D, villages as self-governing entities resume their roles as communities responsible for their own development (PMORALG 2007; Lange 2008; Lund 2007), a role that as we have seen is simultaneously paradigmatic of the new politics of development to which Tanzania is subjected, and which pre-dates African socialism.

As Nikolas Rose and others have shown, the idea of community occupies an important place in the responsibilisation strategies of neoliberal governing, replacing the amorphous social as a domain of policy impact with the reflexive autonomy of communities responsible for governing themselves (1999: 172, 1996: 57; Amin 2005: 619). It is not, however, novel. Community as location and actor in development played a key role in colonial development policy in the decade immediately preceding independence. What changed after independence in 1961 was not the salience of community as development actor, but the equation of fiscal with moral responsibility. As a poor country no longer entitled to support through the Colonial Development and Welfare mechanism, Tanzania could not finance the development of rural communities. Rural people now had to contribute to their own development through income-generating activities, ensuring household food security and the construction of infrastructure (Tanzania National Archives 1961a).

As the community development model was instituted in the years immediately after independence, district files record the difficulties faced by government staff trying to bring this about. Reluctance to contribute cash or labour was not interpreted by officials as political commentary on what under socialism was to be called *kujitegemea* (self-reliance), but as indication of the unreadiness of the rural population to fully commit to the aspirations of development (Blommaert 1997: 140).[5] Government circulars remark on the necessity of education and the need to adopt a unified approach in which technical staff work with rural dwellers on strategies to attack the three well-known enemies – poverty, ignorance and disease. This could not be done by working only through officials. Changing culture and attitudes required the active participation of 'influential people', the middle class who did not hold to backward customs and were receptive to modernity.[6]

---

[5] On the attitudes of villages a community development officer remarks, in English, 'The VDCs (village development committees) are very tough in being convinced by us for teaching people what is meant by community development and what benefit is brought by people in co-operating and bringing good success: so they just argue with us and discourage the people in performing any successful work ... Due to the lazyness [*sic*] of the VDC I could not even manage my work arrangements ...' (Tanzania National Archives, n.d.).

[6] On the need to attack poverty, ignorance and disease, see for example the speech of the Minister for Local Government on 2 July 1961 cited in circulars of the Community Development Division (Tanzania National Archives 1961b).

Community development as modality of intervention segued into the constitution of the village as development actor under Nyerere's socialism, a transition that allowed both for radical community initiatives such as the Ruvuma Development Association, later a model for the creation of *ujamaa* villages, and villages as the targets of top-down control (McHenry 1979; Jennings 2002). Not all villagers shared the government's ambitious aspirations to development. Socialist rule is associated with forced villagisation and the enforced participation of villagers in development projects through by-laws, imprisonment and fines. Such practices persisted in many parts of the country, along with a sustained discourse among government officials and party leaders about peasant backwardness and culture or, where peasants showed initiative and veered towards market relations, their tendency towards self-interest and capitalism (Maghimbi 1995; Costello 1996; Samoff 1979). Agricultural co-operatives were incorporated into party structures and independent organisations, with the exception of professional associations for state employees, and religious organisations restricted. Opportunities for personal advancement during this period were limited in practice to public service and religious institutions, both closely aligned to educational opportunity, and hence with monopolies for the production and reproduction of the middle class, and to professional practice that depended on a relationship of differentiation from villagers (Jennings 2008; Gibbon 2001).

By the late 1990s this system was at breaking point. Self-reliance in a context of rural underproduction and often basic self-sufficiency in food was a failure. Tanzania resumed relations with the IMF and embarked on a rigorous programme of structural adjustment (Rugumamu 1997). Economic stagnation, massive indebtedness and the de facto liberalisation of basic trade through a thriving black market (Bryceson 1993; Tripp 1997) prepared fertile ground for the seeds of political and economic liberalisation systematically sown by Tanzania's renewed relationships with donors under the auspices of development partnerships. Status as a Highly Indebted Poor Country, a donor-financed report by Hellenier (1995), a former diplomat, that advocated greater national ownership in setting development agendas and the scope for new *ex ante* conditionalities created by the World Bank's Comprehensive Development Framework, heralded significant transformations in the business of politics and the organisation of aid (Kelsall 2002; Harrison 2004). Governance concerns and the priority for international financial institution analysts, came to dominate the Tanzanian policy process and the practice of government.

Public-sector reform, fiscal accountability and decentralisation as key policies for Tanzania were implemented through successive multi-donor-funded interventions from the early 1990s with a gradual transition towards direct budgetary support ten years later. These processes have had profound effects, creating a microclimate in which new class relations and organisational forms could thrive. First, the governance agenda promoted by international donors opened up a space for new organisational forms as civil society, a space that was rapidly populated by international NGOs (Mercer 2003). This necessitated a shift from service delivery to new areas of activity of accountability, sensitisation and advocacy specified in donor policy models (Semboja & Therkildsen 1995). Second, substantial amounts of hard currency were made available through government budgets, increased foreign investment and finance for civil-society activity. Finally, university expansion, new forms of private-sector employment and opportunities in the multiplying development agencies operational in Tanzania swelled the professional middle classes and those with associated competencies in office work, organising and documentation. The political economy of capacity-building sustains a real economy of hotels, conference centres, consultants and experts, both international and national. In this context, the forms, artefacts and behaviours associated with development are not only widely circulated, but they come to be powerful signifiers of aspiration. Funding proposals written in the style of development agency documentation now constitute a form through which requests for financial help are couched to potential patrons. I have received several of these, including a request for cash from the owner of a local cooked-food outlet (*mgahawa*) in a small rural district in the style of an application for project funding. The document, in English, is headed 'Appeal for sponsorship of financial aid for empowering the socio-economic development status of the Star restaurant'. Such proposals are not unusual. Sometimes produced with a potential benefactor in mind, they are also commissioned by people with personal 'projects' so as to be prepared in the event of meeting a possible donor in future.

Local NGOs now populate the landscape of peri-urban districts where development is being reframed as the outcome of an interaction between villagers as communities and a new category of non-government development professionals. Jenny, a young community development officer working for local government in Magu, explained the role of different actors to me:

> Our role is to be change agents – my office has to promote change so that people can move from the state they are in to one of sustainable development. This is essential because people need to be made aware now that government does not do anything like in the past and they have to rely on their own resources to bring development.

In Jenny's view, development is not simply a matter of material resources. People's values and practices inhibit their capacities to become fully developmental:

> People have negative attitudes. There are inherited customs which are bad – the old men marrying young schoolgirls, and superstitions such as witchcraft and so on. People need to be made aware. This is what

they have to be sensitised about. To change their behaviour, to change the attitudes of the people.

She explained that because government by itself lacks the resources to bring about the kinds of changes that can make people developmental, NGOs, supported by donors, must play a role in sensitisation, in educating villagers in how to become ready for development.

## Scripting civil society

Local NGOs play this role not because of inherent qualities of civil society or because they are close to the poor as their imagined constituency, but because they are scripted to do so in the development architecture of contemporary Tanzania and places like it.[7] Development finance amounting until recently to more than half of national budgets has heavily steered national policy agendas towards governance objectives, prioritising decentralisation and an increased emphasis on fiscal, rather than political, accountability. The idea of civil society comes into play here as a set of institutions comprising a 'third pillar' between the market and the state that can foster civic engagement and 'make democracy work' (Putnam 1993). From the early 2000s, international donors embarked on their efforts to develop a civil-society sector in Tanzania that could fulfil the accountability and community engagement aspirations of the new approach to aid. Couched in the idiom of partnership as implying both equality and contract, such organisations were to assume formal obligations in relation to the governance agenda (Phillips & Iclan 2004). Initially, international NGOs fulfilled this function, engaging in the policy dialogue around the first Poverty Reduction Strategy Paper as a conditionality for aid (Mercer 2003). Gradually these same organisations, with the financial support of key bilateral and multilateral agencies, worked on building the kinds of national organisations that could operate as NGOs and assume civil-society functions. Operating as an NGO was necessary for these entities to receive funding from other NGOs, hence to be part of a chain of development contracting. Operating as civil society entailed being functionally incorporated into governance relations, through taking on the work necessitated by it, such as engaging in policy dialogue and monitoring accountability.

Existing national popular and non-governmental organisations at the start of the Poverty Reduction Strategy decade could not easily be brought into these kinds of relations. Few in number, associated with elite advocacy groups in major cities, or with strong political and professional interests, most were not amenable to inclusion into this socio-political restruc-

[7] For comparative accounts of this form of civil society in development relations, see Sampson for Albania (1996), Hearn on Africa (2007), Englund on Malawi (2006), Elyachar on Egypt (2003, 2005), Aubrey on Kenya (1997), Medeiros on Bolivia (2001) and Aksartova on the former Soviet Union (2009).

turing. Moreover, the commitment to decentralisation and the demands to reach the rural masses entailed devolving the drivers of civil-society expansion. The NGO Policy (URT 2001) went some way towards this goal, reducing the costs of registration and hence of gaining the official status that allows NGOs to look for funds. A national funding facility, the Foundation for Civil Society, which supports local NGOs working in specific areas of sensitisation, HIV and AIDS, and social protection, was established in 2002. In 1993 there were 224 registered NGOs in Tanzania (Lange et al. 2000: 6). By the second decade of the twenty-first century there were at least five times as many.[8]

The scale of this sustained investment in the promotion of novel social forms has tangible effects that are evident in the district centres comprising this second wave of civil-society extension. This can be clearly seen in Magu town, the administrative centre of a rural district situated on the outskirts of Mwanza, Tanzania's second city. Integrated into the global fish industry centred on Lake Victoria and the dynamic regional economy around it, Magu's favourable integration into Tanzanian political economy is reiterated in policy fields. Magu has long been part of large-scale programming by major donors, notably UNICEF, which attracted a number of significant players to the District during the 1990s. The District is now home to over 50 groups registered as non-governmental or community-based organisations and to an umbrella body, the Magu Civil Society Network (MACSONET), to represent them (Green et al. 2010).

Magu District conforms to the formal architecture of development in terms of civil society marshalled visibly as a sector, that is, as an entity like 'economy' or 'health' that can be articulated with other entities in policy representations of cause and effect. It conforms too in the ways that civil society presents itself on the ground. This presence is tangible in the offices of numerous small-scale organisations found on every street in the town with their bright signboards and elaborate logos painted on the wooden shutters of converted residential houses, recalling the conversion by international NGOs of large residences into offices on the periphery of the town. Although some organisations have large offices crammed with desks and flip charts denoting projects with which they are engaged, and walls pasted with organisational charts and campaign posters from development agencies, many more appear as shuttered buildings with little sign of activity. In between these two extremes are the more usual kind of organisation, whose external face comprises an acronym, an office and some 'volunteers', the manifestation of which is a

---

[8] Obtaining accurate figures on the number of NGOs is difficult. Hearn (2007) suggests that there were 10,000 registered NGOs in 2000. The web pages of the Tanzania Civil Society Database accessible via the Tanzania Development gateway (www.tanzaniagateway.org/civilsociety – accessed 30 June 2014) do not provide total figures but do list NGOs in sectoral categories, from which my estimate is taken. This does not include smaller community-based organisations registered at district level (as at 2011).

room or two with desks and chairs and a chart naming key post holders within the organisation. Civil-society activity is visible in the daily life of the town in other ways, not so much in terms of the projects that organisations claim to be engaged with, which are generally in rural communities, the 'virtuous location' of civil-society activity (Mindry 2001: 1189), but in the town's few photocopy shops and internet cafés. Smartly dressed men and women bring documents for printing, laminating and binding, and pay by the hour to sit hunched over sticky keyboards working on funding proposals.

CSOs are now an established peri-urban form in Tanzania, along with another institutional innovation of the 1990s, the district umbrella organisation or civil-society network. These district networks were an outcome of the organisation-building around the consultation process for the NGO Policy (AKDN 2007, 16), which was designed to produce a national map of verticality and encompassment (Ferguson & Gupta 2002: 982) in which regions and districts mediated between community and the state. Networking is considered to be a characteristically civil-society activity, playing on the association between community activism and social capital (Riles 2001). Sustained by the support of donors with strong civil-society commitments, and because 'networking' has a place in the new relations of accountability between local government and civil society, district umbrella organisations strive to have offices in town centres, staking a claim for the status of civil society in district power relations. The offices of district umbrella organisations display these relations representationally through organisational charts and lists of member organisations. Such listings reveal the emergent mix of the range of organisations claiming affiliation and hence status as district civil society – church organisations, including youth groups, parishes and dioceses; youth networks, themselves established as projects of other organisations and the local NGO as a special kind of small-scale organisation.

## Constituting NGOs in Tanzania

In actuality, civil society as a discursive category in Tanzania is largely confined to development policy materials and documentation in English. Although the category of *asasi za kiraia*, meaning 'citizen organisations', is used as the policy equivalent of civil society in formal spaces such as the Foundation for Civil Society, ordinary people and activists alike classify district CSOs in terms of those they are seen to emulate through the usual descriptor of 'NGO' used by persons speaking either Kiswahili or English. Local NGOs, therefore, are expected to be like the development NGOs on which they are modelled, to have offices, staff and projects, and to be involved in development as a funded field of projects and donor relations. As such they are perceived to be quite distinct from the organisations and pressure groups that characterised Tanzanian political orders in the 1970s and 1960s (Gibbon 2001). Local NGOs display a common organisational structure, with official positions of chair, treasurer and secretary aligned around a developmental purpose usually articulated in the terms of organisational development as vision and mission. They are not expected to be membership organisations (Shivji 2004: 689). The most significant personnel are those in leadership positions, usually founder members, supported by between eight and fifteen associates defining themselves as 'volunteers'.[9] Like the international NGOs whose forms they adopt, these organisations have a name, reducible to an acronym and, where possible, offices identified by signboards as artefacts of official status. Some of these attributes, including their statement of objectives, organisational structure, name and office address, are necessitated by the requirements of NGO registration. Others, the office itself, with its desk and paperwork, the signboards and the dress favoured by staff and volunteers, associate NGO work with development work as modern, professional practice.

NGOs are required to have a constitution setting out their aims and organisational structure (AKDN 2007: 20). This constitution is literal (Strathern 2006: 189). Constitutional statements of aspiration provide the basis for organisational self-identification and, in enabling self-description, for replication among mutually recognisable entities (Strathern 1999: 173). The missions and visions that are part of these documents do not simply identify one organisation among numerous others. They enact the moral constitution of civil-society groupings as quite distinct from private businesses or government institutions. Emphasising this difference is fundamental to the constitution of Tanzanian civil society, as detailed in the NGO Policy, which states that 'NGOs shall have specific characteristics which distinguish them from government organisations or other registered private groupings' (URT 2001, 4). This difference is important in district settings, where many such organisations involve local-government staff and where what such organisations do in competing for contracts could be interpreted as profit-seeking and hence as fundamentally self-interested. Here, as in much of Africa, self-interest equates with negative social values around selfishness, and works against the kind of patrimonial alliance building sought by would-be civil-society entrepreneurs (Swidler 2009; Green 2003). Private development businesses have yet to arise officially in district development because what donors are buying into here is not the efficiency and effectiveness claimed for private-sector consultancy firms, but the moral associations of civil society and assumed relation with beneficiaries (Hearn 2001: 341). The moral dimension of community engagement is valorised in

---

[9] A 2007 survey conducted on behalf of the Aga Khan Development Network in Tanzania found that 27.3 per cent of not-for-profit organisations had membership of between 51 and 100 people. The second largest category of organisations had a membership of between 11 and 25 persons. Significantly, the majority of people who claimed to be members of an NGO 'had membership in 3.4' organisations (AKDN 2007: 28–9).

training materials and civil-society discourse, not only about the suitably deserving status of beneficiaries – orphans, people affected by HIV and AIDS, the disabled, poor people and so on – but in terms of the repertoire of participatory, hence community-oriented, tools with which such organisations are expected to work. Persons paid by CSOs for the duration of project contracts therefore do not present themselves as staff who do not receive salary (*mshahara*), but as volunteers who receive only an allowance (*posho*) (see also Olivier de Sardan 2009; Swidler 2009). It is the moral claim of volunteering in a CSO rather than location or class that informs assertions that such organisations are closer to the poor and understand intrinsically the experience of villagers (Pigg 1992; Mindry 2001). Closeness here, an artefact of interstitiality, legitimates the positioning of CSOs as implementers of community development.[10]

## Capacity-building

Constitutions, and the missions and visions that comprise them, conform to a fairly standard template, a product of NGO registration requirements that demand a specific organisational form, and of the multiple donor initiatives to develop CSOs. This has been accomplished through what is termed in the development field 'capacity-building', the promotion of a set of techniques through which organisational forms can be replicated along with the organisations able to promote them. Tanzanian civil-society expansion is creating a parallel set of specialist organisations designed to meet the capacity needs of these organisations in development. Originally established by international NGOs such as Oxfam, Action Aid, PACT and Hivos as part of their strategies to 'develop civil society' in the 1990s, this new cadre of private providers retains strong links with the organisations that established them. Staff usually comprise people who have themselves been trained by these programmes. Local capacity-builders specialise in building capacity in local areas – they are not themselves situated in districts but in regional centres, as their clients are dispersed across the country. They are likely to be registered as CSOs but operate as small businesses, funded either as part of top-down programmes of capacity development, and hence as contractors to capacity-builders such as PACT, or paid for specific consultancy inputs by smaller client organisations. Enmeshed in chains of contracting, like the organisations they develop, they are ultimately dependent on the spending decisions of international NGOs.

---

[10] Civil society operates as a proxy for community in these interventions, not only in Tanzania, hence support for AIDS-affected children delivered through vertical AIDS funding mechanisms such as PEPFAR – organised, in the absence of alternative institutional structures for social welfare, on the basis of 'community support' – is channelled through CSOs. For the same reasons, CSOs are considered to be the most appropriate media for community education and sensitisation (Swidler & Watkins 2009).

Capacity-building in the NGO sector has consisted of replicating what are regarded as the normative organisational forms for CSOs through training for participants in core areas of activity.[11] The kind of organisation envisaged is 'capacitated' when it can obtain funding and hence achieve 'sustainability' through implementing projects (Swidler & Watkins 2009).[12] In the words of a training manual on strategic planning produced by TRACE, a Dar es Salaam-based capacity provider, itself established as a project of an international NGO:

> The ideal situation for CSOs in Tanzania is to be strategic and therefore proactive in thinking strategically. CSOs need to think beforehand and pursue their funders to assist them financially to develop and implement a strategic plan ... As a young coming up CSOs [sic] you may have to wait for a number of years before you have to build your reputation to be legible [*sic*] for assistance from donors ... (Mwango & Mussadegh n.d.: ix).

Training sessions offered by 'local capacity-builders' exhibit a high degree of standardisation intensified by the use of what come to count as the basic 'tool kits' for various requirements of organisational development. The emphasis of such sessions is on organisational development in three related areas: the organisational structure, which consists of named officers around a mission and vision; strategic planning; and developing a proposal for funding. The standardisation of training and understanding of capacity is accentuated by the limited number of organisations providing training and the relations between new entrants and originators of such programmes. It is also an attribute of globalising technologies of management including, for example, the idea of the project that is 'highly *reproducible* (as) a totality of well defined rules and procedures' (Clegg & Courpasson 2004: 543, original emphasis), and what could be considered as the normative template for not-for-profit organisations transnationally (Hwang & Suarez 2005; Powell et al. 2005; Bazin & Selim 2006: 457). Standardisation is not confined to this kind of intervention but is a sought attribute of development technologies more generally (Hirschmann 1967). Interventions that are replicable and that conform to programme designs practically require standardised approaches, just as standardisation theoretically permits a range of personnel to implement recognised practices across time and space. This implementation is complex because practices are never undertaken in quite the same way, within and outside development. Nevertheless, the representation of standard ways of doing

---

[11] This is termed 'OD' (organisational development) in the training materials, which emphasise having a vision and mission as essential to developing an effective organisation and as a precondition for strategic planning.
[12] Civil-society advocates such as Tina Wallace consider this orientation to arise as a result of donor funding requirements, with the emphasis on formal planning and project management (Wallace et al. 2004).

things to address standard replicable problems is an important part of the conceptual tool kit through which development problems and solutions are not merely 'rendered technical' but are transnationally applicable (Li 2007a, 2007b; Pigg 1992). 'Tool kits' for addressing a range of development issues, from community-level project management to designing PRSs, are readily available on the web pages of development organisations.[13]

The emphasis on replication is not unusual in the highly institutionalised context of international development, indeed government more generally, where standard organisational forms come to be equated with rational functionality irrespective of actual effectiveness (Meyer & Rowan 1977). The standardisation of institutions for the delivery of education at all levels, modalities of what counts as public-sector reform, and the expansion of civil society itself, are examples of this institutional isomorphism evident through development programming in different country settings (see also Frödin 2009). This orientation is likely to be accentuated where 'fast policy' (Peck 2002, 2011) necessitates a heavy reliance on policy templates and where utilisation of consultancy inputs encourages their use. In such situations, of which international development is an exemplar, Meyer and Rowan's analysis is insightful:

> Professions, policies, and programs are created along with the products and services they are understood to produce rationally. This permits many new organisations to spring up and forces existing ones to incorporate new practices and procedures ... Institutionalised products, services, techniques, policies and programmes function as powerful myths, and many organisations adopt them ceremonially (1977: 340).

They continue, 'the building blocks for organizations come to be littered around the societal landscape: it takes only a little entrepreneurial energy to assemble them into a structure' (1977: 345).

## Anticipatory development

Capacity-building is not only an important part of the political economy of development in Tanzania and the wider relations in which it is embedded. In a situation in which development spending and relations prescribed by policy are being devolved to lower levels, capacity-building enables entrepreneurship around development, opening the field to new actors who can access the necessary elements to set up an organisation ready to assume a place in these new contracting relations. A consequence of the availability of capacity, if not funding, is a littering of

---

[13] See for example the World Bank 'OVC (Orphans and Vulnerable Children) Toolkit', the DFID's 'Tools for Development' handbook on development competencies and techniques, and, when dealing with an entire country, the World Bank's exhaustive Poverty Reduction Strategy Paper (PRSP) Sourcebook.

organisational building blocks and a littering of organisations in varying states of activity, along with the widespread popularisation of ideas about development and NGOs as kinds of organisation and activity. Attention to form is extremely important, manifested in the presentation of office space and the emphasis on documentation (Elyachar 2005) such as the mission statements and constitutions that establish an organisation and facilitate registration. Documentation is necessary in order to perform civil society, and the most critical types are the funding proposal and, if successful, the various types of project-monitoring reports through which implementation status is maintained. Finally, mission statements and acronyms enable the integration of registered organisations into the formal map of district governance, through lists presented to local government, and into the representation of national civil society. While these small organisations have offices and representatives to promote them, and a formal place in the architecture of district development, they are not necessarily undertaking development activities. Without funding to carry out activities, or to implement projects for other organisations, they remain dormant, NGOs in waiting, hoping for inclusion in development relations. Whatever their origins, becoming active for CSOs does not entail activism or generating membership or demand, but attaining a place within a set of contracting relations. This evolution from project to organisation to contractor replicates the sought trajectory of the civil-society organisational development, from a funded project of a donor to a contractor implementing projects.

A successful contract facilitates the sought-after professionalisation of an organisation as a contractor in the district development landscape, in which certain organisations bid to be included in externally funded interventions (Mercer & Green 2013). As such contracts are rare, and capacity to obtain funding tends to be limited to organisations that already have experience of implementing projects, and hence to those that were themselves constituted as projects, perhaps the majority of CSO activity is about this kind of situating; what might be termed *anticipatory* development. Anticipatory development refers to the ways in which agents seeking a place in development orders, and associated resource streams, adopt postures premised on the possibility of this emplacement. In relation to the CSOs this is mostly concerned with adopting the appropriate form that enables recognition, registration and, potentially, capacity for funding. The emphasis on form is not simply about recognition by potential funders. In conforming to the institutional design of organisations associated with particular functions, capacity is partially assumed, by volunteers, beneficiaries and members of the public where these organisations seem to conform to popular expectations of local civil-society organisation. In addition to the presentation of exterior forms of enacting civil society through volunteering and setting up offices, the production of documentation is critical. Civil-society documentation is explicitly anticipatory – missions and visions that aspire to engagement in a future-oriented action toward specific outcomes, and the more prosaic funding proposals with their logframe, or logical framework, of cause and effect and carefully crafted budgets. These documentary forms provide the vehicle through which civil society can replicate itself as conforming to particular forms, and a basis for engagement in what is categorised as civil-society activity. Further, in anticipating development as a particular kind of activity through project proposals and budgets (Collier 2006), they reiterate a development imaginary of governance, accountability and sectoral integration.

The emphasis on form as a shortcut to legitimacy, and the association of civil society with particular areas of work around community engagement, opens the field of competition to virtually any organisation that can attain recognition as a civil-society actor. Some organisations are able to use this flexibly, bidding for contracts in different sectoral areas even where the effects of their engagement lead to involvement in activities well beyond their scope of experience. Entrepreneurial flexibility rewarded by the system incentivises organisations to continuously shift what they claim to do and the areas in which they engage. This can be seen more generally in the transition from project to CSO-contractor, displayed in the UNICEF-established youth networks in Magu and Bagomoyo, which currently compete with other NGOs for work in the business of sensitisation around HIV and AIDS, and in the transition in Magu of NGOs working with the environment to HIV and AIDS.[14]

Such shifts in engagement are evident in the examples of two organisations that had made parallel endeavours to adopt the civil-society form. The first, encountered in 2008, was a small-scale orphanage run as the personal project of a middle-class woman in Bagomoyo rural. Such initiatives, often an extended household in which children who have lost one parent are accommodated, are common in Tanzania. Those who run them seek support from district AIDS budgets, from individual benefactors, frequently overseas, and from small-scale donor organisations of the kind that will support informal projects. The orphanage had diversified into wider contracting opportunities through assuming status as a CSO. This had enabled it to bid for funding from a national NGO to implement a participatory research project in a neighbouring fishing village, and ultimately to obtain funding for the purchase of a fishing boat that was intended to be utilised by the fishermen of the village. How this would happen was unresolved when I visited in 2008. The boat was unusable because its net gauge was unsuitable, and neither fishermen nor NGO were willing to make the necessary financial contributions to correct this. The result of this 'shapeshifting' was an orphanage running an unusable fishing boat for beneficiaries who did not benefit and who were not orphans.

[14] In Magu, MAYODEN (Magu Youth Development Network); in Bagomoyo, BAYODEN (Bagomoyo Youth Development Network).

The second organisation that had adopted civil-society form had transitioned from a Pentecostal church in conformity with a parallel organisational template circulating in Tanzanian society – that of the small-scale evangelical pastor-focused church. Feed and Tend International (FTI) was based in Magu District, where its representatives claimed to have constructed an office building at a cost of 8 million Tanzanian Shillings (c. US $6,000, GBP £3,750 at that time). The organisation had a number of volunteers struggling to undertake activities with children defined as vulnerable by the district social welfare office. As well as an acronym and office building, FTI had named officers, including a secretary and treasurer, was undertaking what it claimed were developmental activities, in that they were potentially fundable activities in villages with morally deserving beneficiaries, and a pile of necessary documentation, including a constitution, a mission statement and a vision. FTI's constitution sets out its purpose and mission in English in terms that combine evangelical aspiration with the moral imperative of development. FTI was a hybrid comprised of a range of organisational aspirations within a civil-society skin. Although its vision is to 'Carry out the word of God in the power of the Holy Spirit', the purpose of the organisation is 'to meet physical and spiritual needs through relief and development'. FTI's aims and objectives strive to be more grounded. These are:

> to enable Christians … to cooperate in furthering integral human development, particularly through sharing with the poor and oppressed … to provide educational services, bible colleges, seminaries, public libraries and training institutions, social services, hospitals, dispensaries, clinics, youth centres, children and aged homes, hostels, restaurants, disabled homes; Relief services – food, tents, clothes, building material, water equipment, operation of fishing, agricultural and livestock farms, mining, low cost houses and other poverty alleviating programmes and projects.

FTI's constitution veers between development and evangelical objectives and it had initiated a combination of savings and loan and a pyramid scheme based on contributions from villagers. While those who had contributed cash were losing faith in its capacity to deliver the increased sums they had been promised, its 'volunteers' remained loyal. They had persistent faith in the capacity of FTI as constituting a CSO and, as such, as a genuine actor in district civil society and hence development. Indeed, the secretary of the organisation, handing over a copy of the constitution, was at pains to show that FTI was properly constituted as a CSO and waited only to deliver. FTI was not, in his view, radically different to other CSOs in the District and beyond it. Constituted around a vision, and hence a rationale for interventions among specific beneficiaries, it existed to deliver on civil society's promise.

## Documents and dissemination

Writing and the production of documentation is central to the constitution of what appears as the civil-society sector in Tanzania, and to
individual organisations. Writing is how they present themselves to
others as genuine organisations, from the acronyms and logos to the
constitutions and proposals through which they are structured as well
as displays of activities on office walls. Such displays realise civil-
society engagement in development at the same time as they articulate the
nature of the relation between the organisation and beneficiaries. CSOs,
mostly urban-based, are only occasionally present in the communities
where they undertake funded activities. Organisational presence within
communities is established outside them, not through action or effects,
but through writing as an act of representation. The representation of
activities as part of a 'sector' that transcends organisations and villages
is made possible through certain kinds of writing, as is the distribution
of identical organisational forms through which these organisations are
constituted. This dispersal and replication is supported by contemporary
technologies of dispersal and replication – the photocopier, computer
and internet, as well as the peripheral devices of USB sticks, compact
discs and mobile phones – that allow forms to be stored and disseminated
(Rabinow 2006). It is further enabled by social strategies for the replication of development practices. These include the top-down systems
of capacity-building through dispersal modalities such as the training
of trainers, the funding streams that demand compliance with certain
documentary forms (Wallace et al. 2006), and the institution of the stakeholder workshop as a participatory form through which development
practices come to be circulated and learnt.

Both the social and material technologies of replication have proliferated in Tanzania with increases in donor budgets, the creation of
civil-society funding streams and the significant price reductions in
mobilising technologies such as computers, mobile phones and photo-
copying that have permitted the extension of these services to rural centres.
This extension is a complex social process. Because price prohibits the
accessing of these technologies by individuals, with the recent exception
of mobile phones as tariffs have fallen, the dissemination of communications technologies depends on numerous individual entrepreneurs who
trade in services, often broken down into smallest tradable components
– for example, charging phones, the sale of phone credit and, for those
without handsets, calls from phones. Entrepreneurship is not confined
to the material technologies associated with civil-society expansion. The
sector is ruthlessly competitive, with numerous undifferentiated organisations competing for funding through a combination of generic project
management strategies and the purchase of sector-specific technical

expertise. As well as the formal-service providers dealing in training and organisational development, a number of individual entrepreneurs specialise in the production of civil-society documentation, notably funding proposals. This service is sought after in rural districts, where few people have the experience necessary to construct good, that is fundable, proposals. It is also used by people wanting to have proposals on hand to help in their search for patrons to support more personal projects. Civil-society entrepreneurship is not restricted to countries in which the sector is being established (Rabinow 2006: 49), but is constitutive of not-for-profits more generally where they exist as potential contractors in equivalent relations with government. The not-for-profit sector in the United States, with some twelve million employees, is similarly structured through the marketisation of capacity and organisational development (Powell et al. 2005: 235). It too is characterised by the standardisation of strategies and forms, reliance on consultancy inputs and excessive stylisation (Hwang & Suarez, 2005: 71–81). In countries like Tanzania, where barriers to entry are low for private individuals as long as they have some skills in office practice, personal connections to gain credibility with district staff and cash to invest in document production, the expansion of the not-for-profit sector offers potential opportunities for district professional classes to gain contracting opportunities in community development and become social entrepreneurs.

## Writing relationships to development

The existence of a market in civil society, and associated expertise, not only allows organisations to bid for work with which they have no experience, it also enables new entrants to the development marketplace to access the skills they need to produce the range of documentation required to participate in it. Writing forms the basis of a kind of expertise associated with civil-society capacity, and the basis of much activity in the form of the production of bids for grant funding and the production of tenders for development contracts. Writing not only permits the representation of organisational forms, around which people may or may not align, but it sets out relationships – between form and action, action and impact, organisation and beneficiaries, putting them 'into words' (Callon 2002: 196). This is explicit in the NGO constitutions, which situate the organisation's vision and mission in relation to the intended beneficiaries and Tanzania's development strategy. It is also present in the strategic plans, project proposals, logical frameworks and budgets for activities that CSOs produce as part of their place in the organisation of development. Such documents are not in fact concerned with the representation of actual relations, but with the capture of anticipated relations that constitute the possible basis for a contract, and with it inclusion into the formal relations of development.

In situations where multitudes of small-scale CSOs have come into being to compete for contractual roles within the design of decentralised development, writing a relationship to development is a necessary precondition for contracting and hence for inclusion in development relations. Specialised forms of writing thus constitute the core activity of anticipatory development, at the same time as writing permits the dispersal and extension of development's organisational forms. The materiality of these forms is significant. Like the offices, signboards and business cards as artefacts of development in Tanzania, reports, logframes and proposals carry connotations of lives and work associated with professional status and expertise, and, as the antithesis of the villagers in need of sensitisation, with sophisticated urban identity.[15] In Tanzania, and places like it, engagement with development artefacts allows those seeking the status of development actors to access some aspects of this future engagement in the present. Development artefacts continue to connote status and professional identity in Tanzania. As such, like high-status consumer goods, they become vehicles for 'displaced meaning' (McCracken 1990). Aspiration contributes to the proliferation of district NGOs in Tanzania, as does the desire of peri-urban professional classes to contribute to rural development. Plans, budgets, strategies and visions perform the work of situating civil society representationally as a player in development as a future-oriented project that has yet to be implemented. It is not therefore surprising that civil-society 'volunteers' should perceive themselves as occupying a position proximate to development and hence positioned to incorporate others into development relations. For those outside implementation, where a project exists as a design or strategy, projects and missions provide a boundary between development and un-development, and in so doing, situate civil-society agency (Yakura 2002).[16]

[15] As with 'development' work more generally. For Tanzania see Green (2003), for Nepal see Pigg (1992), and for civil-society practice in the former Soviet Union see Aksartova (2009).
[16] This sense of volunteering is reinforced by the NGO Policy, which stresses the voluntary nature of NGOs (URT 2001).

# 7

**Development
Templates**

Modernising
Anti-Witchcraft
Services
in Southern
Tanzania

This chapter[1] shows how a particular development-influenced imagination of modernisation in relation to public services and market liberalisation is driving transformations in the ways traditional healers undertake their work and interaction with clients. The example of one healer's attempts to modernise the ways people can access the services he provides to suppress the powers of witches permits a privileged insight into the reconstruction of a new modernity in a liberalising Tanzania under the pervasive influence of transnational models of public-sector reform. By focusing on the relations and institutions through which particular constructs of the 'modern' are made real in particular places at particular times it allows for a reappraisal of anthropological theories about modernity as they are made to apply to 'other' people and places.

Some recent anthropological accounts of Africa have emphasised the continuing salience of ideas about witchcraft for understanding contemporary sociality in all its forms. For urban and rural, elite and peasant farmer, *nouveau riche* and dispossessed, witchcraft remains an idiom through which the universe – social, moral, natural – is experienced and acted upon. Such studies claim to challenge conventional modernist assumptions about the persistence of witchcraft into the twenty-first century, making the point that witchcraft, and equivalent discourses of the unseen, are integral aspects of contemporary disparate modernities. These studies show how witchcraft in diverse settings can become a means of making sense of the contradictions of the contemporary capitalist world (Comaroff & Comaroff 1993: xxix), of dealing with the ambivalence of state power under undemocratic regimes (West 2001), of adapting to the demands of structural adjustment (Sanders 2002) or a vehicle for the articulation of personal, local and national

---

[1] The research on which this chapter is based was carried out with Simeon Mesaki. We jointly authored a version of this chapter as a paper in *American Ethnologist* (Green & Mesaki 2005).

political relations (Dolan 2002; Rowlands & Warnier 1988).[2]

As a phenomenon of the contemporary world witchcraft is undoubtedly 'modern', an attribute largely derived from the vagueness and ambiguity of witchcraft discourses that can adapt and become relevant to myriad social environments and social relationships (Geschiere 1997: 10). But while such accounts seek to represent witchcraft as essentially 'modern', they are less concerned with critically interrogating the specific constitution of the modernities of which witchcraft is apparently a part.[3] Where the category 'modernity' is perceived to be more than merely indicative of a contemporaneous state of being it is frequently apprehended, as across anthropology more generally, as encapsulating those somewhat taken-for-granted effects of transnational capitalism on contemporary social relations: the increase in scale of contacts, market incorporation and potentially totalising integration into a global social order (Ferguson 1999; Comaroff & Comaroff 1993). Alternatively, modernity as a category is treated as the abstract episteme of the modernism caricatured by post-modernists such as Jameson (1991), that is, as a related set of narratives and perspectives that privilege Western thought and power, naturalising social relations of capitalism, globalisation and inequality (cf. Latour 1993; Englund & Leach 2000).

Despite the emphasis on the significance and significations of the 'modern' in witchcraft studies,[4] whatever 'the modern' may be represented as being, it is rarely approached as a specific focus of ethnographic inquiry. Perhaps this is not surprising: informants may represent issues around witchcraft as attributes of the present or as a consequence of 'modern' life, but they are less likely to perceive witchcraft practices as constituents of the modern, especially when the constructions of modernity espoused by contemporary African states are likely to be informed by a highly modernist opposition between what is represented as a 'traditional' past associated with 'customs' and a future of planned development in which the irrationality of 'traditional' superstition is reduced to 'culture'.[5] If witchcraft discourses and practices are attributes of the 'modern', and are utilised self-consciously for what are perceived as the 'modern' ends of individual accumulation and personal development (Comaroff & Comaroff 1993; Bond & Ciekawy 2001; Dolan 2002; Green 1997), they are nevertheless categorised by people living in communities where witchcraft is an issue as simultaneously part of indigenous and national 'traditions'. Such practices are likely to be claimed as antithetical

[2] For an overview of recent anthropological studies of witchcraft, see Bond & Ciekawy (2001: 13–17).

[3] Of course, anthropologists have approached the constitution of diverse modernities and notions of the 'modern' ethnographically. See, for example, Miller (1994) for Trinidad and Ferguson (1999) for Zambia.

[4] For a critical perspective on the way that modernity comes to assume explanatory significance in such accounts, see Englund (1996).

[5] On the relation between rationality and a presumed irrational 'culture' as the basis of Otherness, see Scott (2003).

to an imposed modernity and, by extension, to imported means of dealing with witches, hence the dismissal of colonial efforts to use legislation in the battle against *witchcraft* rather than *witches* and the post-colonial state's recourse to the courts in an effort to punish individual witches (Geschiere 1997: 169; 2006; Mesaki 2009). Equally, ideas about witchcraft are liable to be condemned by 'modernisers' as backward, retrogressive and irrational, a position adopted by majority Christian denominations, by Islamic leaders and by 'progressive' governments and their donors in many countries in Africa.

This negative evaluation of witchcraft is reiterated at community level, although in a slightly different form that emphasises the damage done by witches to community aspirations for development. Witchcraft is often viewed as antithetical to a desired modernity because of the ways that witches are thought to attack those individuals striving to achieve modernity for themselves through what have been represented by some anthropologists as distinctly 'untraditional' styles of accumulation and consumption (Bond & Ciekawy 2001; Geschiere 1997; Moore & Sanders 2002).[6] The explicit un-modernity of witchcraft, then, from the community perspective, presents a radical challenge to anthropological efforts to resituate witchcraft in the modern. However, just as anthropologists strive to collapse what is, after all, an essentially modernist dichotomy between 'tradition' and 'modernity' (cf Kapferer 2002: 16) in the case of witchcraft, in order to locate witchcraft within a particular type of present, communities and states in Africa make use of the same dichotomy to make explicit important moral truths about witchcraft in relation to what they perceive as 'modern'. While witchcraft works against modernity and contravenes development, variously defined, the work of specialist practitioners who claim the powers to suppress or eradicate witchcraft is often explicitly associated with the 'modern', both by the ethnographers who have described it (Auslander 1993; Marwick 1950: Richards 1935; Smith 2008) and by practitioners and clients. This is because anti-witchcraft specialists help realise modernity through the suppression of witchcraft and because they have often made use of a particular symbolism of bureaucracy and technology intended to convey associations with the 'modern' to enhance the efficacy of their practice (Fisher & Arce 2001: 87–93; Green 1994; 1997).

I had previously examined the practice of one such anti-witchcraft specialist in an earlier fieldwork carried out in the 1990s. My focus then was on the core symbolism at the heart of the witchcraft-suppression rituals in southern Tanzania, which centred on the purification of alleged witches in a ritual that entailed the shaving off of head and body hair by itinerant shavers. I wrote about the ambiguous location of such practices as both 'traditional', in that they were informed by practice oriented at

---

[6] But see Englund (1996), who makes the point that what is being critiqued by community condemnations of consumption is not consumption *per se*, but failure to meet 'traditional' moral obligations, rendering witchcraft allegations a critique not of 'modernity' but of morality.

constituting relations between people and spirits, and 'modern', in that it played on the symbolic use of 'modern' artefacts to address the anti-modernism of witches (Green 1994, 1997, 2003). Thirteen years later I was able to revisit the practice of that specialist, now in the contested hands of her descendants. What had previously been available in one place only, steeped in the mystique of spirits associated with particular territories, and which demanded an extended stay on the part of those seeking treatment, was now widely advertised through a range of media and could be performed fairly rapidly at several locations in the region. Moreover, these changes were part of an explicit strategy on the part of their initiator to modernise his practice, which covers both shaving witchcraft and what is labelled 'traditional' healing in Tanzania.

'Traditional' healing here refers to the practice of those medical specialists working in the domain of tradition as a relation between people and spirits (cf. Boyer 1990). It does not indicate that such practices are 'traditional' in terms of historic practice, nor in opposition, other than rhetorical, to the 'modern' (Langwick 2011). Dealing with witchcraft is encompassed by traditional healing because of the role of divination in diagnosing witchcraft attack, because such attacks often manifest themselves in illness and because of the relationship between healing and power. This fraught relationship between 'traditional' practice and what constitutes the 'modern', or at least the desirable aspects of it, is one that anti-witchcraft specialists themselves are forced to confront on a daily basis as they deal with the changing demands and expectations of clients caught up in Tanzania's attempts to implement various incarnations of 'modernisation'. The 'modern' in Tanzania, as elsewhere, is a social construct devoid of universal content.[7] Rather, specific constitutions of the 'modern' are invoked at particular times and particular places to envision particular projects of transformation, of modernisation. Transformations in the delivery of anti-witchcraft practice in this instance were driven by the personal vision of their initiator, Shaibu Magungu, and his drive to make his practice modern as a commitment to a personal project of 'development' (*maendeleo*). Magungu's vision of modernity as development is echoed by the users of anti-witchcraft services, who have come to regard them as a precondition for the achievement of their own smaller-scale projects of modernity.

## Dealing with witchcraft in Tanzania

Tanzania is a particularly interesting country for the study of witchcraft. A state founded within development relations and which has been subject to successive regimes of colonial and post-colonial rationalisation, through community development for example, the country has

---

[7] Latour's comment – '...a temporality, in itself, has nothing temporal about it. It is a means of connecting entities and filing them away' (1993: 75) – is relevant here.

been wholly enmeshed within political relations of development assistance structured around poverty reduction and liberalisation policies. A strong national culture nurtured through Kiswahili as the national language, and careful policies designed to stifle 'tribalism', coexist with over one hundred different ethnic groups, all with their own languages and customs. Witchcraft *(uchawi)* transcends local and national culture and is part of daily life in all social settings and in all locations. Although the specific manifestations of *uchawi* and the attributes of witches vary from one place to another and from community to community, *uchawi* shares certain characteristics, and witches attributes, that allow for intelligibility between different witchcraft traditions.

Whether witches are said to be elderly women, as in Sukuma communities, or young children who have inherited witchcraft paraphernalia from their parents,[8] or whether witchcraft powers derive from a physical site within the body,[9] or from substances purchased from other communities to the east,[10] discourses on witchcraft in Tanzania, in consistently addressing themes of envy, greed, cannibalism, death and consumption, are firmly implicated in local and national debates about poverty and development (Green 1994; Sanders 2002),[11] at the same time as demanding strategies for dealing with witchcraft and those alleged to practise it. These strategies vary markedly between the north-western and southern parts of the country. In the north-west, notably among the Sukuma, the country's largest ethnic group, the submerged violence of witchcraft is met with explicit violence commonly directed against the elderly, female and vulnerable who are most likely to be accused.[12] In such areas, expulsion and murder are not uncommon (Mesaki 1994; Bukurura 1994). As the market mediates the access of witches to the medicines and potions with which to commit their secret crimes, it now mediates the execution of witches through the secret hiring of young men willing to hack them to death.

In much of southern Tanzania, and along the coast, ways of dealing with

---

[8] As in some Ulanga and Kilombero communities today. The majority of witches are adults, but it is said that children can become witches through such inheritance. Interestingly, we were told by several people that 'shaving' fosters witchcraft by inheritance, as middle-aged parents get taken for shaving and instruct their children to inherit earlier the things that the adult can no longer use. This situation explains, we were informed, why at least two decades of 'shaving', and access to a range of their anti-witchcraft practitioners over time, has not been able to eradicate witchcraft.

[9] As among the Nyakyusa (Wilson 1963).

[10] The notion that communities to the east have more powerful witchcraft that they sell to their western neighbours is widespread, certainly in southern Tanzania. In Ulanga, people say that witchcraft comes from Ngindo communities to the east, who are in turn said to get it from Mwera and others along the coast, who in turn obtain witchcraft medicines and substances from Pemba Island. People on Pemba are said to get their witchcraft powers even further east, from Arabia and India.

[11] For other countries in Africa see Geschiere (1997), Rowlands & Warnier (1988) or Apter (1993).

[12] Witchcraft here, as elsewhere, is ultimately about murder, the ultimate objective of witches being to kill their victims. In Africa witches are associated with cannibalism, grave-robbing and vampirism of various sorts.

witches are more benign. Witchcraft is conceptualised as a life-threatening activity, and witches embody the antithesis of normal moral values, but witchcraft is viewed as in some sense an affliction that, through the human habit of acquiescence to greed and excess, can affect almost anybody (Green 1997). Witchcraft derived from the power of medicines can be suppressed through the use of other medicines administered by specialists as part of a ritual of cleansing known as shaving witchcraft (*kunyoa uchawi*) or, more recently, as 'getting oneself cleansed' (*kujisafi* or *kusafishwa*).[13] Shaving as a legitimate kind of anti-witchcraft practice in southern Tanzania goes back to at least the beginning of the twentieth century.[14] It is associated with a limited number of specialists who attract clients from a wide area, and some of whom have a long history of this work.

The specific institutional forms through which shaving witchcraft is delivered as a service to communities and individuals have changed in parallel with changes in other institutions. During the British colonial period, the itinerant witchcraft shavers were permitted by the authorities to travel around rural districts offering their services and were even encouraged to shave the adult populations of the villages created as part of the large-scale modernisation programmes justified by the eradication of tsetse and agricultural development. Post-independence policy, similarly based on resettlement through villagisation, also allowed specialists to visit villages. In the early 1980s, the attitude of local authorities changed. Specialists were no longer allowed to shave villages, nor to tour the area looking for clients. Individuals deemed by local authorities to have specific witchcraft problems were, however, permitted to travel to a select number of anti-witchcraft specialists, of whom one in particular became nationally famous. Bibi Kalembwana, of Ihowanja village in Malinyi Division in Ulanga District, acquired a virtual monopoly on anti-witchcraft practices across at least the three contiguous districts of Ulanga, Kilombero and Songea, although a significant proportion of her clients came from further afield, from Iringa, Mbeya, Mwanza and Dar es Salaam (Green 1997; 2003). *Bibi* means senior woman or grandmother, and Kalembwana was and continues to be widely known as simply 'the Bibi', while 'going to the Bibi's' is a euphemism for 'going for shaving'.

Kalembwana's practice was based on a combination of long-established purification procedures and distinctly 'modern' components of bureaucratic practice. The purification aspects of the rite involved shaving off all the head and body hair and the administration of special medicines to suppress the powers of witches. Purification was appropriate for dealing with witchcraft imagined as something dirty and antisocial (Green 1997, 2003b). Similar practices were performed by other well-known witchcraft suppressors, either as individuals or as part of the so-called witchcraft-suppression 'movements', which also have a long history in the area

---

[13] On the conceptualisation of medicines as transformative substances in Pogoro traditional practice, see Green (1996).
[14] See Green (1997), Larson (1976) and Redmayne (1970).

(Redmayne 1970; Willis 1968; Larson 1976).[15] Kalembwana's practice, like that of the anti-witchcraft movements with which it had much in common (Richards 1935; Marwick 1950; Willis 1968; Auslander 1993), did not deal only with alleged witches. Accuser and accused arrived together and received exactly the same treatment. 'Witches' were not identified, nor were they differentiated from those who had accused them of witchcraft.

Clients who came to Kalembwana's homestead for shaving remained in a special camp for several days, during which time they provided labour for her fields and homestead, adhering in the camp to certain prohibitions regarding food, fire, water and sex. They were taken in the early morning to a forested area on the margins of the village where they were made to sit on special medicine sprinkled on the ground, wearing clothing that was not only old in the sense of worn and soiled, but 'traditional', that is, non-Western. It was here that people were shaved, starting with their heads, including their eyebrows, and, after discarding their old clothes, were given more medicine, some cooked in a meal, consisting of chicken and flour that clients had brought with them, which they ate together, accuser and accused. Finally, those who had been shaved were issued with certificates stating they had been shaved by Kalembwana in Ihowanja before being permitted to return to their homes. After undergoing this treatment it was said that anybody who returned to their witchcraft again, even many years later, would certainly die, and tales of such deaths were widely told (Green 1994, 1997, 2003).

Bibi Kalembwana died in 1997, at a time when her monopoly was institutionalised to such an extent that even after rural people were free to travel to specialists in other parts of the country for the first time in years, and local government had ceased to actively send people for shaving as part of dispute resolution mechanisms, hundreds of people a week were regularly making their way to Ihowanja during the dry season. Although other 'traditional' healing services were available at Kalembwana's place, including *kinga* – medicines that could protect people from witchcraft – by far the majority of people came for shaving. The remote location of Ihowanja, at that time a whole day's walk from Malinyi, itself a day's bus journey from the Kilombero District centre, Ifakara, did not deter them. People also regularly made the two-day journey on foot from villages around Mahenge, Ulanga's district capital, and the four-day journey on foot from the rural villages of Songea.

## Major changes in anti-witchcraft services

Given the extent to which Kalembwana's practice was established in the region, its national reputation[16] and strong relations with local author-

---

[15] For a critique of the distinction some analysts have made between witchcraft-suppression practices and the 'movements' that perform them, see Green (1997).
[16] Kalembwana's death was reported in all the national papers at the time.

ities, it might have been expected that anti-witchcraft practices would continue to be centred on Ihowanja, with little change, even after Kalembwana's death. Indeed, for several years prior to this the bulk of day-to-day work had been supervised and carried out by Kalembwana's assistants, her three adult grandchildren among them. This was not to be the case. En route to a development seminar in the western Tanzanian town of Mbeya in September 2000 I was surprised to see a large painted signboard bearing Kalembwana's name at the side of the main road from Dar es Salaam, next to the junction that would have taken the traveller eventually to 'the Bibi's' old village. The sign boldly informed all who read it that Bibi Kalembwana was no longer in Ihowanja but at a place called Mkasu, near Kiberege, along the same road but more than 200 kilometres closer to the national capital. All the services that had previously been available at Ihowanja were, the sign announced, now available there instead. The sign was large like a road sign, with the writing painted in yellow against a dark green background. At the top and bottom of the board were neatly painted national flags, echoing the design of signs announcing the contractors and sponsors of the numerous new construction and road projects in this aid-dependent country.

A further visit to the area two years later held even more surprises. A previously unremarkable piece of scrub on the outskirts of the fairly non-descript village of Kiberege had been transformed into a settlement, with numerous houses and shelters clearly visible from the murram (laterite) road. Along the road itself several small shops and food venues had sprung up around a bus stand constructed from bamboos, next to another large green-painted sign announcing that *this* was the 'headquarters' of Bibi Kalembwana, *mganga wa asili* (traditional healer). This sign featured a three-legged round stool, signifying 'tradition' in relation to power and healing, a national flag, the word *karibu* (welcome) and, in the top right-hand corner, a small image of Mickey Mouse rendered in black and white. Underneath Mickey was written, in bright white lettering, *mambo yote salon*, roughly translatable as 'the everything salon'.[17]

Changes were obviously happening and, judging by the signboards, were intended to be taken note of. Simeon Mesaki,[18] an anthropologist from the University of Dar es Salaam with expertise in witchcraft, had noticed them too and had established a good relationship with their initiator, Shaibu Magungu, Kalembwana's senior grandson, who had previously worked as the Bibi's main assistant in Ihowanja. Magungu was keen that people should understand the changes he was trying to bring to the anti-witchcraft practices he performed. He welcomed our proposal to come and find out more about them. In July and August 2003 we spent six weeks in the districts of Ulanga and Kilombero researching changes in anti-witchcraft practices in the area. These changes turned out

---

[17] In Kiswahili *mambo* refers to things in the abstract, to 'matters' as opposed to 'things' (*vitu*).

[18] Mesaki works on the social context and consequences of witchcraft in rural Sukuma communities. See Mesaki (1993; 1994).

to be significant. Whereas throughout the 1980s and 1990s shaving had been available in very few locations, and shaving by Kalembwana only at Ihowanja, Kalembwana's services were now claimed to be available in another three locations: Mkasu (Kiberege), which functioned as a kind of practice headquarters; Mwaya, a village 40 kilometres south of Mahenge town; and Nangeru village in Songea rural district. Other large signboards announcing the move away from Ihowanja had been placed at key locations where people en route to Ihowanja could potentially be diverted: at the marketplace in Ifakara, by the bus stand in Ifakara, and at the ferry crossing on the Kilombero river, all points at which people going towards Ihowanja would either seek transport or pass through. Each sign was painted in the same shade of green, with the national flag and Kalembwana's name prominently displayed.

Not only were anti-witchcraft services more dispersed and hence more widely available, but the process of dealing with clients had been speeded up substantially. People arriving for shaving no longer had to remain in the camp for several days, unless they were women menstruating and in that case prohibited from entering the special section where shaving takes place. In addition, the requirement that people coming for shaving had to do work for the *mganga*[19] had been lifted. Those arriving in the afternoon or evening were now shaved the next morning where possible or, at Kiberege, where the volume of people coming for shaving made economies of scale desirable, every two days. Kiberege is readily accessible by road from Dar es Salaam via Mikumi, a mere twenty kilometres or so from the end of the tarmac at the Ruaha river hydroelectric station at Kidatu. It is also on the TAZARA, the Tanzania-Zambia railway, which transects Kalembwana's southern Tanzanian client base. This line links communities in Tanzania en route between Dar es Salaam and Makambako (Songea), who benefit from a regular service known as Kipisi,[20] which provides a cheap and predictable link between them. TAZARA makes Kiberege accessible to clients from Songea, from Njombe and from the communities near to Ihowanja,[21] as well as those coming from the capital. Shaving days at Kiberege are timed to coincide with TAZARA timetables.

Efforts had been made to standardise practice at the new outlets offering Kalembwana's services. Magungu, and others, spoke of them as branches (*matawi*), like the branches of a co-operative or a bank. In addition to time spent at Kiberege and Ihowanja, we visited the Mwaya branch, run by Sadat, Magungu's second-born son. The branch at Mwaya was primarily oriented towards serving local people, many of whom come

[19] In Kiswahili *mganga* means 'doctor' in general, but is commonly used to refer to 'traditional' healers: *waganga wa asili*, (original, authentic healers), *waganga wa jadi* (traditional healers) and *waganga wa kienyeji* ('local' or indigenous healers).

[20] Literally, 'the piece'. This is a shortened train that operates only in Tanzania, unlike the full-length trains that go all the way to Zambia.

[21] Who embark at Mlimba, one day's walk from Ihowanja. Conversely, when Ihowanja was the main centre, clients used TAZARA to reach it, embarking at Songea, Kisaki and Ifakara, and alighting at Mlimba.

on foot, as those who can afford to pay for transport prefer to come to the headquarters at Kiberege. The Songea branch, operated by Magungu's younger brother,[22] was similarly oriented towards a local clientele. Fees were standardised, along with practice across each branch operated by Magungu, the total payable for shaving being 2,520 shillings (c. US $2.50, GBP £1.50) at the time of our visit. As in the 1990s the total fee comprised several discrete payments. These were a fee for shaving (2,000 shillings), the cost of the certificate (500 shillings), and 20 shillings in coins that was the portion of the payment destined for offering to the spirits from whose powers the efficacy of the anti-witchcraft medicine derived.[23]

Magungu insisted that he operated three branches in total, and made no claim to count Ihowanja as a branch, although anti-witchcraft services continued to be provided there. The public are less sensitive to such differentiations, and consider all outlets to be part of practices associated with and authorised by Bibi Kalembwana.[24] Their perception partly reflects the effectiveness of Magungu's advertising initiative, which was not limited to the highly visible signboards influenced by development-financed social marketing campaigns. Informants recalled how prior to the opening of each branch notices were pinned on trees along the routes between villages and district centres, and along the paths to outlying villages, informing people that the service would soon be available and where. Magungu had also taken out advertising slots on national radio and in the press. Aspects of his practice were also regularly featured in the lifestyle pages of various national broadsheet and tabloid newspapers.

## Shaving revisited

When people arrived at the Kiberege headquarters or at the Mwaya branch for 'cleansing' they followed a series of signs directing them to Kalembwana's place. This is on the edge of both villages, at the margins of *miombo* forest. At Kiberege visitors were received by a sentry wearing a clean khaki uniform, with a laminated ID tag at his breast pocket. His role was to direct visitors to a large thatched shelter with open sides where a clerk seated behind a desk wrote down their details in a large hard-bound counter book. At Mwaya, which was a much smaller operation, people followed signs to a smaller shelter, after removing their shoes as instructed by a notice, and awaited reception by an assistant of the *mganga*. In both

---

[22] Not in fact a descendant of Kalembwana herself, as this brother shares only a father with Magungu, who is grandson to her through his mother, who was Kalembwana's daughter.

[23] The coin component informs a style of witchcraft accusation still current in Ulanga and Kilombero, when the alleged witch is touched on the head with two coins (now 100 Shilling pieces), referring to the time when single Shillings were in circulation and the anti-witchcraft fee always included two shillings for the spirits. Then, touching the head with two one Shilling coins was understood as an accusation of witchcraft (see Green 1994).

[24] The division of authority and responsibility between the descendants of Kalembwana is currently disputed.

places, visitors were instructed to remain in the shelter set aside for people coming for shaving, not to eat or to drink water after seven o'clock in the evening if they were to be shaved the next morning, and only to take fire from the assistants, not to light fire themselves.[25] People seeking healing were instructed to sleep elsewhere.

People who were to be shaved spent the night in the shelter. In the morning, they were instructed to dress only in 'traditional' clothing, a sheet or a male wrap (*kikoi*) for the men, and for the women two pieces of *kanga* or *kitenge*. They were then led by an assistant of the *mganga*, also wearing traditional cloth, to a special semi-sacred section, bordering the forest, set aside for shaving. Before the female clients entered the special area they discard one piece of cloth, leaving their breasts exposed.[26] Shaving is still performed in Mkasu and Mwaya by Magungu and his son. It is performed in single-sex groups. Women go first and are made to sit on the ground on a special symbol made from powdered medicine, with their hair undressed, ready for shaving. All the head hair, including eyebrows, is shaved. People shave their own body hair, before awaiting the meal of chicken and *ugali* (maize meal) prepared by assistants of the *mganga*. The meal, cooked with more anti-witchcraft medicine, is eaten in groups of those who have brought each other for shaving. Being shaved, discarding soiled clothing, the administration and ingestion of medicine, and eating together are the main themes of the ritual, after which certificates stating that the named individual has been shaved at Bibi Kalembwana's are issued. These elements are the same as in the early 1990s when shaving was performed under the direction of 'the Bibi' herself. The main innovation in this part of the procedure is in the kind of blades used for shaving. Clients coming for shaving now, and in Ihowanja, bring with them two new razor blades, in line with government health and safety recommendations around the prevention of HIV. Used blades and their paper wrappers are discarded, along with piles of hair and clothing, in pits at the edge of the section reserved for shaving.

## Purification as a public service

Magungu had established his new headquarters at Kiberege in 2000, and the branch at Mwaya some two years later. An initial attempt to establish a branch at Luri, a remote high-altitude settlement north of Mahenge town, had failed, due to the difficulties frail or elderly clients had in reaching it. Despite this setback, the Mwaya branch appeared to be fairly well established by 2003, as was Kiberege. Large, thatched shelters for those arriving as witches has been constructed in each place. Special

---

[25] People coming for shaving or treatment cook for themselves.

[26] For an account of the symbolism invoked in shaving rituals, see Green (1997, 2003). For here it suffices to note that such dress evokes funerals at their most polluting, prior to the burial of the body, and the obligation of women to assume the pollution of mourning.

areas had been cleared in the bush for shaving. Both places had established themselves on the national map as primary destinations for people requiring anti-witchcraft services. Kalembwana's Kiberege headquarters are so well known in Dar es Salaam that travellers boarding buses to Kiberege may be asked almost immediately if they are going to see the Bibi. When we arrived and the bus pulled up opposite the sign at the entrance to Magungu's place, the conductor shouted out, not just for our benefit, that we had arrived at the '(hair) salon'.

The popularity of Magungu's new 'branches' had a negative impact on those specialists continuing to offer shaving services at Ihowanja, including Kalembwana's other grandchildren, who remarked on the dramatic decline in numbers visiting for shaving. The reduction in visitors was also commented on by ward staff, bus workers and the youths who had previously been able to earn a living running bicycle 'taxis' ferrying the better-off the 30 kilometres from the bus stand at Malinyi to what was then the more remote Ihowanja. Residents of Ihowanja and Malinyi reckoned in 2003 that fewer than eight people a day, not all of whom were coming for shaving, visited Kalembwana's old village during the dry season. Although recent improvements in transport to Ihowanja from Malinyi, including a regular bus service, will have altered this situation, it was certainly the case that substantial numbers of people continue to visit Kiberege and Mwaya, mostly for anti-witchcraft services, particularly during the dry season. When the new branches first opened it was not unusual for in excess of 70 people to arrive daily for 'shaving' even at the more remote Mwaya. By 2003 Kiberege had a steady volume of clients. At least 30 people a day arrived during the month of August 2003 and shaving was conducted in large groups of around 70 or more people. The total number of people seeking access to witchcraft-suppression practices was probably equivalent to 1990 levels, despite the shift in the location of services and enormous changes in the political and institutional environment that had removed the previous role of local government in witchcraft disputes, a role which, in authorising disputants to go to Kalembwana for 'shaving', had contributed to the consolidation of Kalembwana's monopoly on anti-witchcraft services during the 1980s.

Residents of villages in Ulanga and in Kilombero with whom we discussed the changes, many of whom had personal experience either of Ihowanja or of the newer branches, were of the opinion that there was no essential difference in terms of content between being shaved in the old days in Ihowanja and currently elsewhere under Kalembwana's name. The basic structure and content of the ritual is the same as it was when I had first visited Ihowanja in 1990. People are given three types of anti-witchcraft medicine, essential prohibitions about fire, food and clothing continue to apply, and they still have to bring a live chicken, salt and a portion of flour with them prior to shaving.[27] A portion of the

---

[27] The chicken has to be a 'traditional' one in the sense of being a local breed (*wa kienyeji*). *Kuku wa kisasa* (imported, literally 'modern', chickens) are not acceptable.

payment in coins continues to be set aside for the spirits whose power ultimately renders the ritual effective. The main changes in *kunyoa uchawi* (shaving witchcraft) are not then concerned with the content of the service so much as the mode of delivery. The significant changes here are in the dispersal of services, the faster throughput for clients seeking the service, and the greater emphasis on client choice about the existence and location of services. People commented on the shorter stay necessary and the fact that services were now available locally, nearer to people's home villages. This move was much appreciated. Ending the requirement to provide labour on the Bibi's *shamba* (fields) as a compulsory contribution was also significant. Magungu and his son both said that labour was no longer necessary because it added to the burden of people who already had serious difficulties because of being involved in a witchcraft dispute.[28] This presentation of changes in the delivery of shaving support a representation of shaving as a service that is oriented towards the needs of clients and that is concerned with caring. The wording on the certificates had also been amended slightly from that used in the 1990s. Whereas previously certificates had confirmed that people were indeed 'shaved for *witchcraft*' by Kalembwana, those issued today by Magungu at his various branches mention only 'shaving'.

Perceptions of what shaving is have also altered. In the 1990s being shaved was regarded as a profound personal event of ritual significance, involving a long journey and an extended stay at a remote location, and was novel enough to be a topic of continual discussion in many villages. More than twenty years of shaving at Ihowanja has permitted its evaluation in somewhat different terms. While the ritual significance of shaving continues to be acknowledged, in particular the importance of medicine (Green 1996), shaving has come to be perceived as a public service (*huduma ya umma*) and as such as a normal part of the institutional landscape in Ulanga and Kilombero. The representation of shaving as a public service was not confined to those directly engaged in providing it, descendants of Kalembwana and other *waganga* involved in what they regard as the delivery of anti-witchcraft services. Ordinary people also spoke of shaving in the language of service delivery to explain what shaving does and why it is necessary. Shaving can suppress the powers of witches. This is necessary to address the suspicions of kin and neighbours of people enmeshed in bitter quarrels and suspected of witchcraft.

That cleansing (*kujisafi/kusafishwa*) or 'being shaved' (*kunyolewa*) can be performed for all those who require it, either at Ihowanja or

---

[28] This view was challenged by district staff in Ulanga and in Kilombero. They say that the ending of labour for people going to be shaved was a political decision from the authorities. Whatever the original reason, it is interesting to note how ending this onerous requirement has fed into the new discourse about services and supporting clients. Witchcraft accusations commonly follow a funeral. Consequently people coming for shaving are not only reeling from the emotional shock of being accused of witchcraft, but are likely, particularly if they are accusing others who are accompanying them, to have been recently bereaved. For a fuller account of the dynamics of accuser and accused relationships, see Green (1997).

elsewhere, has contributed to the institutionalisation[29] of *kujisafi*, and the perception of anti-witchcraft practices as an essential public service, like health, education, law and order, and government. In the popular view, what Kalembwana does is reduce the number of witches, making it possible for others to build their lives and resources without fear of inciting the envy of witches. This perception of the services offered by Kalembwana and Magungu was shared by many local-government staff in Kilombero District at the time, including senior officials, who appreciated the contribution shaving made to law and order through resolving witchcraft disputes in the villages.[30]

## The drive for 'modernisation'

Magungu as an individual is a self-avowed moderniser, constantly seeking to improve his personal life and his surroundings. He has built a large modern house on the land at Mkasu and in 2012 was exploring ways of bringing electricity to the compound. He retains an interest in improving and modernising the delivery of his anti-witchcraft, as well as traditional healing services. Part of his stated rationale for relocation to Kiberege was to make certain improvements possible. These concerned making services more efficient and giving clients a choice of service location. Magungu made use of 'modern' public-information strategies like advertising, through a range of media, to achieve this. He had also produced a planning document that set out detailed objectives for the development of his practice, with a view to attracting external finance for improvements. The perception of *kunyolewa* as a public service had implications for the changes brought about in its delivery that intentionally parallel the ongoing drive for a particular kind of 'modernisation' in other public services as part of an externally financed programme of public-sector reform.

The reform of public services has been a key component of development assistance in Tanzania since the mid-1990s in the attempt to make government more efficient and accountable, as well as to increase the affordability of services. Programmes of reform across the public sector, ranging from the civil service to health, education and local government,

---

[29] Witchcraft-suppression services are institutionalised in several senses here. First, in terms of their relationship with local institutions, such as the various local-government structures that previously authorised disputants to go for shaving and which currently register and license 'traditional' healers. Second, witchcraft-suppression practices are institutionalised in Goffman's (1961: 16) sense of the term, as they take place in highly structured and controlled social settings, governed by the authority of inheritors of various powers to 'shave'. Finally, witchcraft-suppression practices are an established, and dynamic, constituent of the social institution of witchcraft in the districts of Ulanga, Songea and Kilombero.

[30] District staff in Ulanga were more ambivalent. Current policy is to encourage individuals reluctant to agree to shaving to pursue a legal claim against their accusers in a protracted process of revenge via the courts, with mixed success. The majority of people involved in witchcraft disputes agree voluntarily to go for shaving.

are being implemented in a package of measures that aims to enhance the responsiveness of services to local needs and to 'modernise' delivery. Modernisation in this context does not rest on technological innovations or on infrastructural investment, but on techniques of governance as the management and control of resources (Harrison 2001: 465). What is predominantly claimed to be built through development transfers is not the roads or factories that characterised development as modernisation in the 1960s and 1970s, but 'capacity' and institutions. Like the antecedent discourse of the old modernisation premised on technological inputs and mechanisation, the new modern is premised on ideas of technology centred on improving social organisation and relations; that is, on technologies of the social. Techniques of the new public management of which public-sector reform is part emphasise the importance of establishing rational and efficient systems and of the implementation of mechanisms that allow for the ongoing tracking of inputs, outputs and outcomes (Harrison 2001: 474; Miller & Rose 1990).

Public-sector reform is not only a system for delivering public services. Like other neoliberal governance reforms it is also an explicit transfer of moral and political values. Public-sector reform is as much concerned with the management of the public as with managing public resources. Consequently, such reforms imply an assumed reconstitution of political subjects as users of public services in quite specific ways. The new subject is a citizen of a multi-party democracy living in a free-market society who uses their purchasing power to select between the services on offer and to hold service providers democratically to account. Notions of choice, value, efficiency and the idea of a contract between service providers and service users have informed the design of public-sector reform programmes, which promote concepts such as public-private partnership and 'competition' (Minogue et al. 1998).

The discourse of reform as the axiomatic basis of relations between government and donors in Tanzania is now strongly identified with efforts to bring about 'development' (*maendeleo*), currently defined in terms of the locally adapted but internationally determined goals or eliminating poverty (Kelsall 2002). The association of reform as improvement (*maboresho*) and *maendeleo* entangles idea about reform with notions of progress and, rhetorically at least, with the reduction of poverty. But it also implicates ideas about reform with the institution of the project (*miradi*) as the accepted modality for achieving development in Tanzania. The notion of the project, derived from an extensive history of aid-dependency through projects and programmes, has come to refer to a range of initiatives at all levels through which people, as individuals or organisations, seek to improve something, to achieve *maendeleo.* As projects are about improvement and development, when applied to the individual or family the notion conveys income generation and the expectation of profit. It is this that, after all, is the means to achieving *maendeleo.*

The concept of 'project' also conveys the donor-assisted initiatives directed at public improvement that are prevalent in the country, across government and non-government sectors, and which extends to encompass the numerous personal patron-client, benefactor-assisted transnational dyads that characterise the economic asymmetry inherent in Tanzania's relationship with richer nations. It is assistance (*msaada*) and investment that transforms visions of progress into a project as the means of making it happen, and at the level of organisations involved in seeking assistance it is the construction of the project as a documented programme of investments and outcomes that is the first step towards making a project, as a specific web of social relations, a reality. Magungu's effort to transform the delivery of 'traditional' services is informed by these ideas about development as project and by the new conception of modernisation in development assistance as reform in public services. It is not, then, surprising that Magungu had written up his proposals for ongoing improvements as a project document, with a view to attracting funds from unspecified donors at some future date. For the present he has focused on reforming the ways in which his services are delivered, treating clients more as consumers and giving them the option of locally available, more efficient services.

Magungu's attempt to modernise his practice is not unusual among traditional healers in what amounts to a very dynamic part of Tanzanian's health system. Traditional healers in Tanzania have a record of innovation in client services and relations, while retaining a strong commitment to 'traditional' modes of diagnosis and medication (Gessler et al 1995: 152).[31] The receptiveness of traditional healers to what appears as 'modern' where appropriate underlies their enthusiasm for the Traditional Medicine Act of 2002, which sought to foster the integration of traditional practitioners into the formal medical system (Langwick 2011). The inclusion of healers who base their treatment on divination, who collaborate with spirits and who are likely to become possessed in the course of their medical duties, may at first sight seem to contradict the 'modernising' objectives of public-sector reform. It does not. Integration into the health system integrates 'traditional' healing into the management frameworks of the new modernisation, incorporating the 'traditional' sector in the vertical management chain of the total health-sector programme, even if this positioning is ultimately conceptual.[32]

---

[31] These centre on various modes of divination that may entail possession by spirits. For an overview of modes of practice and diagnosis among healers in Dar es Salaam, see Swantz (1990).

[32] Traditional healing in Tanzania has always had a symbiotic relationship with the hospital system (Green 2000; Langwick 2011). Traditional healers try to refer patients to hospital when they feel that they are unlikely to benefit from treatment on offer, a stance actively promoted by district medical officers.

## Development and witchcraft

The relation between development and modernisation as a desire for improvement is central also to the understandings of those who feel they have no choice but to make use of use of witchcraft-suppression services. 'Development' as a personal achievement conveying increased wealth and a better standard of living, manifested in improved housing and displays of consumer goods, as well as what is considered an urban sensibility that looks down on backward rural customs, is a national aspiration, fuelled by a national culture that has systematically promoted various incarnations of 'development' since well before independence. 'Development' as *maendeleo* is coterminous with popular representations of the modern in the sense of contemporary (*kisasa*), because it is through personal development (*maendeleo ya mtu binafsi*) that one can achieve the necessary wherewithal to purchase 'contemporary' things. Poverty is antithetical to development in this sense, just as it contravenes the representation of modernity that the state is trying to promote through its reform programmes, which are intended to support its overarching goal of reducing poverty.

As in other communities in Africa, witchcraft discourses here are partly discourses on success, failure and inequality as manifested through the visible indices of consumption and tragedy. Witchcraft can be used to explain unusual events with negative consequences, deaths and accidents. It is also invoked to account for the failure of others to achieve what they set out to accomplish, evidenced by a spoilt crop, a ruined business, a blighted career. Witchcraft, caused by the malicious use of medicines that empower witches to harm, can be guarded against through special protective medicines (*kinga*) widely available from 'traditional' healers. There is also a market in medicines that can enable individuals to achieve and succeed in business (*dawa ya biashara*), in farming and in court cases, and to attain promotion (*kupandisha cheo*).

For most people living in poor rural communities, success in the personal struggle for development is seen realistically to depend largely on factors beyond an individual's control. Arbitrary employment decisions, the vagaries of farming, and market fluctuations all render life unpredictable for the majority, as do the numerous demands for support from kin. It is here that witchcraft comes into its own as an explanation of why people have not managed to achieve, and why others have fallen victim to poverty. Poverty leaves people bitter and jealous when they see what others are trying to do, and moves some beyond victimhood to the practice of witchcraft. Witches are thus as likely to come from among the poorest of the poor as to be successful in their own right, just as their victims may be the better off who have inspired the envy of witches or the poor who have already been thwarted by witchcraft in their efforts to get out of poverty. That witchcraft discourse here can account for poverty or wealth and set up rich or poor as attacker or victim is a clear example of the ambiguity that Geschiere has suggested contributes to the tenacity of such discourses in much of Africa (1997: 10). In southern Tanzania the ambiguity that contributes to the perpetuation of witchcraft simultaneously contributes to the perpetuation of witchcraft-suppression practices, ensuring the ongoing existence of a diverse client group in need of services. The existence of anti-witchcraft practices that can credibly deal with witchcraft and that can do so relatively harmlessly doubtless contributes to the local institutionalisation of witchcraft (cf. Douglas 1991: 726–30) as a serious practice but one that can be invoked without the immediate violence of western Tanzanian responses.

If witchcraft works against development, it follows that anti-witchcraft practices are pro-development, an essential service that enables individuals in communities to begin to work towards achieving development for themselves. Witchcraft-suppression services delivered in a distinctly modern manner remain based on traditional practices around shaving, medicine and purification. The modernity of such practices is not now merely symbolic, as earlier accounts of witchcraft-suppression practices, my own included, suggested (Green 1994, 1997; Auslander 1993; Richards 1935; Marwick 1950). The routinisation and bureaucratisation associated with them is to some extent necessitated by the volume of clients and demands of patient management. It is also a consequence of the close and symbiotic relationship between the 'traditional' and formal medical sectors, leading, as in South America, to the increased 'medicalisation' of non-Western indigenous medical practice as it strives to model itself on the formal system (Pedersen & Baruffati 1989). Practices of certification and record keeping characterise current practice across a range of 'traditional' medical services (Gessler et al. 1995: 151).

Witchcraft-suppression practices in this part of southern Tanzania are situated within a national popular discourse about poverty, modernity and development. It is this discourse, as much as the dispute among Kalembwana's descendants, that has fuelled the transformation of anti-witchcraft practices into a public service intended to provide clients with accessible and efficient points of delivery. Witchcraft-suppression practices performed under Magungu's management using the name of Kalembwana have, through advertising and promotion, become part of the burgeoning market for traditional healing in which the client is reconstituted as a consuming agent who selects between services on offer. The construction of the client as a consumer of services meshes with the post-liberalisation economic ideology of the free market (*soko huria*) and the target subjectivities reconstituted through public-sector reform. It is necessitated in part by the formal ending of Kalembwana's monopoly on anti-witchcraft practices created through the involvement of local government in witchcraft disputes. In post-socialist Tanzania, local authorities at district and village level are no longer permitted to involve themselves in such disputes, other than to report people accusing others of witchcraft.

That the new user of anti-witchcraft services is primarily a consumer who has a choice is reflected in the new language used to describe the witchcraft-suppression process. In the 1990s, when people were generally sent to Ihowanja by village governments and party officials, or taken, sometimes by force, by irate neighbours, the process was known as *kunyolewa*, connoting the passivity and lack of agency involved in 'being shaved' (Green 1994). In 2003 the process is widely referred to as *kujisafi*, to 'cleanse oneself', the reflexive *ji* implying the agency of the active subject. This is not to suggest that the element of obligation no longer applies. It does, in the sense of moral compulsion to go in the event of an accusation or dispute, but whereas in the past people could be taken for shaving without their consent, the current institutional context emphasises freedom of choice and that those who go for cleansing on their own initiative have gone voluntarily.

These changes in the perception of witchcraft-suppression services and in the assumed subjectivities of users render the name 'salon' for the places where shaving is available more than simply humorously ironic. Brightly painted hair salons are fast becoming a feature of even remote rural towns and larger villages in Tanzania. As a visible indicator of the new consumption oriented towards the self in the liberalised economy, their utilisation has become the subject of discourses about moral responsibility and obligation (Stambach 2000: 261–2), as well as providing an example of the kinds of private services available to paying consumers with choice who can afford to use them. The representation of what is offered as an 'everything salon' signifies more than shaving. After people have been shaved they are permitted to seek other kinds of 'traditional' treatments and services, including divination, medicines and treatments through which everything – recovery, succeeding in business, falling in love, getting a good harvest – is indeed possible. The brightly painted signboard and Mickey Mouse indicate an aspirational modernity, that such practices, though authentically indigenous and 'traditional', as indicated by the stool, are up to date (*kisasa*).[33] Importantly, the signs also convey a humorous openness about shaving, which, freed from restrictive government regulation, can come out in the open as a resource that serves the people.

If 'modernisation' has produced the salon here, it has not produced 'the clinic' (Foucault 1973). Witchcraft-suppression services have not become wholly enmeshed in a new system of knowledge, nor have the modes of delivery become components of a reformed way of viewing the client subjects' subjectivity. Witchcraft continues to demand purification and medicines to suppress inherent human desires, although these can be administered slightly differently than previously. That this seems to be

---

[33] *Kisasa*, for obvious reasons, also conveys foreignness, hence items from abroad, even if 'old', and merits the tag of 'modern', in contrast to the indigenous and 'traditional'.

the case is probably because of the conceptualisation of the witch as an individual with excessive desire and human impulse, a construction that can work with the new consumer as a subject of witchcraft-suppression services. Witchcraft-suppression practices remain essentially unchanged despite their modified package of delivery.

# 8

## Making Middle Income

## New Development Citizenships in Tanzania

Sub-Saharan Africa is being reconfigured from a zone of vulnerability to a region of economic opportunity. As international relations are restructured in a reordering world, Chinese investment, global demand for minerals and unprecedented rates of economic growth at around 7 per cent annually seem poised to consolidate this new positioning (Mohan & Power 2009). This situation is not solely the result of shifts in the global political economy. It is equally the consequence of an historical transformation in the ways in which national elites perceive their place at home and in the international economic order (Hickey 2013). Successful African states are seeking recognition as players in the game of economic development, an ambition articulated in their goal to achieve middle-income status in little more than a decade. While middle-income status here does not imply anything like the income levels or GNP per capita equivalents of rich or even established middle-income countries, it is nevertheless a striking aspiration for countries such as Uganda and Tanzania that, until very recently, were counted as among the poorest in the world.

Categorisation as 'poor' since the 1980s as a condition for inclusion within the political relations of international development assistance entailed a degree of external control of national policies and economic trajectories (Green 2006; Harrison 2001; Lie 2011). This control is easing. As emerging powers assume greater influence through the provision of finance largely untied to policy concerns (Greenhill et al. 2013), and economies grow as a result of revenue streams derived from the extraction of natural resources, African countries are freer to assert their own priorities while continuing to accept substantial external funding to meet the targets for social development set by the international community (Hickey 2013; Wangwe 2010).[1] As in the years after independence for countries such as Zambia, Ghana and Nigeria (Ferguson 1999; Guyer 2007), African states and their growing

[1] Increased autonomy is constrained in practice by ongoing reliance on donor finance for social development investments and new relations with foreign private corporations in the extractive sector (Emel et al. 2011).

middle classes can once again aspire to attaining middle-income status.

Middle-income strategies as national political projects are premised on far-reaching changes in the relations in which African countries are enmeshed and the organisation of their economies, which imply profound shifts in the practices and relations of citizens (Moyo et al. 2010). Becoming middle income is not only concerned with economic growth and increasing per capita income. It is equally a cultural project in which African nations seek to be resituated within 'a global structure of common difference' (Wilk 1996: 111). Achieving middle-income status involves a series of actual and discursive transitions: from poverty to economic growth, from subsistence agriculture to modern farming, from low to high levels of education, from what are regarded as 'traditional' occupations to 'employment',[2] and from informality – of settlements and economic practices – to formalisation (Varley 2013). The idea of the urban plays a significant role in these representations (Ong 2012; Roy 2011). No longer equated with extreme deprivation, archaic technical practices and predominantly rural social forms, with the predominance of status over contract and the persistence of 'traditional' cultures – except as artefacts of informed cultural identification, as in 'traditional' dance (Askew 2002) – middle-income Africa seeks to escape from the geographical entrapment through which it was previously confined to a state of poverty, through conceptual alignment with countries including Brazil, China and Vietnam that exemplify successful economic transition beyond the continent.

Becoming middle income is not confined to the official statements and discourses produced by political and policy elites, both external and internal, although these are influential. The substantial economic changes that national strategies demand are set in motion through the practices and aspirations of ordinary citizens as they enact new ways of living in the twenty-first century (Snyder 2002; Moore 1993). Aspiring to becoming middle income is no longer restricted to the realm of the imagination, as suggested by some anthropological analyses of economic relations in Sub-Saharan Africa in the immediate aftermath of structural adjustment (e.g., Weiss 2002; Hansen 1994; Geschiere & Rowlands 1996). Transformations in the economies of Sub-Saharan African countries, and the range of economic opportunities available to some citizens, are having a dramatic effect in reshaping African societies and everyday social practice. The group most able to enact new forms of daily life are those who we might categorise as middle class, persons who have some access to the purchasing power necessary to make different choices in the way they live their everyday lives, from the kinds of utensils they use in the homes to the foods they eat and the clothes their children wear, and who view themselves as situated between poor farmers and the cosmopolitan elites at the centre of power in the major cities.

In Tanzania this growing middle class defines itself practically through

---

[2] Hence reframing the non-availability of formal kinds of work becomes 'unemployment'.

its relation, actual or sought, to formal waged forms of employment (Swidler & Watkins 2009), higher levels of education, and their perusal of what is perceived to be an urban lifestyle in terms of housing preferences and consumption. The association with urban practices is not simply an issue of style. Middle classes are likely to define themselves partly through their mediated relation to agricultural production. While middle classes may own land or engage in agricultural enterprises, they prefer not to work the land themselves but to rely on hired labour (*kibarua*).[3] Hired labour, generally organised on a piecework basis, is culturally and economically differentiated from waged employment. *Kibarua* is manual, low-status work implying no ongoing commitment between labourer and hirer. Waged work, in contrast, is associated with relations of obligation to employees regarding social entitlements, even if these are more symbolic than actual for many formal-sector employees. It is highly valued because of its place within imaginaries of entitlement encompassed within the conceptual packaging of the formalisation and 'decent work' agendas, and hence within the transnational imaginaries of middle-income citizenship.[4]

Economies such as Tanzania's, in which over 70 per cent of the population are engaged in agriculture (Mkenda et al. 2010), cannot sustain a middle class through formal or even non-agricultural employment. Tanzanian middle classes in rural areas seek to support themselves through diverse income portfolios, including access to wage labour and making use of investments to engage in business related to agriculture, rather than hands-on involvement in actual farming. They also invest in maintaining middle-classness through spending on the kind of education for themselves and their children that, it is hoped, may provide access to waged employment. Maintaining middle-classness has obvious implications for inequality in Tanzania, in terms of access to education and in relation to changes in access to resources entailed by the enclosure-orientation of middle-class investment strategies directed towards rental income. The drive to become middle income cannot, however, be explained only in terms of the desire for differentiation (Daloz 2007). Although middle-class cultural practice is inevitably an axis of differentiation associated with higher incomes and imported goods, and hence with the encompassing domain of that which is categorised as 'modern' (*kisasa*), it is not so much concerned with the demarcation of the traditional practices of the past as with incorporation into a global frame in which middle-income Tanzanians seek recognition as citizens of the world (Snyder 2002; Wilk 1996). Becoming middle income is part of a sweeping transformation in the 'norms and forms of the social

---

[3] For a comparative analysis of the more extreme attitude of the educated rural middle classes in India towards hands-on agricultural labour, see Jeffrey et al. (2008).

[4] 'Decent work' is an International Labour Organization (ILO)-promoted policy category that packages commitments to entitlements within the contractual relation between employer and employee. On the changing imaginaries of entitlement in relation to formal-sector employment in Africa, see Miller (2005).

environment' (Rabinow 1995) and in the architectures of everyday life that have been rendered more available through economic liberalisation. Ideas about what constitutes the normal for various kinds of people inform expectations about 'comfort, cleanliness and convenience' (Shove 2003), as well as understandings of rights, entitlements and citizenship, that are structuring everyday practices and ordinary consumption.

This chapter explores the cultural logics of the quest for middle income through an account of socio-economic transformation in Ulanga District in southern Tanzania since the 1990s. Rather than claim economic change as the effect of hegemonic forces or external pressure from market logics or globalisation,[5] I hope to show how the desires and aspirations of the emergent middle class are central to the enactment of what amounts to a particular instantiation of a 'new economy' in East Africa (Thrift 2000). Most commonly associated with analyses of new management practices and the information technology sector, or with new practices for the commodification of value (Löfgren & Willim 2005), the concept of new economy has to date been applied to the global North and South in terms of its integration within relations of globalised production. Irrespective of relations to, or otherwise, with globalisation (see Amin 2002), the concept is suggestive in highlighting central aspects of the transformations currently underway in countries like Tanzania. This economic reordering is characterised by major transitions in the practice of everyday life and expectations of normality, in relations between rich and poor, rural and urban, between place and identity, and between place and economic activity.

Core features of new economic relations include geographic dispersal, a change in the constitution of place, the utilisation of communication technologies and contracting, changed modalities for the governance of productive enterprise, and the formation of specific subjectivities and aptitudes (Thrift 2000; Sennet 2006). The enactment of a new economy in Tanzania is made possible by a number of factors, within and beyond Tanzania, including changed infrastructures brought about through foreign investment and new technologies, and through important political changes. The contribution of socialist public-sector policies and development aid are also relevant. While the policy discourse of achieving middle income fetishises the core ingredients of the market reform 'cookbook', the new African economy in formerly socialist Tanzania is realised through the investments associated with the public spending of previous policy regimes.

## Economic transformation in Tanzania

Ulanga District is a rural district in Morogoro region, southern Tanzania. It is bordered on its southern side by the country's largest

---

[5] For a recent example of this perspective in relation to Tanzania, see Norris & Worby (2012).

game reserve, the Selous, and to the north by the rice-producing Kilombero valley, which was about to become part of a major investment programme creating an agricultural growth corridor along a south-western sweep of the country.[6] Until quite recently Ulanga was associated with underdevelopment, low incomes and low levels of agricultural productivity (Green 2003). This situation is changing. Ulanga, like other rural districts, is being brought into changed relations of national economic development through improvements in infrastructure, increased demand for agricultural products and the extension of mineral extraction on the Selous borderlands. Despite the formal narrative of neoliberal efficiency achieved through a shrinking state, the public sector in Tanzania is steadily expanding as donor-financed development spending sustains investments in schools and health centres across rural districts, as well as the increase in the scale of local government necessitated by donor-funded decentralisation. This, plus the accompanying proliferation of local-government administrative units such as villages and wards, in parallel to the national process of 'districtization' (Kelsall 2000),[7] fuels the rise in the numbers of public servants in rural areas. It also contributes to a substantive change in the geography of Tanzania – the growth in the number of small towns and townships. In the past ten years or less, places that were administrative outposts for the delivery of government services have become centres with resident populations of waged workers, transport hubs and shops selling a wide range of goods that were previously only available in large towns and cities (Bryceson 2011).

The effects of this transition are strikingly evident in Mahenge town, Ulanga's district capital. From a population of 4,000 in 1998, just before I commenced my first fieldwork, the area comprising Mahenge town had a population of around of almost 24,000 by the time of the 2012 census.[8] Between 2003 and 2012 the number of designated villages in the District increased from 65 to 91. The number of public servants serving the District rose significantly during the same period, from 1,256 to 2,162.[9] The area of the town has expanded considerably, with housing, construction and guest-houses occupying what was until recently agricultural land, even

[6] Announced in 2010, the Southern Agricultural Growth Corridor of Tanzania (SAGCOT) programme is based on the notion of public private partnerships and strong commercial involvement, and is to run until 2030.

[7] A process whereby new districts are created for political purposes, not for administrative efficiency or enhanced democratisation. Tanzanian districts generally have very low populations. Creating new districts involves establishing the complex systems and infrastructures of local government, including an elected council, revenue-collection infrastructure and representative offices of core sectoral ministries that deliver local services.

[8] The two wards that comprise what is Mahenge town, Vigoi and Mahenge, have a total population of 23,975 according to the 2012 census.

[9] The number of serving civil servants is around 3,000. This is a small number, but what is significant is the proportional increase relative to the adult population of the district. According to the 2012 census the total Ulanga district population was 265,203 (nbs.go.tz), of whom the majority were under 18. The adult earning population is very small.

close to the town centre. What were once separate villages distinct from the town, places like Nawnege and Mbagula, have become its peri-urban peripheries. The scale of the expansion is indicated in the administrative structures of local government.

Although not yet categorised as urban, a status reserved for larger conurbations, the area administered as Mahenge town now comprises two village units, each with an executive officer and village government. District leadership is keen on Mahenge achieving urban status.[10] A proper 'urban' bus station, with passenger bays and shelters, has recently been brought into use at the edge of the town centre to receive and dispatch the two buses a day that link Mahenge to Ifakara, the capital of Kilombero District, and then to Dar es Salaam. The District Executive Director, in post until 2012, was keen to extend modalities of urban planning to townships in the District and to promote urban aesthetic forms. For him this included redesigned urban housing for local-authority staff and the promotion of multi-storey construction. Such 'modern' buildings, together with the modern shops that he imagined would one day occupy their lower floors, would identify Mahenge as a 'proper town'. The archetypical modern shop is the supermarket, connoting distinctly modern middle-class styles of consumption. Whereas in 2003 the entire District had 204 shops large enough to be registered with local government, already a massive increase from the days of state marketing through regional co-operative societies, in 2012 there were 479 – including general stores, hair salons and mobile-phone shops – of which some 150 are in Mahenge.[11] Three shops – two small and one attached to a petrol station – present themselves as 'super-markets'.

As in other countries in Africa, mobile telecommunications have a visible presence, intensified by the pervasive advertising campaigns and colourful branding of big providers like Vodacom and Airtel. In the early 2000s, few people could afford their own handsets, relying on paying for use of other people's phones or owning a 'line' (a SIM card) that they could insert in other people's handsets. In 2012, even Nokia handsets were relatively affordable, retailing at around 20,000 shillings (c. US $20 or GBP £12.50 at the time).[12] Price differentials between rural centres and cities have also fallen. Innovations in transfer of funds by mobile phone (pioneered in Kenya by Safaricom's M-Pesa service) are revolution-ising doing business and relations with distant kin. Kiosks specialising in money transfer have constant queues throughout the day. The post office in Mahenge town, formerly home to the only public telephone in

---

[10] This would be as a town not a municipality (*manispaa*), which is a local-government category for larger conurbations.

[11] For analyses on the relationship between hair salons and economic liberalisation in Tanzania, see Stambach (2000) and Weiss (2002).

[12] I bought a used imported handset for the equivalent of US $90 (c. GBP £55) in 2005 from one of the two handset stores in Ifakara, in the neighbouring district. At that time handsets could not be purchased in Mahenge. In 2012 at least five shops in the town centre sell handsets, the cheapest of which retail at around US $20 (c. GBP £12).

the District, is largely silent as demand for its services is replaced by mobile money and the mass uptake of telephones. The changed state of the economy is indicated by another social shift, the peripheralisation of second-hand clothes sellers in the town centre and market-place. Whereas second-hand clothes stalls dominated retail trade in Tanzania and Zambia in the early years of liberalisation (Hansen 1994), new clothing is widely available, sold from shops in the centre of the town. Second-hand clothing has been relocated to market stalls on the margins, spatially reiterating the division between middle-income consumers who frequent the town shops and the local population who depend on small-scale agriculture.

## From socialism to inclusive growth

Economic transformation in Tanzanian rural districts reiterates the direction of change set out in national policies that prioritise rapid growth through openness to foreign investment, development of the minerals sector, and agricultural modernisation. Core national policies come together in the 2011 National Five Year Development Plan, which effectively supersedes the donor artefact of the Poverty Reduction Strategy (PRS) (URT 2011). Five-year development plans were abandoned in the aftermath of structural adjustment as the Tanzanian state conceded to the policy demands of international donors. Their reinstatement highlights Tanzania's changed place in the global arena and the reinvigorated political confidence of its leadership, as well as the ironies of Tanzania's current situation. A government instrument fundamental to the central planning of socialism is now marshalled to further an explicitly neoliberal agenda that is enabled in practice through high levels of government expenditure and de facto state control of core sectors of the economy (Cooksey 2012).

The 2011 Five Year Development Plan is subtitled 'Unleashing Tanzania's Latent Growth Potentials'. It delineates the country's middle-income ambition and the means through which it will be achieved. Building on various sector development plans intended to foster the creation of a 'modern' economy,[13] particularly in agriculture, changes in tenure to enable individuals to have titles that can function as collateral, and attempts to formalise property relations and business conduct, the Plan is informed by an explicitly comparative stance that situates Tanzania in relation to other middle-income countries.[14] Comparative intent is clearly articulated in the 2004 'Tanzania Mini Tiger Plan', which places

[13] Along the lines described for Peru by Mitchell (2005). Hernando de Soto's Institute for Liberty and Democracy organisation has provided consultancy services to the Government of Tanzania on economic formalisation.

[14] For accounts of ongoing reform interventions in Tanzania, see Cooksey (2003) and Lysons & Msoka (2010).

Tanzania on the trajectory of successful Asian states. This positioning justifies ambitions in the Plan to increase numbers of graduates and professionals. The imaginary of the Plan presents Tanzania as a country in which agriculture is transformed into an entrepreneurial activity as 'modern' farmers enhance the productivity of their asset base while those who are not farmers are highly educated in readiness for participation in formal-sector professional employment.

The representation of Tanzania set out in the five-year plan presents a striking contrast with the aspirations under the socialist policy regime, which lasted from shortly after independence from Britain in 1961 to the transition to political and economic liberalisation in the early 1990s. Details of Tanzania's more recent history are too complicated to describe in the space available here. In essence, the same political party, *Chama Cha Mapinduzi* (CCM), the Party of the Revolution, formed from the merging of TANU and the Zanzibar Afro-Shirazi Party (ASP) in 1977, has retained power despite the formal transition to a multi-party political system (Whitehead 2012). The radical shift in policy and politics from socialism to all-out market fundamentalism has occurred within the same political party. Development assistance has provided the legitimating models for economic re-ordering in Tanzania at the same time as it has provided the finance, formally and informally, for individuals to enact new economic relations.[15]

The socialist period in Tanzania is associated with the political ideology and leadership of the first president, Julius Nyerere, credited with formulating a uniquely Tanzanian version of 'African socialism'. This had various components, including attempted collectivisation of rural production, forced villagisation, the nationalisation of private enterprise, and state centralisation through the extension of party organisation down to 'ten-house cells' (McHenry 1979; Maghimbi 1995; Coulson 2013; Bryceson 2011; Schneider 2007). Whatever the limitations of Nyerere's socialism in practice, and its role in exacerbating the poverty of Tanzanians, his intentions, informed by the writings of anti-colonial theorists, were undoubtedly egalitarian. Sensitised by the example of the growth of inequality in other newly independent states and by socialist politics, Nyerere was determined that Tanzania should be a nation built on principles of equality and justice. Ending colonial relations of exploitation should not simply introduce new occupants for roles vacated by servants of colonial power. Aware of Fanon's caution concerning the domination of African elites over the masses on whose behalf they claimed power, Nyerere believed that urban areas should not be privileged over the rural, nor professionals over the peasants, for whose benefit development should be organised (Saul 2012).

---

[15] For example, the current Governor of the Bank of Tanzania is a former World Bank adviser and Professor of Economics at the University of Dar es Salaam. He is the lead author of an influential World Bank report on African growth.

Nyerere's ideas about equality are set out in his collected speeches published as *Freedom and Socialism* (1974) and in the 1967 declaration of the party's commitment to explicitly socialist policies. The Arusha Declaration views development as a consequence of the efforts and commitment of the people rather than a result of money or international aid. Agriculture is regarded as the foundation of national development because the majority of the people make their living from the land. Land, and other productive assets, should be owned by the state for the people and not become the basis of relations of exploitation, which was to be prevented. A code of conduct for leaders, reiterated in the Party Guidelines (*mwongozo*) of 1971, was informed by socialist principles. Leaders were expected not to behave in ways that mirrored the temptations of either feudalism or capitalism, both of which Nyerere acknowledged as temptations in the predominantly rural social ordering of Tanzania. They were not permitted to have two salaries or to own houses for rent. The Leadership Code, revised in 1981, encapsulates the essence of Nyerere's interpretation of socialist theory concerning the relation between ownership of property and exploitation (Hydén 1980: 157–63). It was repealed in 1991 (Sundet 1994).[16]

The 2011 Development Plan can be read as a through-the-looking-glass version of the Arusha Declaration. Its reversed reality presents a vision for the development of agro-enterprise rather than a vision for the development of agricultural communities. Although agriculture retains its place as the foundation for economic development, the driver of development is no longer the peasant organised through collective relations of production, but the private sector envisaged as a broad coalition of enterprise from small farmer to multinational corporations.[17] Inequality is not a problem to be specifically addressed. The intention is, rather, to bring all Tanzanians into the possibilities for 'inclusive growth'. These possibilities will be created through investments in infrastructure, agricultural modernisation and the formation of special economic development zones like the regional growth corridor planned to run through the south-western part of Tanzania, including the very northern edge of Ulanga and much of Kilombero District. The Plan is not concerned with redressing imbalances between rural and urban. On the contrary, it seeks to extend the economic opportunities conveyed by the urban to encompass other areas. The investments described in the Plan convey a vision of huge infrastructure projects, modernised agriculture and urban sophistication. Images of gleaming high-rise office buildings, electricity pylons and construction workers in hi-tech attire adorn its front cover.

---

[16] Nyerere stepped down in 1985 and the presidency was assumed by Ali Hassan Mwinyi.

[17] As part of Africa's 'Green Revolution'. See Thompson (2012) for further details.

## Making the middle class

The private-sector orientation of the 2011 Plan, the concerns with formal-isation and infrastructure, and with employment and higher education, speak forcefully to the concerns of the growing middle class who define themselves in practice through affiliation to urban modes of livelihood (cf. Varley 2013). This middle class is expanding as greater numbers of people reside in urban and peri-urban areas and are engaged in non-agricultural livelihoods,[18] and as the children of established middle-class parents come to create their own middle-class income strategies (Lewinson 2007). This group of middle-class Tanzanians owes its position, at least partially, to relations within the former socialist administration, which ensured access to the limited educational opportunities that were a guaranteed route into public-sector employment. It was this group of public servants that sought to increase the value of low salaries under socialism by engaging in small business, ushering in, as Tripp has shown, the economic realignments of liberalisation (1997). This realignment occurred at multiple levels, as the same strategies were replicated by the high- as well as the low-paid, by senior officials and lowly civil servants, as well as teachers and nurses throughout the country. The strategies pursued by senior figures gained a new legitimacy after the ending of the Leadership Code and the examples set by Presidents Mwinyi and Mkapa and their wives regarding personal investments. It is not unusual in Tanzania today to find academics at public universities owning student accommodation, or the boss of a research institute owning a conference centre. More usually, of course, public-sector workers have much smaller enterprises, ranging from the kinds of ventures described by Tripp, from specialising in the sale of cooked food to renting out rooms, chairs in hair salons or, a relatively new phenomenon in Tanzania, *boda boda*s, or motorcycle taxis.[19]

Two factors influence the ways in which the middle class engages in enterprise in Tanzania today. First, the availability of credit through the private-sector micro-finance institutions, such as Faidika, Finca and Bayport, that are expanding in Sub-Saharan Africa (Roy 2010) and through the proliferating savings and credit co-operative societies (SACCOS) heavily promoted by President Kikwete after his election in 2005. Both types of institution serve richer farmers and salaried employees. Second, the need to link educational attainment with employment necessitates increased spending on accessing a range of educational opportunities

---

[18] Or what they consider to be less agricultural livelihoods. In actuality, what is happening in Tanzania is the increasing mix and diversification of income strategies in both rural and urban areas. See Bryceson (2002) and Ellis & Mdoe (2003).

[19] Investing in housing was, and is, also popular. See Briggs & Mwafupe (2000) for Dar es Salaam.

locally and internationally. For the upper echelons of the elite this means accessing institutions with global reputations in the United States or United Kingdom. For those of somewhat lower status it can mean degree opportunities in Indonesia or South Africa. For the majority of the middle class the priority is accessing the kinds of private secondary schools that are likely to lead to admission to universities in Tanzania. The expansion of publicly funded secondary education under the auspices of the poverty-reducing aid regime has not in actuality resulted in an expansion of educational opportunity. The proliferation of low-quality local secondary schools in rural areas under the ward secondary school policy has driven demand for higher quality private education, creating an additional marker of differentiation that is simultaneously a point of passage for entry into middle-class status. At the same time, rural parents aspire to sending their children to ward secondary schools in the belief that they will be able to access employment imagined as a life of income security and engagement with the 'modern' economy, quite distinct from farming (*kilimo*).

Despite the state's attempts to transform rural citizens into 'modern' farmers, the cultural devaluation of agriculture and peasants by successive development-oriented regimes (Chachage 1988) maintains the connection between non-agricultural employment and middle-class status. Students at ward secondary schools strive to adopt distinctly urban styles of dress, hair and consumption. Educated young people without realistic chances of professional employment enact middle-income identities through dress and taste, capability with technologies like internet phones, and such practices as 'volunteering' in development non-governmental organisations (NGOs) (Weiss 2002). These identities are not primarily about actual income. Like the television show *Big Brother Africa*, featuring a representative of sophisticated urban youth from most countries on the continent, and watched by millions for the best part of a decade, such enactments situate young people within a transcontinental frame that speaks to global references, making claims about what they perceive to be appropriate ways of living in contemporary middle-income Africa.

Twenty-five years after the formal end of socialist policies, Tanzania is poised between state centralisation and market free-for-all legitimated by neoliberal globalisation. Frenzied free-market rhetoric, the proliferation of shops and the visibility of entrepreneurial branding notwithstanding, the country remains financially dependent on development assistance to meet its national budget. Ownership of land continues to be vested in the state under the administration of village governments. Public services comprise the bulk of formal-sector employment. Apparent continuities in the organisation of the economy mask far-reaching changes in the organisation of economic relations, specifically in the range of opportunities available to those with disposable income and the extent of differentiation between the middle class and those directly engaged in agricultural production. These changes are articulated through the established cultural repertoire of rural and urban as idioms of differentiation (Ferguson 1999; Moore 1993).

If Tanzania's 'old' economy was characterised by a rural/urban divide dominated by the public servants and party apparatchiks who benefitted from public investments skewed towards a few large cities, its new economy is characterised by a divide between small-scale rural producers, many of who work as farm labour on the farms of other small farmers, and middle-income persons who pursue income strategies that enable them to sustain an indirect relation to farming. In the new economy the urban can be performed irrespective of location. Rural centres are re-categorised as urban. Relations between the middle classes and rural producers are no longer remote and mediated through middle-class positions in the 'bureaucratic bourgeoisie' (Samoff 1979; Shivji 1976), but are highly personalised relations of exploitation. Unlike the 'bureaucratic bourgeoisie', who were supported by the state, the new middle class has to support itself through restructured relations with rural producers. These relations offer opportunities for small farmers to produce goods and services, transforming rural economies and small towns, and shrinking the gap between the country and the city.

## The new economy in Ulanga

The impacts of these transitions are visible in Ulanga, where the economy is moving towards its 'new' form in which the role played by the middle class is critical. This role is determined partly by aspiration and the need for additional income. It is enabled by the socio-technical possibilities of contemporary Africa brought about through the conjunction of development interventions, the expansion of financial services and mobile technologies.

Government policies on imports and relations with India and China have led to reductions in the price of manufactured goods, including the technologies that bring the mobilisation of the new economy within reach of the ordinary public servant in rural districts. One of the most noticeable effects of these policies is a substantial change in options for local transport in rural and in urban areas, evidenced in the ways in which the three-wheeler taxi (known as *Bajaj* – a brand name used generically) is remaking the geography of the country's biggest city. Since around 2010, motorcycles made in India and China that sell for the equivalent of around US $700 (c. GBP £425) have become available in the District, dramatically altering the ways in which people and goods move through and beyond it.[20]

Motorcycles are not new in rural Tanzania. What is new is motorcycles cheap enough to be purchased by private individuals rather than

[20] These items came in after President Kikwete was elected in 2005 but were unavailable in Ulanga until recently.

distributed to a small number of government staff and NGO employees as perks of externally funded development programmes. The 50 or so massed motorcycles lined up in the central space outside the old market building at the centre of Mahenge town, and against which young men lean proprietorially, are not parked by owner drivers who have come in from outlying farms. They are owned by members of the middle class living in the town who rent them out, usually to young men, as *boda boda* motorcycle taxis. Drivers pay owners a weekly rental of upwards of 10,000 shillings per day (around US $8, GBP £5), meet their own fuel costs and pay for routine maintenance, irrespective of passenger numbers. Owners are generally salaried workers who may have taken a loan from finance companies or an employee's SACCOS to make the purchase. *Boda boda* fares are negotiated between driver and passenger. They are not fixed. *Boda boda* have to compete in practice on the two main road routes with bus prices. Most passengers make low-cost local journeys and the number of *boda boda* taxis increases daily. Profits are small. Nevertheless, becoming a *boda boda* driver is appealing to young men because it is a kind of work, fast, technological and non-agricultural, that is paradigmatic of the 'new' middle-income Tanzania.[21]

*Boda boda* alter the options for local transportation in the area, and in the process, transform the experience of space and time (Massey 2005) in rural Tanzania. In making it possible to reach places that were previously only accessible on foot, they shrink journey times, and facilitate the transportation of produce out and manufactured goods in to what were remote rural villages. Small village shops in 'out of the way places' (Tsing 1993) can now stock the kinds of goods formerly restricted to the district centre, including bottled beer and 'soda' (manufactured soft drinks). Rural infrastructure programmes have contributed to this transformation. All-season bridges, in reconnecting villages, alter the economic relations in which parts of the district are situated. Formerly marginal places are in the process of being remade as *on the way* to other places, effectively relocating the western rice-plains within the districts to which they are adjacent and practically opening up vast expanses of land to speculative arrangements and new forms of tenure.[22] This is most pronounced in the rice valleys between Luprio, in Ulanga District, and Ifakara, in neighbouring Kilombero, where greater numbers of Mahenge people who can afford the transport costs establish rice farms, often on an annual rental basis, which they manage remotely, either by 'placing someone', a relative or a local resident, to manage their venture, or by making regular visits. No longer remote and inaccessible, they can be incorporated into the dispersed livelihood strategies of others living outside them, while

[21] Thrift associates the new economy with speed. Other occupations for the unskilled that were seen as suitably 'new' and non-agricultural include the sale of phone-credit vouchers, although this has to a large extent been taken over by small shops and phone kiosks.

[22] A process already underway as a result of the TAZARA (Tanzania and Zambia) railway, which passes through the Kilombero valley (Monson 2009).

those who live in them find their own economic practices reoriented towards newly adjacent centres. Villages as locations of tradition where the contemporary has yet to happen are resituated within coeval relations through this (re)placing (Pigg 1993; Wilk 1995).

The remote management of farm and other enterprises is made possible by two other technologies: mobile phones, which are now widely used because of the fall in the price of handsets and call packages, and the more recent innovation of mobile money-transfer, mentioned above. This allows one person to send another person a set amount of money, which they can collect at a kiosk in all urban and most small rural centres. The recipient can collect as soon as the transfer information appears on their phone. What this enables people to do, apart from send remittances and help kin in an emergency, is to pay for goods and services without having to be there in person. Although bank transfer was always possible in Tanzania, it depended on the recipient having a bank account and on there being a bank in the vicinity. Getting people to carry money to someone remotely, for example via bus workers, was considered high risk. Mobile money obviates these concerns, opening up possibilities for pulling in goods and services from virtually anywhere in the country. While for some this involves connections with major cities, trade and transfers within the District are also critical because local opportunities have lower entry costs and because moving around the District remains time-consuming and difficult. A person managing an annual rice crop in the valley from his desk in the district council can send the cash to the person he has placed on the field with which to purchase inputs such as weed-killer, or to pay for labour, without having to go there himself. What would formerly have involved a journey totalling as many as three days, much of it on foot, can be achieved in an instant, fundamentally altering the possibilities for income opportunities, both for the person 'placed' and the person with capital.

Technologies and mobilities alter other opportunities too, notably in the organisation of trade in agricultural products. Speculative trade in food crops, involving seasonal buying and selling of rice and maize in order to profit from the predictable annual increases in prices that structure the grain economy in the region, is a long-standing route to accumulation for the rural salariat in Ulanga and in places like it (Bryceson 1993). Whereas formerly this was difficult to engage in for small players, who could not afford the transport costs of amassing the crop or the time to negotiate with sellers, unless they had relations with known farmers who would set aside produce for them, motorcycle transport and, where that is unavailable, the bicycle taxi, opens up remote farms to potential buyers for relatively low cost, while mobile money enables deals to be struck and made, and storage or transport arranged, from far away. For most waged public-sector worker involvement in the food trade is relatively small scale. Unlike large agricultural traders, they are not aiming to buy produce for sale in major cities, but to profit from the seasonal changes in the price of maize and rice for markets to meet local demand within a limited area. This approach reduces their costs of doing business, as transport costs are kept to a minimum. Some food entrepreneurs aim to avoid them altogether, buying a proportion of a crop before it is harvested and paying for it to be stored in the vicinity until it is sold to traders coming in to the area. As with the *boda boda* business, the extension of the food trade is opened up by the availability of credit for waged employees.

Middle-income strategies build on widely shared ideas about the proper utilisation of money that are held by rich and poor alike. Money somehow loses its value if it is not in circulation. Consequently, money must be set to work and made productive through being involved in ventures that will enable it to generate more money. High inflation and cultural ideals around the need for generosity (Platteau 2010) make securing value dependent on money being continually used to reproduce itself, out of the reach of others who consider they have entitlements to it. Whereas the poor have to rely on high-risk options, such as beer brewing or the sale of cooked food like *vitumbua* (rice cakes), to make their money make money (Green 1999), those who have money can use it to secure control over resources that others need in order to make their money. Middle-income persons take advantage of changes in land legislation to formalise tenure and buy land enabling future rental.[23] They rent out rooms, *boda boda*, barber 'chairs' in hair salons, sewing machines and the like as preferred options for making money make money. As in similar situations of economic uncertainty, people with money to invest strive to minimise the risks inherent in productive enterprise, particularly agriculture, opting to trade in crops rather than produce them (Gregory 1997). This logic underlies the kinds of ventures that are popular middle-income investments, such as renting out motorcycles to youths who want to earn their living as *boda boda* drivers. As with the urban *dala dala* minibus businesses, the majority of which are owned by middle-class individuals, all the risks are borne by the operators (Rizzo 2011). The enhanced capacity of those with money to make money productive fuels stereotypical representations that middle-income persons hold about the poor, a distinction that comes to be associated with local people whose habits regarding work are compared unfavourably with those of employed incomers.

## Supermarket style

If new economies are determined through the conjunction of technologies and relations, they are, as Thrift has shown, equally impacted by the styles

---

[23] Subject to the decisions of village governments. While village governments can give individuals title to land, ultimate ownership rests with the state, and unused land can theoretically revert to village governments.

that contribute to their constitution (2002). For Thrift, the matter of style encompasses the subjectivities inculcated through engagement within new technologies and relation, and the styles through which the cultures of the new economy are enacted. Enacting middle income involves ways of dressing, hair-styling and comportment, the kinds of work with which one associates, the food that one eats, as well as aptitudes and orientations towards middle-income cultural performance. These dimensions of a new economy are materially instantiated in the form of another socio-technical innovation proliferating across middle-income Africa, the supermarket (Miller 2005). The three small supermarkets in Mahenge, all opened since 2011, are apt icons of Tanzania's transition.

The cultural form of the supermarket has been present for over 30 years in East Africa. There were at least four small, privately owned supermarkets in Dar es Salaam in the years immediately preceding liberalisation. These first-generation supermarkets were situated in or adjacent to the neighbourhoods favoured as residential areas by high-paid foreigners and diplomats. Usually small, because of the constraints on capital accumulation and private-sector enterprise under the socialist regime, and owned by Asian business families, they aimed to replicate the styling of self-service and produce associated with supermarkets internationally, as well as the range of goods sold, including processed foods, the implements required for adopted Euro-American styles of food preparation and imported toiletries, cleaning products and cosmetics. In Tanzania, as in other post-socialist settings, the supermarket and its product range is powerfully evocative of a new era of personal and market freedoms (Stillerman & Salcedo 2012; Miller 2005).

After liberalisation, larger supermarkets from Kenya and South Africa sought to enter the Tanzanian market, opening a number of regular branches followed by a small number of superstores.[24] The most prominent of these is the enormous Shoprite superstore, appropriately situated in the country's first indoor shopping mall, Mlimani City, built on land that was formerly attached to the main campus of the University of Dar es Salaam.[25]

The privately owned supermarkets remain under family ownership but have expanded, opening more branches and adapting the aesthetic styles of the international chains. Locally owned supermarkets such as Shoppers' Supermarket and Shrijee's do most of their business in high-income neighbourhoods.[26] Differentiation between supermarkets, certainly in Dar es Salaam, is not so much based on price as on the range of goods available. Chains like the Kenyan Uchumi and South African

---

[24] In 2013 there were three in Dar es Salaam, a city of just over 4 million people.

[25] Mlimani City was formally opened by President Kikwete in 2006.

[26] As in countries like Egypt, Chile and Brazil, these neighbourhoods and malls become destinations for lower-income groups seeking high-income goods, thus constituting new kinds of public-private space (Abaza 2001; Salcedo 2003; Stillerman & Salcedo 2012). This is occurring on a small scale at Mlimani city, which is well served by public transport.

Shoprite supply the kinds of products that are fast becoming everyday items for the middle classes. Some privately owned outlets specialise in stocking imported food products for well-paid foreign workers. Large supermarkets, irrespective of ownership, are not the preferred retail destination for ordinary citizens, who buy unpacked food by volume from market traders and small shops that sell basic, low-price products in small quantities. Supermarkets, with international or foreign brands, packaged goods, and items considered by most as luxuries, specialise in goods for occasional consumption by the middle classes and those, such as toiletries, memory sticks and marker pens, that are becoming essential to its performance. The 'occasional' category includes varieties of biscuits, manufactured juices and alcohol, while the 'essential' includes new kinds of detergents and household products, toiletries like shampoos and deodorants, sanitary protection and disposable nappies.

Supermarkets in Tanzania are places for the purchase of special, higher status, international goods. They are also places in which the purchase of goods is strongly differentiated from other kinds of retail spaces, small shops (*maduka*), kiosks (*kigenge/kibanda*) and market stalls. In shops and market stalls, buyers face sellers across a display of goods that the seller will pick out for the client. Price may or may not become a point of negotiation. In the case of market traders, the volume of product may be adjusted upwards to give better value (Pietila 2008). Rural shops, including those in small towns, conform to a fairly standard architectural layout, with shelving on which goods are stacked around the back walls and the shopkeeper sitting or standing behind a counter. If this is glass fronted, it may be used for the display or storage of goods. Shops in small towns and rural centres often have iron grilles separating customers from shopkeepers. Items are handed to the customer through a gap in the grille.

The most common type of small rural shop does not specialise in particular types of products. Rather, it sells a range of everyday items in constant demand by all households; salt, soap bars, sugar, tea leaves, matches, exercise books, sugar, body oil and batteries. Cooking oil and kerosene are sold by measures of different sizes, the smallest of which is one spoonful. Customers provide their own containers. In areas with a higher-income presence , such as small towns, the range of items encompasses a wider range of staples, perhaps different kinds of branded soap, body lotions, hair oils, jam and instant coffee, and the basic items, such as cooking oil, may be sold packaged and in larger quantities. Typically, goods such as soap, sugar and salt are sold loose, without packaging. Branding is minimal. If a shop sells cooking oil by price difference this relates to the unit of sale by quantity rather than the kind of oil on offer. In this economy of quantities, contra Callon et al. (2002), the customer is not expected to have an interest in the qualities of the goods on offer, which are dealt with functionally. Goods are therefore not available for inspection by the customer. Moreover, as the customer is defined through their need of goods, and hence as someone who cannot be trusted not to steal them, customers must be separated, by grilles and counters, from the shopkeepers and their products.

## Self-service urbanism as a practice of citizenship

Large supermarkets present an obvious contrast with the regular *duka*, a contrast accentuated by the architecture and organisation of the newly constructed hypermarkets, with bright fluorescent lights, rows of cash registers, wide aisles and product displays. The supermarket is not merely an architectural form. It involves a particular enactment of the practice of provisioning entailing a unique relation between customer and products in the form of self-service (du Gay 2004). In countries where super-market products contrast markedly with the everyday goods consumed by most households, the supermarket is also the location where people can establish relations of various sorts with these exotic things. It is not profitable for large supermarket companies to operate in small rural centres where retail volumes are low and transport costs considerable. Supermarkets in small rural towns are therefore not the large stores with rows of shelving leading to registers at the end of multiple aisles. They are the standard *duka* reconfigured through the prism of supermarket style in terms of the kinds of goods that are available and the relation between product, shopkeeper and consumer.

Mahenge's claim to being on the way to urban status is sustained by the construction of new buildings and what comes to stand for urban layout, the bus station on the periphery and a recently opened modern fuel station at the entry to the town. This has a large covered forecourt with garish signage announcing petrol, diesel and supermarket open 24 hours. Although the supermarket had yet to become operational in mid-2012, this did not detract from its statement of intent to provide up-to-the-minute services. Modern service stations in towns and on highways all advertise 24-hour service and mini-marts. Two other shops located in the town centre proclaim themselves as supermarkets. One, which I shall call Mama Ulanga's, is a converted former tea shop that operates from the small square unit of a standard *duka*. A glass door, tiled floor and electric lighting suggest the store's aspiration to urban style. Service is conven-tional, with the owner passing goods to customers from behind a counter.

Mama Ulanga stocks mainly imported alcoholic beverages, Scotch whisky made in India and the United Kingdom, juice, soft drinks, biscuits and shrink-wrapped packages of Indian snacks. Everyday items such as salt, cooking oil and exercise books are not sold. In contrast, Sumaku Supermarket, across the street, is more innovative in its adaptation of supermarket aesthetics to the small-shop form[27]. The outcome of careful observation by the owner of the style of Dar es Salaam supermarkets

[27] Sumaku's, like Mama Ulanga, is a pseudonym.

and his understanding, based on a decades of experience of running a *mgahawa*, a local food outlet, and of the social context of Mahenge town, Sumaku's strives to become a destination that will have constant turnover of low-cost high-volume trade as well as being a magnet for the middle-class population of local-government workers, many of whom come from outside the District. Sumaku's therefore stocks the everyday items bought by most people – tea, sugar, salt and cooking oil – as well as replicating the essence of the supermarket experience for the consumer. Sumaku's owner achieves this through stocking a combination of high- and low-end products, suitably packaged for the kind of people who regard themselves as supermarket consumers. Salt and sugar are not sold loose, as in every-day shops, but in packages at various price points.[28]

Like Mama Ulanga's, Sumaku's stocks what are thought of as quintes-sential supermarket goods, including the juices and packaged products, but extending to new kinds of household goods such as toilet brushes, which are prominently displayed, manufactured bread, and products like disposable nappies, meeting the emergent needs of the urban middle-class consumer. The low-income customer is catered for with more affordable exotic luxuries, evocative brands of soft drink like Lucozade and Red Bull, which are newly available in Tanzania, ordinary sodas (Coke and Fanta), Snickers bars and pieces of cake. As with new entrants to the food trade, the small-scale supermarket is made practicable through the new options for communications and remote management, allowing the restocking of perishables like baked goods in small quantities by sending cash to a relative who sends back stock to Mahenge with one of the returning buses.

Sumaku's supermarket occupies a small unit that is similar in size to those of other shops in the town. The use of space is radically different. Open to shoppers with no counter separating them from the shopkeeper or from the goods on sale, customers have potentially unmediated access to goods, which they can take from the shelves and examine. To enable this, and to make the supermarket a proper supermarket, Sumaku's owner has obtained genuine supermarket shelving for the centre of the shop, making up tiny aisles along which customers can replicate the supermarket experience by browsing. Not all customers do this. Items will be fetched from the shelves for customers who prefer the standard relationship between person and product. Customers unfamiliar with the supermarket form have to be instructed how to shop in this new environment. Such instruction renders explicit the novelty of the supermarket experience

---

[28] These food outlets are hybrids between tea shops and cafeterias. Menus are virtually standard across Tanzania. Such outlets serve tea, tea with milk, rice cakes or *mandazi* (dough-nut-like fried bread), and perhaps *sambusa* (samosas) as snacks, and what is considered to be food for meals involving rice or *ugali* (maize meal) and a smaller side dish of vegetable or meat. Everyday food is also a mode of differentiation, with meat and tea with milk conveying higher income, and snack foods like chips (fries) thought of as urban and luxurious. Chips, and small meat skewers, are often prepared separately outside the main kitchen. Cooking chips and skewers, like *boda boda* driving, is a young peri-urban male occupation.

and the radically different ways of being in relation to how one interacts with the shopkeeper, and shopkeeper with customer, and how the potential customer interacts with the products presented for their inspection. Shelves lining the walls are crammed with colourful displays of a huge variety of branded products in their distinctive packaging. Such displays are directed at the new knowledgeable consumer, sensitive to product differentiation and for whom price is not the prime determinant of product choice.[29] Sumaku stocks a hierarchy of laundry detergents, from the unbranded powder sold by weight in unmarked clear plastic bags through to small sachets of the nationally produced Toss and Foma to expensive international brands sold in better packaging and larger quantities. Such items are not bought very often. Their display creates the ambience of sophistication and possibility that supermarket shopping is structured to enable. Shopping at Sumaku's restructures the experience of interacting with shopkeeper and with products, situating choice in place of need and hence reordering the relation between shopkeeper and customer, reframed from patron to partner in the transaction.

If visiting the supermarket permits the enactment, albeit transiently, of a new form of modern citizenship in which the subjects are knowledgeable equals in enterprise exchanging products and services within the market framing of a formalised economy, places like supermarkets provide the milieu where these subjectivities can be performed. In providing the products and services constitutive of middle-income cultural practice, they contribute to the consolidation of new 'norms and forms' (1995) in middle-income Tanzania. These norms and forms are not limited to consumption and livelihood practices, but extend to relations with traditional and state authorities. It is not coincidental that the NGO Twaweza! – which aims to enhance relations of accountability between providers and users of public services – delivers the informational messages thought to empower citizens to take action through the packaging on 'fast-moving consumer goods'.

## Economic change in Tanzania

The picture of change in Tanzania is complex and ambiguous. It is not one of catastrophic dislocation described in anthropological accounts of African economic transformation in the early 1990s (e.g. Geschiere & Rowlands 1996). Although globalisation, large-scale foreign investments, localised land-grabbing and the rise of the mining sector are impacting on inequality in some parts of the country, economic transformation in Tanzania is not constituted through such instances of dramatic dispossession but through

[29] Neither Mama Ulanga's nor Sumaku's display price labels on products. This is partly because price is not the major determinant for their customers and the shops are never very busy, so people will ask the price of items. It is also because neither shop owner is so familiar with the conventions of urban supermarkets.

the everyday transactions between small farmers and the middle class. In Ulanga, the middle-income imaginary of the 'mini-tiger' world of small-scale agricultural entrepreneurs has yet to come into existence. What has happened is a change in the organisation of the agricultural economy in which public servants use cash income and access to credit to become intermediary micro-entrepreneurs, providing markets for agricultural produce, getting involved in input supply businesses (because there is government subsidy to build the private sector), and getting involved in seasonal trade in basic food staples. Despite new opportunities created by changes in land tenure that promote buying and seasonal renting, middle-class investment strategies seek to minimise risk and so limit investments in agricultural production to small areas where returns are more certain, including renting or bought farms towards the Kilombero valley. In the villages in the vicinity of Mahenge, low agricultural productivity, dispersed plots and high transport costs render agricultural investment unattractive. Middle-income strategies thus seek to enclose other kinds of resources on which they can levy fees. Small farmers in the vicinity of Mahenge find their own income strategies enabled, temporarily at least, by this expansion. Middle-income presence increases local demand for food crops, and for other produce such as eggs, chickens, milk and pork, providing incentives for innovation in the local agricultural economy.

Services made available through middle-income enterprise, particularly transport, impact on local economic capabilities and alter the experience of living in out-of-the-way places. Marginal villages and their inhabitants are brought into a wider set of economic possibilities. While the terms of this inclusion are not necessarily optimal for small farmers, they nevertheless widen the scope of income-earning opportunities. Such changes bring considerable risk, of which the most immediate is the alienation of land by those seeking to consolidate middle-class advantage through the purchase of land from which they can derive rental income. The social implications of this process are uncertain. There is no doubt that pathways of dispossession are created through it, especially in relation to land, but it must be emphasised that the land situation is not straightforward in regard to selling and that small farmers and village governments retain considerable control over land they have been allocated, including the right to refuse private sales. Perhaps the most significant social consequence of this economic reordering in Tanzania is a social reorientation towards the middle-income group, away from the small farmers cultivated by initial CCM policies and away from the state-supported bureaucratic bourgeoisie. This reorientation cultivates the nascent private sector while at the same time sustaining small farmers, whose livelihoods come to depend on their relations with middle-income clients.

In Mahenge and small rural townships the material instantiation of middle-income urbanism is demonstrated in styles of housing, with glass windows and, although there is neither sewage system nor piped water, flushable toilets situated inside the house. Although styles of construction and consumer goods convey associations with class, differentiating poor from better-off households, and local from more explicitly cosmopolitan styles, economic liberalisation has made the kinds of goods through which such differences are literally constructed more available, democratising the materials of middle-income self-construction. People aspiring to living the life of contemporary Tanzanians are gradually adopting novel ways of organising domestic space irrespective of their style of housing, transforming the presentation of domestic public space from outside the house, in the yard, to the inside, where large sofas are used to receive guests and to display a new urban-influenced civility. Middle-income styles provide models of domestic organisation and personal comportment that are influencing how people live their everyday lives. As housing made from thatch and timber is gradually replaced by brick construction in most villages, and iron-sheet roofs become commonplace rather than exceptional, urban styles of furnishing are coming to signify aspirations to developed status in a proportion of rural homes. Middle-income categories of life experience encompass life itself, with diseases such as 'pressure' – high blood pressure – previously associated with the middle class, fast becoming national afflictions (Strahl 2003).[30] Although middle-income Tanzanians have close connections, past or present, with the state, they depend on a diverse portfolio of investments and connections to support themselves and meet the costs of differentiating education necessary for social reproduction in the post-adjustment order. These include appropriating the surpluses produced by small farmers, and making money from mediating access to goods and services that small farmers need. Middle-income lifestyles and economic strategies enact this interstitially, enabled by the transformations of the new economy in which a hands-off relation with agriculture permits middle classes to appropriate the production of others. Narratives of economic inclusion are founded on the consolidation of inequality.

[30] Another new disease is 'sugar' (diabetes).

# Conclusion

In 2011 the Government of Tanzania issued a Five Year National Development Plan, setting out clear ambitions to become a middle-income country by 2025 through a transformed national economy led by private-sector growth. The orientation towards structural transformation and away from social sectors, alongside changing relations with key donors who had become disillusioned with direct budgetary support, could be taken as an indication that the direction of development in Tanzania is changing. It some respects it is. The Tanzanian state is rapidly moving towards an economic policy that prioritises immanent (Cowen & Shenton 1996: 51) development in the sense of enabling the extension of capitalist relations of production to promote rapid economic growth (URT 2011; Wangwe 2010). This is to be achieved through openness to foreign investment, particularly in minerals and natural-resource extraction, investments in large-scale infrastructure, and commercial farming. Development is thus being practically redefined in Tanzania, as elsewhere in Africa, as openness to capitalist structural transformation. A return to the national development plan as an instrument of economic management shelved during the recent development era sends clear signals to donors that Tanzania is losing patience with the soft conditionalities of the poverty reduction process.

As economic growth becomes a more prominent ambition and the focus of public investment, in infrastructure for example, the kind of donor-funded social development oriented towards low cost service provision becomes peripheralised as a priority and politically. Legitimated by the narrative of inclusive growth, poverty reduction as an effect of social sector programming takes second place to investments geared towards economic productivity. The national plan supersedes the poverty reduction strategy practically, a shift marked by the situation of responsibility for the Plan within a strengthened Planning Commission, under the Office of the President, while poverty reduction is marginalised in a weakened Poverty Eradication Division within the Ministry of

Finance associated with progress monitoring and donor conditionalities. The current phase of the Tanzania Social Action Fund, which previously provided co-financing for local-government community infrastructure and group projects, symbolises the kinds of changes taking place in development in Tanzania, and indeed elsewhere in Africa, where development solutions funded by donors must support the kinds of policies claimed to enable growth. The Tanzania Social Action Fund continues to using village participatory structures and local government systems to implement its programmes, but these are now directed towards the identification of individuals who can be individually supported for a defined term in order to achieve their own projects of development.

The organisation of public services in health, education and agricultural extension remain the responsibility of decentralised district authorities, which are allocated block grants from central government and can theoretically raise additional revenue. Districts retain responsibility for implementing the national development policy in villages in their areas and for ensuring that residents participate in prioritising activities and contributing labour and cash to capital projects such as the construction of schools and clinics. Local and national civil-society organisations (CSOs) struggle to obtain the recognition that enables them to compete for funding to implement the programmes of others or to obtain a contract to monitor the spending of district government.

The organisation of development in Tanzania is increasingly professionalised, involving specialised mastery of techniques and styles as well as the kind of knowledge considered 'technically' relevant. As we have seen, volunteering in a CSO in rural districts has become a 'professional' activity. Development in Tanzania remains founded on differentiation between beneficiaries and others, while development continues to offer symbolic and material resources that both accentuate difference and enable its real beneficiaries to pursue their personal projects of development. The chapters in this book clearly demonstrate that this is not a recent phenomenon. The constitution of development as a form of social organisation in Tanzania cannot simply be claimed as an effect of neo-liberalism or structural adjustment. It is, rather, integral to the constitution of the Tanzanian state itself, conceived as a project of moral internationalism founded on notions of trusteeship and self-help. These core notions were rendered convincing through substantial financial flows. They become reframed in the late twentieth century in terms of development partnerships, international targets, sustainability and expertise. Consequently, the organisation of development in Tanzania demonstrates a remarkable durability of forms throughout the colonial and post-colonial periods. This durability derives from the core organisational principle of community development as the basis for organising rural inclusion into a state constituted for the organisation of development conceived not as an endeavour of state developmentalism, but as a dependant on relations with other states. The continuity of community development forms in

Tanzania is striking. Practically anticipated in the German commune system and in indirect rule premised on the native treasury, it was elaborated through later British colonial policy, which provided the framework through which the independent government would conceptualise the relations between the state and rural society. Community development forms through village institutions and notions of devolved responsibility could be segued into the neoliberal policy-framing of the Local Government Reform Programme, leaving the fundamental hierarchical organisation of development relations, in which communities participate in development through planning to be included in the budgets of upper tiers of government, fundamentally unaltered.

Development continues to be conceptualised as primarily a problem of rural populations who must be made responsible for its attainment. The role of the state in managing national development is to establish and facilitate this vision. Enacting development implies particular relations between state and agents of development and between development agents and subjects. As we have seen, the particular forms of the Tanzanian state have been sustained through internationally financed development interventions that have sought to sustain specific models of community as potentially self-reliant and capable of transformation, at the same time as Tanzanian exemplars of community forms have provided templates for development imaginaries of beneficiary engagement. Such imaginaries have a long history within the moral philosophies informing the rationalities of intentional development as state actions designed to ameliorate the social dislocations caused by capitalist expansion (Creed 2006; Li 2007a: 51). The assumed values of community were perceived to be most at risk by development and thus had to be protected or reinstated. Community could also become the basis for development itself as long as there was a transformation in values and attitudes that could situate persons in relation to new economic opportunity. These ideas became the explicit foundation of colonial community development policy after 1945 and of the independent states approach to community development. Although collectivisation as an economic and social policy was short-lived under *ujamaa* socialism the strong moral value placed on collective endeavour remains evident in Tanzanian development policy and in donor programming. In recent years the national agriculture development programme has provided agricultural machinery in the form of power tillers and tractors to villages or groups of villagers, while the social action fund supported group enterprises such as keeping 'modern' cattle.

The idea of community as driver of development was also present in the policy of indirect rule that anticipates the fiscal responsibility of decentralisation. Decentralisation of responsibility without accompanying resources proved problematic for the newly independent state. It remains the paradox not only of donor-financed decentralisation but of development more generally, and not only in Tanzania. It is not surprising that development increasingly oriented towards sustainability and 'capacity-building' appears to its intended beneficiaries as merely 'projects of words' and that reform fails to bring about the kinds of changes claimed for it. Development in Tanzania is neither wholly internal nor wholly external. Partially an effect of Tanzania's constitution as a state within development relations it is consolidated through the durability of the institution of community development. Community development works for those persons who can claim a role in developing communities, as local CSOs or official beneficiary representatives. It works for the officials of district governments whose work is including villages in district plans that are actually plans of how the District will meet the national policy vision. It works for government and donors in that it shifts responsibility for development and a proportion of the financing away from central government. Finally, it creates communities as development subjects, perpetually waiting for a catalyst in the form of 'capacity', a project (*mradi*) or 'help' from *wafadhili* (donors) that will transform development from a kind of anticipatory activity such as building or planning into a description of where they are.

Development does however have substantial political, cultural and material effects. It establishes a system for the articulation of difference along an axis of development in which adjacency to development is the sought-after position. It provides potential access to material and symbolic resources for furthering one's personal projects of development, and it organises relations between rural citizens and the state. Further, in creating incentives for the perpetuation of development, through off-the-peg policies and the replication of template programming legitimated by development expertise, development works against the emergence of responsive politics and policy making informed by local contexts which could meet the real needs of countries in Sub-Saharan Africa. This issue was, of course, recognised by Frantz Fanon (2001) at the dawn of African independence who predicted the evolution of southern economies based on extractive industries, tourism and the expansion of a comprador class. The extension of development relations furthers these opportunities, consolidating inequality while providing substantial benefits to those within and beyond particular recipient countries who are able to situate themselves within them.

# REFERENCES

Abaza, Mona, 2001, 'Shopping Malls, Consumer Culture and the Reshaping of Public Space in Egypt', *Theory, Culture & Society*, 18 (5): 97–122.

Abrahams, R.G. (ed.), 1985, *Villagers, Villages and the State in Modern Tanzania*, Cambridge, Centre of African Studies.

Abrahams, R.G. (ed.), 1994, *Witchcraft in Contemporary Tanzania*, Cambridge, Centre of African Studies.

Aga Khan Development Network (AKDN), 2007, *The Third Sector in Tanzania: Learning More About Civil Society Organisations, Their Capabilities and Challenges*, Dar es Salaam, AKDN.

Agrawal, Arun, 1995, 'Dismantling the Divide Between Indigenous and Scientific Knowledge', *Development and Change* 26: 413–39.

Aksartova, S., 2009, 'Promoting Civil Society or Diffusing NGOs? US Donors in the Former Soviet Union', in Hammack, D. & Heydemann, S. (eds), *Globalization, Philanthropy and Civil Society: Projecting Institutional Logics Abroad*, Bloomington, IN, Indiana University Press: 160–90.

Amin, A., 2002, 'Spatialities of Globalisation', *Environment and Planning A*, 34 (3): 385–99.

— 2005, 'Local Community on Trial', *Economy and Society*, 34 (4): 612–33.

Anders, G., 2005, 'Good Governance as Technology: Towards an Ethnography of the Bretton Woods Institutions', in Mosse, David & Lewis, David (eds), *The Aid Effect: Giving and Governing in International Development*, London, Pluto: 37–60.

Anderson, B., 2010, 'Pre-emption, Precaution, Preparedness: Anticipatory Action and Future Geographies', *Progress in Human Geography*, 34 (6): 777–98.

Arce, Alberto & Long, Norman, 1993, 'Bridging Two Worlds: An Ethnography of Bureaucrat-Peasant Relations in Western Mexico', in Hobart, Mark (ed.), 1993, *An Anthropological Critique of Development: The*

*Growth of Ignorance*, London, Routledge: 179–208.

Aubrey, L., 1997, *The Politics of Development Cooperation: NGOs, Gender and Partnership in Kenya*, London, Routledge.

Askew, K., 2002, *Performing the Nation: Swahili Music and Cultural Politics in Tanzania*, Chicago, IL, University of Chicago Press.

Augé, M., 1995, *Non-Places: Introduction to an Anthropology of Supermodernity*, London, Verso.

— trans. Jacobs, A., 1998, *A Sense for the Other: The Timeliness and Relevance of Anthropology*, Stanford, CA, Stanford University Press.

Auslander, M., 1993, '"Open the wombs!" The Symbolic Politics of Modern Ngoni Witchfinding', in Comaroff, J. & Comaroff, J.L. (eds), *Modernity and Its Malcontents: Ritual and Power in Postcolonial Africa*, Chicago, IL, University of Chicago Press: 167–92.

Bartunek, Joel, 1993, 'Scholarly Dialogues and Participatory Action Research', *Human Relations*, 46 (10): 1221–34.

Bayart, J.-F., 1993, *The State in Africa: The Politics of the Belly*, 2nd edn, London, Longman.

Bazin, L. & Selim, M., 2006, 'Ethnography, Culture and Globalization: Anthropological Approaches to the Market', *Critique of Anthropology*, 26 (4): 437–61.

Bebbington, A., 1994, 'Theory and Relevance in Indigenous Agriculture: Knowledge, Agency and Organization', in Booth.

Berry, S., 1993, *No Condition is Permanent: The Social Dynamics of Agrarian Change in Sub-Saharan Africa*, Madison, University of Wisconsin Press.

Beidelman, Thomas O., 1982, *Colonial Evangelism: A Socio-Historical Study of an East African Mission at the Grassroots*, Bloomington, IN, Indiana University Press.

Beveridge, W., 1942, Report of the Inter-Departmental Committee on Social Insurance and Allied Services, London, National Archives.

Blommaert, J., 1997, 'Intellectuals and Ideological Leadership in *Ujamaa* Tanzania', *African Languages and Cultures*, 10 (2): 129–44.

Boex, J., & Martinez-Vazquez, J., 2006, *Local Government Finance Reform in Developing Countries: The Case of Tanzania*, London, Palgrave Macmillan.

Bond, G.C. & Ciekawy, D.M., 2001, *Witchcraft Dialogues: Anthropological and Philosophical Exchanges*, Athens, OH, Centre for International Studies.

Booth, David, 1994, 'Rethinking Social Development: An Overview', in his (ed.), *Rethinking Social Development: Theory, Research and Practice*, Harlow, Longman: 3–34.

Bornstein, E., 2005, *The Spirit of Development*, Stanford, CA, Stanford University Press.

Bowker, G. & Star, S.L. 2000, *Sorting Things Out: Classification and Its Consequences*, Boston, MA and Cambridge: MIT Press.

Boyer, P., 1990, *Tradition as Truth and Communication: A Cognitive*

*Description of Traditional Discourse*, Cambridge, Cambridge University Press.

Brett, A., 2003 Participation and Accountability in Development Management, *Journal of Development Studies*, 40 (2): 1–29.

Briggs, J. & Mwafupe, D., 2000, 'Peri-Urban Development in an Era of Structural Adjustment in Africa: The City of Dar es Salaam, Tanzania', *Urban Studies*, 37 (4): 797–809.

Brosius, P., 2006, 'Seeing Communities: Technologies of Visualisation in Conservation', in Creed, G.W. (ed.), *The Seductions of Community: Emancipations, Oppressions, Quandaries*, Santa Fe, NM, School of American Research Press.

Brown, H. & Green, M. (forthcoming), 'Performing Work in Africa's New Economies: Volunteering as Status, Practice and Labor in Development Architectures', *African Studies Review*.

Bryceson, D., 1993, *Liberalising Tanzania's Food Trade: Public & Private Faces of Urban Marketing Policy 1939–1988*, London, James Currey.

— 2002, 'The Scramble in Africa: Reorienting Rural Livelihoods', *World Development*, 30 (5): 725–39.

— 2011, 'The Birth of a Market Town in Tanzania: Towards Narrative Studies of Urban Africa', *Journal of Eastern African Studies*, 5 (2): 274–93.

Bukurura, S., 1994, 'Sungusungu and the Banishment of Suspected Witches in Kahama', in Abrahams, R.G. (ed), *Witchcraft in Contemporary Tanzania*, Cambridge, Centre of African Studies: 61–9.

Burke, F., 1964, 'Tanganyika: The Search for *Ujamaa*', in Friedland, W.H. & Rosberg, C.G. (eds), *African Socialism*, Palo Alto, CA, Stanford University Press: 195–237.

Cahill, C., 2007, 'The Personal is Political: Developing New Subjectivities Through Participatory Action Research', *Gender, Place and Culture*, 14 (3): 267–92.

Callahan, M., 1993, 'Nomansland: The British Colonial Office and the League of Nations Mandate for German East Africa, 1916–1920', *Albion: A Quarterly Journal Concerned with British Studies*, 25 (3): 443–64.

Callon, M., 2002, 'Writing and (Re)writing Devices as Tools for Managing Complexity', in Law, J. & Mol, A. (eds), *Complexities: Social Studies of Knowledge Practices*, Durham, NC, Duke University Press: 191–217.

Callon, M., Meadel, C., Rabhariosa, V., 2002, 'The Economy of Qualities', *Economy and Society*, 31 (2): 194–217.

Campbell, J., 2001, 'Participatory Rural Appraisal as Qualitative Research: Distinguishing Methodological Issues from Participatory Claims', *Human Organization*, 6 (4): 380–89.

— 2002, 'A Critical Appraisal of Participatory Methods in Development Research', *International Journal of Social Research Methodology*, 5 (1): 19–29.

Caplan, P., 1992, 'Socialism from Above: The View From Below', in Forster,

P. & Maghimbi, S. (eds), *The Tanzanian Peasantry: Economy in Crisis*, Aldershot, Avebury: 103–23.

Chachage, C.L.S., 1988, 'British rule and African civilization in Tanganyika', *Journal of Historical Sociology*, 1 (2): 199–223.

Chakrabarty, D., 2000, *Provincializing Europe: Postcolonial Thought and Historical Difference*, Princeton, NJ, Princeton University Press.

Chaligha, A., 2008, Local Autonomy and Citizen Participation in Tanzania: From a Local Government Reform Perspective, REPOA Special Paper, Dar es Salaam: Mkuki na Nyota).

Chambers, R., 1983, *Rural Development: Putting the Last First*, London, Longman.

— 1994, 'The Origins and Practice of Participatory Rural Appraisal', *World Development*, 22 (7): 953–69.

Chatterjee, P., 2004, *The Politics of the Governed: Reflections of Popular Politics in Most of the World*, New York, Columbia.

Cleaver, F., 1999, 'Paradoxes of Participation: Questioning Participatory Approaches to Development', *Journal of International Development*, 11 (4): 597–612.

— 2007, 'Understanding Agency in Collective Action', *Journal of Human Development*, 8 (2): 223–44.

Clegg, S. & Courpasson, D., 2004, 'Political Hybrids: Tocquevillean Views on Project Organizations', *Journal of Management Studies*, 41 (4): 525–47.

Collier, Stephen, 2005, 'Budgets and Biopolitics', in Ong, Aiwa & Collier, Stephen (eds), *Global Assemblages: Technology, Politics and Ethics as Anthropological Problems*, Oxford, Blackwell: 373–90.

Collins, P., 1974, 'The Working of Tanzania's Rural Development Fund: A Problem in Decentralization', in Rweyemamu, A.H. & Mwansasu, B.U. (eds), *Planning in Tanzania: Background to Decentralisation*, Nairobi, East African Literature Bureau, 87–120.

Colonial Office, 1944, 'Mass Education in African Society', Colonial Advisory Committee on Education in the Colonies, *Colonial*, 186.

Comaroff, J. & Comaroff, J.L., 1991, *Of Revelation and Revolution*, Vol. 1, *Christianity, Colonialism and Consciousness in South Africa*, Chicago, IL, University of Chicago Press.

— 1993, Introduction to their (eds), *Modernity and Its Malcontents: Ritual and Power in Postcolonial Africa*, Chicago, IL, University of Chicago Press.

Cooke, B. & Cox, W., 2005, *Fundamentals of Action Research*, London, Sage.

Cooke, Bill and Kothari, Uma (eds), 2001, *Participation: The New Tyranny?* London, Zed.

Cooksey, Brian, 2003, Marketing Reform? The Rise and Fall of Agricultural Liberalisation in Tanzania, *Development Policy Review*, 21 (1): 67–91.

— 2012, Politics, Patronage and Projects: The Political Economy of

Agricultural Policy in Tanzania, Working Paper 40, Dar es Salaam, PEAPA.

Cooksey, Brian and Kikula, Idris, 2005, When Bottom-up Meets Top-down: The Limits of Local Participation in Local Government in Tanzania, REPOA Special Paper No 17, Dar es Salaam, Mkuki na Nyota.

Cooper, F., 2005, *Colonialism in Question: Theory, Knowledge, History*, Berkeley, CA, University of California Press.

Cooper, F. & Packard, R., 1997, 'Introduction' in their (eds), *International Development and the Social Sciences: Essays on the History and Politics of Knowledge*, Berkeley, CA, University of California Press: 1–41.

Corbridge, S., Williams, G., Srivastava, M. Veron, R., 2005, *Seeing the State: Governance and Governmentality in India*, Cambridge, Cambridge University Press.

Cornwall, Andrea, 2004, 'Introduction: New Democratic Spaces? The Politics and Dynamics of Institutionalised Participation', *IDS Bulletin* 35 (2): 1–10.

— 2006, 'Historical Perspectives on Participation in Development', *Commonwealth and Comparative Politics*, 44 (1): 62–83.

Cornwall, Andrea & Fleming, Sue, 1995, 'Context and Complexity: Anthropological Reflections on PRA', *PLA Notes*, 24, 8–12.

Cornwall, A & Jewkes, R, 1995, 'What is Participatory Research?' *Social Science and Medicine*, 41(12): 1667–76.

Costello, M., 1996, 'Administration Triumphs Over Politics: The Transformation of the Tanzanian State', *African Studies Review*, 39 (1): 123–48.

Coulson, A., 2013, *Tanzania: A Political Economy*, 2nd edn, Oxford, Clarendon Press.

Cowen, Michael & Shenton, Robert W., 1996, *Doctrines of development*, London, Taylor & Francis.

Craig, D. & Porter, D., 1997, 'Framing Participation: Development Projects, Professionals and Organisations', *Development in Practice*, 77 (3): 229–36.

— 2006, *Development Beyond Neoliberalism? Governance, Poverty Reduction and Political Economy*, London, Routledge.

Creed, G.W., 2006, 'Reconsidering Community', in Creed, G.W. (ed.), *The Seductions of Community: Emancipations, Oppressions: Quandaries*, Santa Fe, NM, School of American Research Press: 3–22.

Crewe, Emma & Harrison, Elizabeth, 1998, *Whose Development? An Ethnography of Aid*, London, Zed.

Crozier, A., 1979, 'The Establishment of the Mandates System 1919–25: Some Problems Created by the Paris Peace Conference', *Journal of Contemporary History*, 14 (3): 483–513.

Culwick, A.T. & Culwick, G.M., 1935, *Ubena of the Rivers*, London, George Allen & Unwin.

— 1938/39, 'A Study of Population in Ulanga, Tanganyika Territory', *The Sociological Review*, 30 (4): 365–79.

Curtis, D., 1995, 'Power to the People: Rethinking Community Development', in Nelson, N. & Wright, S. (eds), *Power and Participatory Development: Theory and Practice*, London, Intermediate Technology Publications: 115–24.

Daloz, J.-P., 2007, 'Elite Distinction: Grand Theory and Comparative Perspectives', *Comparative Sociology*, 6: 27–74.

de Haan, Arjan, 2009, *How the Aid Industry Works: An Introduction to International Development*, Boulder, CO, Kumarian Press.

de Koning, K., 1995, 'Participatory Appraisal and Education For Empowerment?' *PLA Notes* 24: 34–7.

Development Partners Group Tanzania, 2014, www.tzdpg.or.tz (accessed 26 June 2014).

Dezalay, Yves & Garth, Bryant G., 2002, *The Internationalization of Palace Wars: Lawyers, Economists, and the Contest to Transform Latin American states*, Chicago, IL, University of Chicago Press.

Dill, B., 2009, 'The Paradoxes of Community-Based Participation in Dar es Salaam, Tanzania', *Development and Change*, 40 (4): 717–43.

Dolan, C., 2002, 'Gender and Witchcraft in Agrarian Transition: The Case of Kenyan Horticulture', *Development and Change*, 33 (4): 659–81.

Douglas, M., 1966, *Purity and Danger: An Analysis of Concepts of Pollution and Taboo*, London, Routledge and Kegan Paul.

— 1970 (ed.), *Witchcraft Confessions and Accusations*, London, Tavistock.

— 1986, *How Institutions Think*, New York, Syracuse University Press.

— 1991, 'Witchcraft and Leprosy: Two Strategies of Exclusion', *Man* (NS), 26 (4): 723–36.

du Gay, P., 2004, 'Self Service: Retail, Shopping and Personhood', *Consumption, Markets and Culture*, 7 (2): 149–63.

Eckert, A., 2004, 'Regulating the Social: Social Security, Social Welfare and the State in Late Colonial Tanzania', *Journal of African History*, 45 (3): 467–89.

Edwards, M., 1994, 'Rethinking Social Development: The Search for "Relevance"', in Booth.

Ellis, F., & Mdoe, N., 2003, 'Livelihoods and Rural Poverty Reduction in Tanzania', *World Development*, 31 (8): 1367–84.

Elyachar, J., 2003, 'Mappings of Power: The State, NGOs and International Organizations in the Informal Economy of Cairo', *Comparative Studies in Society and History*, 45 (3): 571–604.

— 2005, *Markets of Dispossession: NGOs, Economic Development and the State in Cairo*, Durham, NC, Duke University Press.

Emel, J., Huber, M. & Makene, 'Extracting Sovereignty: Capital, Territory and Gold Mining in Tanzania', *Political Geography*, 30 (2): 70–79.

Englund, H., 1996, 'Witchcraft, Modernity and the Person: The Morality of Accumulation in Central Malawi', *Critique of Anthropology*, 16 (3): 257–79.

— 2006, *Prisoners of Freedom: Human Rights and the African Poor*,

Berkeley, CA, University of California Press.

Englund, H. & Leach, J., 2000, 'Ethnography and the Meta-Narratives of Modernity', *Current Anthropology*, 41 (2): 225–48.

Eriksen, S., 1997, 'Between a Rock and a Hard Place? Development Planning in Tanzanian Local Governments', *Third World Planning Review*, 19 (3): 251–69.

Escobar, A., 1991, 'Anthropology and the Development Encounter: The Making and Marketing of Development Anthropology', *American Ethnologist*, 18 (4): 658–82.

— 1995, *Encountering Development: The Making and Unmaking of the Third World*, Princeton, NJ, Princeton University Press.

Eyben, R. & Ladbury, S., 1995, 'Popular Participation in Aid-Assisted Projects: Why More in Theory than Practice?' in Nelson, N and Wright, S (eds), *Power and Participatory Development*, London, Intermediate Technology Publications: 192–200.

Fairhead, J., 1993, 'Representing Knowledge: The "New Farmer" in Research Fashions', in Pottier, J. (ed.), *Practising Development. Social Science Perspectives*, London, Routledge: 186–204.

Fatton, R., 1985, 'The political ideology of Julius Nyerere: The structural limitations of "African Socialism"', *Studies in Comparative International Development*, 20 (2): 3–24.

Fanon, Frantz, 2001 [1961], *The Wretched of the Earth*, London, Penguin.

Feierman, S., 1990, *Peasant Intellectuals: Anthropology and History in Tanzania*, Madison, WI, University of Wisconsin Press.

Ferguson, J., 1990, *The Anti-Politics Machine: 'Development,' Depoliticization and Bureaucratic Power in Lesotho*, Cambridge, Cambridge University Press.

— 1995, 'From African Socialism to Scientific Capitalism: Reflections on the Legitimation Crisis in IMF-Ruled Africa', in Moore, D. and Schmitz, G. (eds), *Debating Development Discourse: Institutional and Popular Perspectives*, Basingstoke, Macmillan: 129–47.

— 1997, 'Anthropology and Its Evil Twin: "Development" in the Constitution of a Discipline', in Cooper, F. and Packard, R. (eds), *International Development and the Social Sciences*, Berkeley, University of California Press: 150–75

— 1999, *Expectations of Modernity: Myths and Meanings of Urban Life on the Zambian Copperbelt*, Berkeley, CA, University of California Press.

— 2006, *Global Shadows: Africa in the Neoliberal World Order*, Durham, NC, Duke University Press.

Ferguson, J. & Gupta, A., 2002, 'Spatializing States: Towards an ethnography of Neoliberal Governmentality', *American Ethnologist*, 29 (4): 981–1002.

Frödin, O., 2009, 'Generalised and Particularistic Thinking in Policy Analysis and Practice: The Case of Governance Reform in South Africa', *Development Policy Review*, 27(3): 287–306.

Finucane, J.R., 1974, *Rural Development and Bureaucracy in Tanzania: The Case of Mwanza Region*, Uppsala, Scandinavian Institute of African Studies.

Fisher, E. & Arce, A., 2001, 'The Spectacle of Modernity: Blood, Microscopes and Mirrors in Colonial Tanganyika', in Arce, A. and Long, N. (eds), *Anthropology, Development and Modernities: Exploring Discourses, Counter-tendencies and Violence*, London, Routledge: 74–99.

Fisher, W., 1997, 'Doing Good? The Politics and Antipolitics of NGO Practices', *Annual Review of Anthropology*, 26: 439–64.

Fjeldstad, O.H. & Semboja, J. 2000, Dilemmas of Fiscal Decentralisation: A Study of Local Government Taxation in Tanzania, *Forum for Development Studies*, 27 (1): 7–41).

Foucault, M., 1973, *The Birth of the Clinic: An Archaeology of Medical Perception*, London, Routledge.

— 2000 'Governmentality', in Faubion, J (ed.), *Power: Essential Works of Foucault 1954–1984*, London, Penguin: 201–22.

Fraser, Nancy, 1992, 'Rethinking the Public Sphere: A Contribution to the Critique of Actually Existing Democracy', in Calhoun, C. (ed.), *Habermas and the Public Sphere*, Cambridge, MA, MIT Press: 109–42.

Freund, W.M., 1981, 'Class Conflict, Political Economy and the Struggle for Socialism in Tanzania', *African Affairs*, 80 (321): 483–99.

Friedman, J., 1992, *Empowerment: The Politics of Alternative Development*, Oxford, Clarendon.

Gabay, C., 2012, 'The Millennium Development Goals and Ambitious Developmental Engineering', *Third World Quarterly*, 33 (7): 1249–65.

Gardner, K. & Lewis, D., 2000, 'Dominant Paradigms Overturned or Business as Usual? Development Discourse and the White Paper on International Development', *Critique of Anthropology*, 20 (1): 15–29.

Gatter, P., 1993, 'Anthropology in Farming Systems Research: A Participant Observer in Zambia', in Pottier, J. (ed.), *Practising Development: Social Science Perspectives*, London, Routledge: 152–86.

Geschiere, P., 1997, *The Modernity of Witchcraft: Politics and the Occult in Postcolonial Africa*, Charlottesville, VA, University of Virginia Press.

— 2006, 'Witchcraft and the Limits of the Law: Cameroon and South Africa', in Comaroff, J. & Comaroff, J.L. (eds) *Law And Disorder in the Postcolony*, Chicago, University of Chicago Press: 219–46.

Geschiere, P. & Rowlands, M., 1996, 'The Domestication of Modernity: Different Trajectories', *Africa*, 66 (4): 552–4.

Gessler, M., Msuya, D., Nkunya, M., Schar, A., Heinrich, M., Tanner, M., 1995, 'Traditional Healers in Tanzania: Sociocultural Profile and Three Short Portraits', *Journal of Ethnopharmacology*, 48 (3): 145–60.

Gibbon, P., 2001, 'Civil Society, Locality and Globalization in Rural Tanzania: A Forty-Year Perspective', *Development and Change*, 32 (5): 819–44.

Giblin, J., 2005, *A History of the Excluded: Making Family a Refuge from State in Twentieth-Century Tanzania*, Oxford, James Currey.

Goffman, E., 1961, *Asylums: Essays on the Social Situation of Mental Patients and Other Inmates*, Harmondsworth, Penguin.

Goldman, M., 2006, *Imperial Nature: The World Bank and Struggles for Social Justice in the Age of Globalization*, New Haven, CT, Yale University Press.

Gould, J., 2005, 'Timing, Scale and Style: Capacity as Governmentality in Tanzania', in Mosse, D. & Lewis, D. (eds), *The Aid Effect: Giving and Governing in International Development*, London, Pluto: 61–84.

Gould, Jeremy & Ojanen, Julia, 2005, 'Tanzania: Merging in the Circle', in Gould, J (ed.), *The New Conditionality: The Politics of Poverty Reduction Strategies*, Zed: 17–65.

Goulet, Denis, 1989, 'Participation in Development: New Avenues', *World Development*, 17 (2): 165–78.

Green, M., 1994, 'Shaving Witchcraft in Ulanga, *Kunyolewa* and the Catholic Church', in R.G. Abrahams (ed.), *Witchcraft in Contemporary Tanzania*, Cambridge, African Studies Centre: 23–45.

— 1996, 'Medicines and the Embodiment of Substances among Pogoro Catholics, Southern Tanzania', *Journal of the Royal Anthropological Institute*, 2 (3): 485–98

— 1997, 'Witchcraft Suppression Practices and Movements: Public Politics and the Logic of Purification', *Comparative Studies in Society and History*, 39 (2): 319–45.

— 1999, 'Trading on Inequality: Gender and the Drinks Trade in Southern Tanzania', *Africa*, 69 (3): 83–114.

— 2000, 'Public Reforms and the Privatization of Poverty: Some Institutional Determinants of Health Seeking Behaviour in Southern Tanzania', *Culture, Medicine and Psychiatry*, 24 (4): 403–30.

— 2003, *Priests, Witches and Power: Popular Christianity after Mission in Southern Tanzania*, Cambridge, Cambridge University Press.

— 2006, 'Representing Poverty and Attacking Representations: Perspectives on Poverty from Social Anthropology', *Journal of Development Studies*, 42 (7): 1108–29.

— 2009, 'Doing Development and Writing Culture: Exploring Knowledge Practices in International Development and Anthropology', *Anthropological Theory*, 9 (4): 395–417.

— 2011, 'Calculating Compassion: Accounting for Some Categorical Practices in International Development', in Mosse, D. (ed.), *Adventures in Aidland: The Anthropology of Professionals in International Development*, London, Berghahn: 33–58.

Green, M. & Hulme, D., 2005, From Correlates and Characteristics to Causes: Thinking about Poverty from a Chronic Poverty Perspective, *World Development*, 33 (6): 867–80.

Green, M. & Mesaki, S., 2005, 'The Birth of the "Salon": Poverty, "Modernization," and Dealing with Witchcraft in Southern Tanzania', *American*

*Ethnologist,* 32 (30): 371–88.

Green, M. & Waterhouse, R., 2006, *PPA Evaluation and Recommendations for the Poverty Monitoring System in Tanzania,* London, Social Development Direct.Green, M., Mercer, C., Mesaki, S., 2010, Faith Based Organizations and Development in Magu and Newala Districts Tanzania, Birmingham, RAD Working Paper 49.

Greenhill, R., Prizzon, A., Rogerson, A., 2013, *The Age of Choice: How are Developing Countries Managing in the New Aid Landscape?* London: Overseas Development Institute.

Gregory, C.A., 1997, *Savage Money: The Anthropology and Politics of Commodity Exchange,* London, Routledge.

Guyer, J., 2004, *Marginal Gains: Monetary Transactions in Atlantic Africa,* Chicago, IL, University of Chicago Press.

— 2007, 'Prophecy and the Near Future: Thoughts on Macroeconomic, Evangelical and Punctuated Time', *American Ethnologist,* 34 (3): 409–21.

Gwassa, G., 1969, 'The German Intervention and African Resistance in Tanzania', in Kimambo, I.N. & Temu, A.J. (eds), *A History of Tanzania,* Nairobi, East African Publishing House: 85–122.

Hall, Budd, 1992, 'From Margins to Center? The Development and Purpose of Participatory Research', *The American Sociologist,* 23 (4): 15–28.

— 2001, 'I Wish This Were a Poem of Practices of Participatory Research', in Reason, P & Bradbury, H (eds), *The SAGE Handbook of Action Research: Participative Inquiry and Practice,* London, Sage, 171–9.

— 2005 'In From the Cold? Reflections on Participatory Research from 1970–2005, *Convergences,* 38 (1): 5–24.

Hannerz, U., 1996, *Transnational Connections: Culture, People, Places,* London, Routledge.

Hansen, K., 1994, 'Dealing with used Clothing: Salaula and the Construction of Identity in Zambia's Third Republic', *Public Culture,* 6: 503–23.

Hardt, Michael & Negri, Antonio, 2000, *Empire,* Cambridge, MA, Harvard University Press.

Harper, R., 2000, 'The Social Organization of the IMF's Mission Work: An Examination of International Auditing', in Strathern, M (ed.), *Audit Cultures: Anthropological Studies in Accountability, Ethics and the Academy:* 23–53.

Harrison, G., 2001, 'Post-Conditionality Politics and Administrative Reform: Reflections on the Cases of Uganda and Tanzania', *Development and Change,* 32 (4): 657–79.

— 2004, *The World Bank and Africa: The Construction of Governance States,* London, Routledge.

— 2008, 'From the Global to the Local? Governance and Development at the Local Level: Reflections from Tanzania', *Journal of Modern African Studies,* 46 (2): 169–89.

Hart, G., 2001, 'Development Critiques in the 1990s: Culs de Sac and Promising Paths', *Progress in Human Geography*, 25 (4): 649–58.

Hasset, D., 1985, 'The Development of a Village Co-operative Enterprise in Mchinga 2 Village, Lindi Region', in Abrahams, R.G. (ed.), *Villagers, Villages and the State in Modern Tanzania*, Cambridge, Centre of African Studies: 16–54.

Haugerud, A., 1995, *The Culture of Politics in Modern Kenya*, Cambridge, Cambridge University Press.

Havnevik, Kjell J., 1993, *Tanzania: The Limits to Development From Above*, Uppsala: Nordic Africa Institute.

Hearn, Julie, 2001, 'Taking Liberties: Contesting Visions of the Civil Society Project', *Critique of Anthropology*, 21 (4): 339–60.

— 2007, 'African NGOs: The New Compradors?' *Development and Change*, 38 (6): 1095–1110.

Helleiner, G., Killick, T., Lipumba, N., Ndulu, B. & Svendsen, K.-E., 1995, Report of The Group of Independent Advisers on Development Cooperation Issues between Tanzania and its Aid Donors, Copenhagen, Royal Danish Ministry Of Foreign Affairs.

Henkel, H. and Stirrat, R. 2001, 'Participation as Spiritual Duty: Empowerment as Secular Subjection', in Cooke, B. and Kothari, U. (eds), *Participation: The New Tyranny?* London, Zed: 168–84.

Herzfeld, M., 1992, *The Social Production of Indifference: Exploring the Symbolic Roots of Western Bureaucracy*, Chicago, IL, University of Chicago Press.

Heydemann, S. & Hammack, D., 2009, 'Philanthropic Projections: Sending Institutional Logics Abroad', in Hammack D. & Heydemann, S. (eds), *Globalization, Philanthropy and Civil Society: Projecting Institutional Logics Abroad*, Bloomington, IN, Indiana University Press: 3–31.

Hickey, S., 2013, 'Beyond the Poverty Agenda? Insights from the New Politics of Development in Uganda', *World Development*, 43: 194–206.

Hickey, S. & Mohan, G., 2005, 'Relocating Participation within a Radical Politics of Development', *Development and Change*, 36 (2): 237–62.

Hirschmann, A., 1967, *Development Projects Observed*, Washington DC, Brookings Institution.

Hobart, Mark (ed.), 1993, *An Anthropological Critique of Development: The Growth of Ignorance*, London, Routledge.

Hogendorn, J. & Scott, K., 1981, 'The East African Groundnut Scheme: Lessons of a Large-Scale Agricultural Failure', *African Economic History* 10: 81–115.

Holford, J., 1988, 'Mass Education and Community Development in the British Colonies, 1940–1960: A Study in the Politics of Community Education', *International Journal of Lifelong Education*, 7 (3): 163–83.

Hulme, D., 2007, The Making of the Millennium Development Goals: Human Development meets Results-Based Management in an Imperfect World, BWPI Working Paper 16, Brooks World Poverty Institute, University of Manchester.

Humphrey, C., 2002, *The Unmaking of Soviet Life: Everyday Economies after Socialism*, Ithaca, NY, Cornell University Press.

Hussein, K., 1995, 'Participatory Ideology and Practical Development: Agency Control in a Fisheries Project, Kariba Lake', in Nelson, N. & Wright, S. (eds), *Power and Participatory Development*, London, Intermediate Technology Publications: 170–80.

Hwang, H. & Suarez, D., 2005, 'Lost and Found in the Translation of Strategic Plans and Websites', in Czarniawska, B. & Sevon, G. (eds), *Global Ideas: How Ideas, Objects and Practices Travel in the Global Economy*, Herndon, Copenhagen Business School Press: 71–93.

Hydén, G., 1980, *Beyond Ujamaa in Tanzania: Underdevelopment and an Uncaptured Peasantry*, University of California Press.

IBRD (International Bank for Reconstruction and Development), 1961, The Economic Development of Tanganyika: Report of a Mission Organized by the International Bank for Reconstruction and Development at the Request of the Government of Tanganyika and the United Kingdom, Baltimore, Johns Hopkins University Press.

Iliffe, J., 1969, *Tanganyika Under German Rule*, Cambridge, Cambridge University Press.

— 1979, *A Modern History of Tanganyika*, Cambridge, Cambridge University Press.

International Development Center of Japan (IDCJ), 2006, The Study on Improvements of Opportunities and Obstacles to Development (O&OD) Planning Process, Progress Report, Dar es Salaam, Japan International Cooperation Agency.

Jameson, F., 1991, *Postmodernism: Or, the Cultural Logic of Late Capitalism*, London, Verso.

Jeffrey, C., 2008, 'Waiting', *Environment and Planning D: Society and Space*, 26 (6): 954–8.

Jeffrey, C., Jeffrey, P., Jeffrey, R., 2008, *Degrees Without Freedom: Education, Masculinities, and Unemployment in North India*, Stanford, CA, Stanford University Press.

Jennings, M., 2002, 'Almost an Oxfam in Itself: Oxfam, *Ujamaa* and Development in Tanzania', *African Affairs*, 101 (405): 509–30.

— 2003, 'We Must Run While Others Walk: Popular Participation and Development Crisis in Tanzania 1961–9', *Journal of Modern African Studies*, 41 (2): 163–87.

— 2007, '"A very real War": Popular Participation in Development in Tanzania During the 1950s and 1960s', *International Journal of African Historical Studies*, 40 (1): 71–95.

— 2008, *Surrogates of the State? Non-Governmental Organisations, Development and Ujamaa in Tanzania*, Bloomfield, CT, Kumarian Press.

Kapferer, B., 2002, 'Outside All Reason: Magic, Sorcery and Epistemology in Anthropology', *Social Analysis*, 46 (3): 1–30.

Kapoor, I., 2002, 'The Devil's In the Theory: A Critical Assessment of

Robert Chambers' Work on Participatory Development', *Third World Quarterly*, 23 (1): 101–17.

Kearney, M., 1996, *Reconceptualizing the Peasantry: Anthropology in Global Perspective*, Boulder, CO, Westview Press.

Kelsall, T., 2000, 'Governance, Local Politics and Districtization in Tanzania: The 1998 Arumeru Tax Revolt', *African Affairs*, 99 (397): 533–51.

— 2002, 'Shop Windows and Smoke-Filled Rooms: Governance and the Repoliticisation of Tanzania', *Journal of Modern African Studies*, 40 (4): 597–619.

Kesby, M., 2005, 'Retheorizing Empowerment-Through-Participation as a Performance in Space: Beyond Tyranny to Transformation', *Signs: Journal of Women in Culture and Society*, 30 (4): 2037–65.

Klodawsky, Fran, 2007, '"Choosing" Participatory Research: Partnerships in Space-Time', *Environment and Planning A*, 39 (12): 2845–60.

Koponen, J., 1988, *People and Production in late Precolonial Tanzania,* Monographs of the Finnish Society for Development Studies 2, Helsinki, Finnish Society for Development Studies.

— 1994, *Development for Exploitation: German Colonial Policies in Mainland Tanzania, 1884–1914*, Helsinki, Finnish Historical Society.

Kopytoff, I., 1964, 'Socialism and traditional African societies', in Friedland, W.H. & Rosberg, C.G. (eds), *African Socialism*, Stanford, CA, Stanford University Press: 53–62.

Lange, S., 2008, 'The Depoliticisation of Development and the Democratisation of Politics in Tanzania: Parallel Structures as Obstacles to Delivering Services to the Poor', *Journal of Development Studies*, 44 (8): 1122–44.

Lange, S., Wallevik, H., Kiondo, A., 2000, *Civil Society in Tanzania*, Bergen, Christian Michelesen Institute.

Langwick, Stacey A., 2011, *Bodies, Politics, and African Healing: The Matter of Maladies in Tanzania*, Indiana University Press.

Larson, L., 1976, A History of the Mahenge (Ulanga) District, c.1860–1957, PhD thesis, University of Dar es Salaam.

Latour, B., 1990, 'Drawing Things Together', in Lynch, M. and Woolgar, S. (eds), *Representation in Scientific Practice*, Cambridge, MA, MIT Press: 19–68.

— 1993, *We Have Never Been Modern*, Harlow, Pearson.

Latour, B. & Woolgar, S., 1986, *Laboratory Life: The Construction of Scientific Facts*, Princeton, NJ, Princeton University Press.

Law, J., 2004, *After Method: Mess in Social Science Research*, London, Routledge.

Law, J. & Mol, A., 2008, 'Globalisation in Practice: On the Politics of Boiling Pigswill', *Geoforum*, 39 (1): 133–43.

League of Nations, 1923, 'British Mandate for East Africa', *American Journal of International Law*, 17 (3), Supplement, Official Documents: 153–7.

Leal, Patrick, 2007, 'Participation: The Ascendancy of a Buzzword in the Neo-liberal Era', *Development in Practice*, 17 (4–5): 539–48.

Leftwich, Adrian, 1992, 'Is There a Socialist Path to Socialism?' *Third World Quarterly*, 13 (1): 27–42.

— 1995, 'Bringing Politics Back In: Towards a Model of the Developmental State', *The Journal of Development Studies*, 31 (3): 400–27.

Lewis, J, 2000, *Empire State Building: War & Welfare in Colonial Kenya,1925–52*, Oxford, James Currey.

Lewinson, A., 2007, 'Viewing Postcolonial Dar es Salaam through Civic Spaces: A Question of Class', *African Identities*, 5 (2): 199–215.

Li, Tanya Murray, 2007a, *The Will To Improve: Governmentality, Development and the Practice of Politics*, Durham, NC, Duke University Press.

— 2007b, 'Practices of Assemblage and Community Forest Management', *Economy and Society*, 36 (2): 263–93.

Lie, J.H.S., 2011, Developmentality: The New Aid Architecture and the Formation of Partnership between the World Bank and Uganda, PhD thesis, Department of Social Anthropology, Bergen, University of Bergen.

Lofchie, M., 1993, 'Trading Places: Economic Policy in Kenya and Tanzania', in Callaghy, TM & Ravenhill, J (eds), *Hemmed In: Responses to Africa's Economic Decline*, New York, Colombia University Press: 398–462.

Löfgren, O. & Willim, R., 2005, 'Introduction: The Mandrake Mode', in their (eds), *Magic, Culture and the New Economy*, Oxford, Berg: 1–18.

Long, Norman & van der Ploeg, Jan, 1994, 'Heterogeneity, Actor and Structure: Towards a Reconstitution of the Concept of Structure', in Booth.

Ludden, D., 1993, 'Orientalist Empiricism: Transformations of Colonial Knowledge', in Breckenridge, C. & van der Veer, P. (eds), *Orientalism and the Postcolonial Predicament: Perspectives on South Asia*, Philadelphia, PA, University of Pennsylvania Press.

Lugard, F., 1965 [1922], *The Dual Mandate in British Tropical Africa*, 5th edn, London, Frank Cass.

Lund, J., 2007, 'Is Small Beautiful? Village Level Taxation of Natural Resources in Tanzania', *Public Administration and Development*, 27: 307–18.

Lysons, M. & Msoka, T., 2010, 'The World Bank and the Street: (How) Do "Doing Business" Reforms Affect Tanzania's Micro Traders?' *Urban Studies*, 47 (5): 1079–97.

McCracken, G., 1990, 'The Evocative Power of Things: Consumer Goods and the Preservation of Hopes and Ideals', in his *Culture and Consumption: New Approaches to the Symbolic Character of Consumer Goods and Activities*, Bloomington, IN, Indiana University Press.

McHenry, D., 1979, *Tanzania's Ujamaa villages: The Implementation of a Rural Development Strategy*, Research Series 39, Berkeley, CA, Institute of International Studies, University of California.

McMillan, D.E., 1995, *Sahel Visions: Planned Settlement and River Blindness Control in Burkina Faso*, Tucson, AZ, University of Arizona Press.

Maghimbi, S., 1990, Rural Development Policy and Planning in Tanzania, PhD thesis, University of London.

— 1992, 'The Abolition of Peasant Co-operatives and the Crisis in the Rural Economy in Tanzania', in Forster, Paul & Maghimbi, Sam (eds), *The Tanzanian Peasantry: Economy in Crisis*, Harlow, Avebury: 216–35.

— 1995, 'The Rise and Fall of Nyerere's Populism (Ujamaa)', in Forster, Peter & Maghimbi, Sam (eds), *The Tanzanian Peasantry: Further Studies*, Aldershot, Avebury: 23–36.

Mamdani, M., 1996, *Citizen and Subject: Contemporary Africa and the Legacy of Late Colonialism*, London, James Currey.

Mandel, R., 1997, 'Seeding Civil Society', in Hann, C. (ed), *Postsocialism: Ideals, Ideologies and Practices in Eurasia*, London, Routledge: 279–95.

Mapolu, H., 1986, 'The State and the Peasantry', in Shivji, I. (ed.), *The State and the Working People in Tanzania*, Dakar, CODESRIA.

Marsden, D., 1994, 'Indigenous Management and the Management of Indigenous Knowledge', in Wright, S (ed), *Anthropology of Organizations*, London, Routledge: 41–55.

Marsland, Rebecca, 2006, 'Community Participation the Tanzanian Way: Conceptual Contiguity or Power Struggle?' *Oxford Development Studies*, 34 (1): 65–79.

Marston, S.A., Jones, J.P., Woodward, K., 2005. 'Human Geography Without Scale', *Transactions of the Institute of British Geographers*, 30 (4): 416–32.

Marwick, M., 1950, 'Another Modern Anti-Witchcraft Movement in East Central Africa', *Africa*, 20 (2): 100–112.

Massey, Doreen, 2005, *For Space*, London, Sage.

Max, J.A. 1991, *The Development of Local Government in Tanzania*, Dar es Salaam, Educational Publishers and Distributors.

Medeiros, C., 2001, 'Civilizing the Popular? The Law of Popular Participation and the Design of a New Civil Society in 1990s Bolivia', *Critique of Anthropology*, 21 (4): 401–25.

Mercer, C., 1999, 'Re-conceptualising State-Society Relations in Tanzania: Are NGOs "Making a Difference"?' *Area*, 31 (3): 247–58

— 2002, 'The Discourse of *Maendeleo* and the Politics of Women's Participation on Mount Kilimanjaro', *Development and Change*, 33 (1): 101–27.

— 2003, 'Performing Partnership: Civil Society and the Illusions of Good Governance in Tanzania', *Political Geography*, 22 (7): 741–63.

Mercer, C. & Green, M., 2013, 'Making Civil Society Work: Contracting, Cosmopolitanism and Community Development in Tanzania',

*Geoforum*, 45: 106–15.

Mesaki, S., 1993, Witchcraft and Witch-killings in Tanzania: Paradox and Dilemma, PhD thesis, University of Minnesota.

— 1994, 'Witch killing in Sukumaland', in Abrahams, R.G. (ed.), *Witchcraft in Contemporary Tanzania*, Cambridge, African Studies Centre.

— 2009, Witchcraft and the Law in Tanzania, *International Journal of Sociology and Anthropology*, 1 (8): 132–8.

Meyer, J. & Rowan, B., 1977, 'Institutionalized Organizations: Formal Structure as Myth and Ceremony', *American Journal of Sociology*, 83 (2): 340–63.

Miller, Daniel, 1994, *Modernity: An Ethnographic Approach – Dualism and Mass Consumption in Trinidad*, Oxford, Berg.

Miller, Darlene, 2005, 'New Regional Imaginaries in Post-Apartheid Southern Africa: Retail Workers at a Shopping Mall in Zambia', *Journal of Southern African Studies*, 31 (1): 117–45.

Miller, P. & Rose, N., 1990, 'Governing Economic Life', *Economy and Society*, 19 (1): 1–31.

Mindry, D., 2001, 'Nongovernmental Organizations, "Grassroots" and the Politics of Virtue', *Signs: A Journal of Women in Culture and Society*, 26 (4): 1187–1211.

Minogue, M., Polidano, C., Hulme, D., 1998, Introduction to their (eds), *Beyond the New Public Management: Changing Ideas and Practices in Governance*, Cheltenham, Edward Elgar: 1–16.

Mitchell, Timothy, 2002, *Rule of Experts: Egypt, Techno Politics, Modernity*, Berkeley, CA, University of California Press.

— 2005, 'The Work of Economics, How a Discipline Makes its World', *Archives Européennes de Sociologie*, 46 (2): 297–320.

Mitlin, D., Hickey, S., Bebbington, A., 2007, 'Reclaiming Development? NGOs and the Challenge of Alternatives', *World Development*, 35 (10): 1699–1720.

Mkenda, A, Luvanda, E. & Ruhinduka, R., 2010, Growth and Distribution in Tanzania: Recent Experience and Lessons, Report Submitted To REPOA, Dar es Salaam.

Mohan, Giles & Stokke, Kristian, 2000, 'Participatory Development and Empowerment: The Dangers of Localism', *Third World Quarterly*, 21 (2): 247–68.

Mohan, Giles & Power, M., 2009, 'Africa, China and the "New" Economic Geography of Development', *Singapore Journal of Tropical Geography*, 30 (1): 24–28.Monson, J., 1998, 'Relocating Maji Maji: the Politics of Alliance and Authority in the Southern Highlands of Tanzania, 1870–1918', *Journal of African History*, 39 (1): 95–120.

— 2009, *Africa's Freedom Railway: How a Chinese Development Project Changed Lives and Livelihoods in Tanzania*, Bloomington, IN, Indiana University Press.

Moore, H.L. & Vaughan, M., 1994, *Cutting Down Trees: Gender, Nutrition and Agricultural Change in the Northern Province of Zambia*,

*1890–1990*, London, James Currey.Moore, H.L. & Sanders, D.T., 2002, *In Magical Interpretations, Material Realities: Modernity, Witchcraft and the Occult in Postcolonial Africa*, London, Routledge.

Moore, M., 1998, 'Death Without Taxes: Democracy, State Capacity and Aid Dependency in the Fourth World', in Robinson, M. & White, G. (eds), *Towards the Democratic Developmental State: Politics and Institutional Design*, Oxford, Oxford University Press: 84–121.

Moore, Sally Falk, 1977, 'Political Meetings and the Simulation of Unanimity: Kilimanjaro 1973', in Moore, S.F. & Myerhoff, B., *Secular Ritual*, Amsterdam: Van Gorcum: 53–73.

— 1988, 'Legitimation as a Process: The Expansion of Government and Party in Tanzania', in Cohen, R. & Toland, J. (eds), *State Formation and Political Legitimacy*, Political Anthropology vol. 6, New Brunswick, Transaction Publishers: 155–72.

— 1993, 'Post Socialist Micro Politics: Kilimanjaro 1993', *Africa*, 66 (4): 587–606.

— 2001, 'The International Production of Authoritative Knowledge: The Case of Drought Stricken West Africa', *Ethnography*, 2 (2): 161–89.

Moore, S.F. and Myerhoff, B. (eds), 1977, *Secular Ritual: A Working Definition of Ritual*, Amsterdam, Van Gorcum: 152–68.

Morgan, J., 1964, *Colonial Development: A Factual Survey of the Origins and History of British Aid to Developing Countries*, British Aid 5, London, Overseas Development Institute.

Moss, T.J., Pettersson, G., van de Walle, N., 2006, An Aid-Institutions Paradox? A Review Essay on Aid Dependency and State Building in Sub-Saharan Africa, Working Paper 74, Washington DC, Center for Global Development.

Mosse, David, 1994, 'Authority, Gender and Knowledge: Theoretical Reflections on the Practice of Participatory Rural Appraisal', *Development and Change*, 25 (3): 497–526.

— 2001. 'Social Research in Rural Development Projects', in Gellner, D. & Hirsch, E. (eds), *Inside Organisations: Anthropologists at Work*, Oxford, Berg.

— 2004, 'Is Good Policy Unimplementable? Reflections on the Ethnography of Aid Policy and Practice', *Development and Change*, 35 (4): 639–71.

— 2005a, *Cultivating Development: An Ethnography of Aid Policy and Practice*, London, Pluto.

— 2005b, 'Global Governance and the Ethnography of International Aid', in Mosse, D. & Lewis, D. (eds), *The Aid Effect: Giving and Governing in International Development*, London, Pluto: 1–36.

— (ed.), 2011, *Adventures in Aidland: The Anthropology of Professionals in International Development*, Vol. 6, Oxford: Berghahn.— 2013, The Anthropology of International Development, *Annual Review of Anthropology*, 42, 227–46.

Mosse, David et al. (KRIBP project team), 1995, 'Social Analysis in Participatory Rural Development', *PLA Notes*, 24: 27–33.

Mosse, David & Lewis, David (eds), 2005, *The Aid Effect: Giving and Governing in International Development*, London, Pluto: 37–60

Moyo, M., Simson, R., Jacob, A., de Mevius, F., 2010, *Attaining Middle Income Status: Tanzania – Growth and Structural Transformation Required to Reach Middle Income Status by 2025*, London, International Growth Centre.

Mueller, S.D., 1980, 'Retarded Capitalism in Tanzania', in Miliband, R. & Saville, J., *Socialist Register*, London, Merlin: 203–27.

Mwango, H. & Mussadegh, M., n.d., *A Guide to Strategic Planning Process for Organisations*, Dar es Salaam, TRACE.

Narayan, D., 1998, *Voices of the Poor: Poverty and Social Capital in Tanzania*, Washington DC, World Bank.

— 1999, Bonds and Bridges: Social Capital and Poverty, Policy Research Working Paper 2167, Washington DC, World Bank.Narayan, D. & Srinivasan, L, 1994, Participatory Development Tool Kit: Materials to Facilitate Community Empowerment, Washington DC, World Bank.

Narayan, D. & Pritchett, L., 1999, 'Cents and Sociability: Household Income and Social Capital in Rural Tanzania', *Economic Development and Cultural Change*, 47 (4): 871–97.

Narayan, D., Patel, R., Schafft, K., Rademacher, A., Koch-Schulte, S., 2000, *Voices of the Poor: Can Anyone Hear Us?* New York, Oxford University Press and World Bank.

Norris, A. & Worby, E., 2012, 'The Sexual Economy of a Sugar Plantation: Privatization and Social Welfare in Northern Tanzania', *American Ethnologist*, 39 (2): 354–70.

Nyerere, J.K., 1967, 'The Arusha Declaration', in J.K. Nyerere, 1968, *Freedom and Socialism*, Nairobi: Oxford University Press: 231–250.

— 1968, *Ujamaa: Essays on Socialism*, London, Oxford University Press.

— 1974, *Freedom and Socialism / Uhuru na Ujamaa: A Selection from Writings and Speeches 1965–1967*, Nairobi, Oxford University Press.

Oakley, Peter et al., 1991, *Projects with People: The Practice of Participation in Rural Development*, Geneva, International Labour Organization.

O'Connell, S.A. & Soludo, C.C., 2001, 'Aid Intensity in Africa', *World Development*, 29 (9): 1527–52.

Olivier de Sardan, J.-P., 2009, The Eight Modes of Local Governance in West Africa, Africa Power and Politics Research Programme APPP Working Paper 4, London, ODI (for Africa Power and Politics Programme).

Ong, A., 2012, 'Introduction: Worlding Cities or the Art of Being Global', in Ong, A. & Roy, A. (eds), *Worlding Cities: Asian Experiments and the Art of Being Global*, Oxford, Blackwell: 1–26.

Osborne, Thomas, 2004, 'On Mediators: Intellectuals and the Ideas Trade in the Knowledge Society', *Economy and Society*, 33 (4): 430–47.

Pain, R. & Francis, P., 2003, 'Reflections on Participatory Research', *Area*,

35 (1): 46–54.

Pallotti, A., 2008, Tanzania: Decentralising Power or Spreading Poverty? *Review of African Political Economy*, 35 (116): 221–35.

Payer, C., 1983, 'Tanzania and the World Bank', *Third World Quarterly*, 5 (4): 791–813.

Peck, J, 2002, 'Political Economies of Scale: Fast Policy, Interscalar Relations and Neoliberal Workfare', *Economic Geography*, 78 (3): 331–60.

— 2011, 'Global Policy Models, Globalizing Poverty Management: International Convergence or Fast-Policy Integration?' *Geography Compass*, 5 (4): 165–81.

Pederson, D., & Baruffati, V., 1989, 'Healers, Deities, Saints and Doctors: Elements for the Analysis of Medical Systems', *Social Science and Medicine*, 29 (4), 487–96.

Phillips, S. & Edwards, M., 2000, 'Development, Impact Assessment and the Praise Culture', *Critique of Anthropology*, 20 (1): 47–66.

Phillips, L. & Ilcan, S., 2004, 'Capacity Building: The Neoliberal Governance of Development', *Canadian Journal of Development Studies*, 25 (3): 393–409.Pietila, T., 2008, *Gossip, Markets and Gender: How Dialogue Constructs Moral Value in Post-Socialist Kilimanjaro*, Madison, WI, University of Wisconsin Press.

Pigg, Stacy Leigh, 1992, 'Investing Social Categories Through Place: Social Representations and Development in Nepal', *Comparative Studies in Society and History*, 34 (3): 491–513.

— 1993, 'Unintended Consequences: The Ideological Impact of Development in Nepal', *Comparative Studies of South Asia, Africa and the Middle East*, 13 (1–2): 45–58.

— 1997, '"Found in Most Traditional Societies": Traditional Medical Practitioners between Culture and Development', in Cooper & Packard: 259–90.

Platteau, J., 2010, Redistributive Pressures in Sub-Saharan Africa: Causes, Consequences and Coping Strategies, Paper Presented at IIAS Conference, Accra, 15–17 July.

Pottier, J., 1993a, 'Introduction: Development in Practice – Assessing Social Science Perspectives', in his (ed.) *Practicing Development: Social Science Perspectives*, London: Routledge.

— 1993b, 'The Role of Ethnography in Project Appraisal', in his (ed.), *Practising Development:* 13–33.

— 1997, 'Towards an Ethnography of Participatory Appraisal and Research', in Grillo, R.D. & Stirrat, R.L. (eds), *Discourses of development: Anthropological perspectives*, Oxford, Berg: 203–28.

Powell, Robert & Bird, Graham, 2010, 'Aid and Debt Relief in Africa: Have They Been Substitutes or Complements?' *World Development*, 38 (3): 219–27.

Powell, W., Gammal, L., Simard, C., 2005, 'Close Encounters: The Circulation and Reception of Managerial Practices in the San Francisco Bay

Area Nonprofit Community', in Czarniawska, B. & Sevon, G. (eds), *Global Ideas: How Ideas, Objects and Practices Travel in the Global Economy*, Frederiksberg, Copenhagen Business School Press: 233–58.

Pratt, Cranford, 1999, 'Julius Nyerere: Reflections on the Legacy of His Socialism', *Canadian Journal of African Studies*, 33 (1): 137–52.

President's Office Regional Administration and Local Government (PORALG), 2002, *National Framework for Participatory Planning and Budgeting in Local Government Authorities*, Dodoma, United Republic of Tanzania.

Prime Minister's Office Regional Administration and Local Government (PMORALG), 2007, *Joint Government Development Partner Programme Evaluation*, Dar es Salaam, Local Government Reform Programme.

Putnam, R., 1993, *Making Democracy Work: Civic Traditions in Modern Italy*, Princeton, NJ, Princeton University Press.

Putnam, R., Leonardi, R., Nanetti, R., 1994, *Making Democracy Work: Civic Traditions in Modern Italy*, Princeton, NJ, Princeton University Press.

Rabinow, P., 1989, *French Modern: Norms and Forms of the Social Environment*, Chicago, IL, University of Chicago Press.

— 2006, 'Midst Anthropology's Problems', in Ong, A. & Stephen, C. (eds), *Global Assemblages: Technology, Politics and Ethics as Anthropological Problems*, Oxford, Blackwell: 40–54.

Rahnema, M., 1992, 'Participation', in Sachs, W. (ed.), *The Development Dictionary: A Guide to Knowledge as Power*, London, Zed: 116–31.

Redmayne, A., 1970, 'Chikanga: An African Diviner with an International Reputation', in Douglas, M. (ed.), *Witchcraft Confessions and Accusations*, London, Tavistock.

Richards, A., 1935, 'A Modern Movement of Witchfinders', *Africa*, 8 (4): 448–61.

Richards, Paul, 1995, 'Participatory Rural Appraisal: A Quick and Dirty Critique', *PLA Notes*, 24: 13–16.

Rigby, Peter, 1977, 'Local Participation in National Politics, Ugogo, Tanzania', *Africa*, 47 (1): 89–107.

Riles, A., 2001, *The Network Inside Out*, Ann Arbor, University of Michigan Press.

Rizzo, Matteo, 2006, 'What was Left of the Groundnut Scheme? Development Disaster and Labour Market in Southern Tanganyika 1946–1952', *Journal of Agrarian Change*, 6 (2): 205–38.

— 2011, '"Life is War"! Informal Transport Workers and Neoliberalism in Tanzania, 1998-2009', *Development and Change*, 42 (5): 179–206.

Robbins, J., 2004, *Becoming Sinners: Christianity and Moral Torment in a Papua New Guinea Society*, Berkeley, CA, University of California Press.

Robins, S., Cornwall, A., Von Lieres, B., 2008, 'Rethinking "Citizenship" in the Postcolony', *Third World Quarterly*, 29 (6): 1069–86.

Rose, N., 1996, 'Governing "Advanced" Liberal Democracies', in Barry,

A., Osborne, T., Rose, N. (eds), *Foucault and Political Reason: Liberalism, Neo-liberalism and Rationalities of Government*, London, Routledge, 37–64.

— 1999, *Powers of Freedom: Reframing Political Thought*, Cambridge, Cambridge University Press.

— 2000, 'Community, Citizenship and the Third Way', *American Behavioural Scientist*, 43 (9): 1395–1411.

Rowlands, M. & Warnier, J.-P., 1988, 'Sorcery, Power, and the Modern State in Cameroon', *Man* (NS), 23 (1): 118–32.

Roy, A., 2010, *Poverty Capital: Microfinance and the Making of Development*, London, Taylor & Francis.

— 2011, 'Urbanisms, Worlding Practices and the Theory of Planning', *Planning Theory*, 10 (1): 6–15.

Rugumamu, Severine, 1997, *Lethal Aid: The Illusion of Socialism and Self Reliance in Tanzania*, Trenton, Africa World Press.

Sachs, J., 2005, *The End of Poverty: Economic Possibilities for our Time*, New York, Penguin.

— 2009, *The End of Poverty: How We Can Make it Happen in Our Lifetime*, New York, Penguin.

Said, E., 1995, *Orientalism: Western Conceptions of the Orient*, London, Penguin.

Salcedo, R., 2003, 'When the Global Meets the Local at the Mall', *American Behavioural Scientist*, 46 (8): 1084–1103.

Samoff, J., 1979, 'The Bureaucracy and the Bourgeoisie: Decentralization and Class Structure in Tanzania', *Comparative Studies in Society and History*, 21 (1), 30–62.

— 1981, 'Crises and Socialism in Tanzania', *Journal of Modern African Studies*, 19 (2): 279–306.

Sampson, S., 1996, 'The Social Life of Projects: Importing Civil Society to Albania', in Dunn, E. & Hann, C. (eds), *Civil Society: Challenging Western Models*, London, Routledge.

— 2002, 'Beyond Transition: Rethinking Elite Configurations in the Balkans', in Hann, CM (ed.), *Postsocialism: Ideals, Ideologies and Practices in Eurasia*, London, Routledge: 297–316.Sanders, D.T., 2002, 'Save our Skins: Structural Adjustment, Morality and the Occult in Tanzania', in Moore, H.L. & Sanders, D.T. (eds), *Magical Interpretations, Material Realities: Modernity, Witchcraft and the Occult in Postcolonial Africa*, London, Routledge: 160–83.

Sapsed, J. and Salter, A., 2004, 'Postcards from the Edge: Local Communities, Global Programs and Boundary Objects', *Organization Studies*, 25 (9): 1515–34.

Saul, J., 2002, 'Poverty Alleviation and the Revolutionary-Socialist Imperative: Learning from Nyerere's Tanzania', *International Journal*, 57 (2): 193–207.

— 2012, 'Tanzania Fifty Years on (1964–2011): Rethinking Ujamaa, Nyerere and Socialism in Africa', *Review of African Political Economy*,

39 (131): 117–25.

Schneider, L., 2007, 'High on Modernity? Explaining the Failings of Tanzanian Villagisation', *African Studies*, 66 (1): 9–38.

Scoones, I. & Thompson, J., 1994, 'Knowledge, Power and Agriculture: Towards a Theoretical Understanding', in their (eds), *Beyond Farmer First: Rural People's Knowledge, Agricultural Research and Extension Practice*, London, Intermediate Technology Publications: 16–32.

Scott, D., 1995, 'Colonial Governmentality', *Social Text*, 43: 191–220 (reprinted in Inda, J (ed.), 2005, *Anthropologies of Modernity: Foucault, Governmentality, and Life Politics*, Oxford, Blackwell: 23–49).

— 2003, 'Culture in political theory', *Political Theory*, 31 (1): 92–115.

Scott, J., 1998, *Seeing Like a State: How Certain Schemes to Improve the Human Condition have Failed*, New Haven, CT, Yale University Press.

Semboja, J. & Therkildsen, O., 1995, *Service Provision Under Stress: The State, NGOs and Peoples Organisations in Kenya, Uganda and Tanzania*, Copenhagen, Centre for Development Research.

Sennet, R., 2006, *The Culture of the New Capitalism*, Newhaven, CT, Yale University Press.

Shao, J., 1986, 'The Villagization Program and the Disruption of the Ecological Balance in Tanzania', *Canadian Journal of African Studies*, 20 (2): 219–39.

Shivji, I., 1976, *Class Struggles in Tanzania*, New York, Monthly Review Press.

— 2004, 'Reflections on NGOs in Tanzania: What We Are, What We Are Not and What We Ought To Be', *Development in Practice*, 14 (5): 689–95.

Shove, E., 2003, *Comfort, Cleanliness and Convenience: The Social Organization of Normality*, Oxford, Berg.

Shrestha, N., 1995, 'Becoming a Development Category', in Crush, J (ed.), *Power of Development*, London, Routledge.

Simon, D., 1995, 'The Demise of "Socialist" State Forms in Africa: An Overview', *Journal of International Development*, 7 (5): 707–39.

Skage, I.A., Søreide, T., Tostensen, A., 2013, 'When Per Diems Take Over: Training and Travel as Extra Pay: Real World Challenges', in Søreide, T. & Williams, A. (eds), *Corruption, Grabbing and Development*, London, Cheltenham, Edward Elgar: 196–206.

Smith, H. (ed.), 1966, *Readings on Economic Development and Administration in Tanzania*, Oxford University Press for Institute of Public Administration, Dar es Salaam.

Smyth, Rosaleen, 2004, 'The Roots of Community Development in Colonial Office Policy and Practice in Africa', *Social Policy & Administration*, 38 (4): 418–36.

Snyder, K., 2002, 'Modern Cows and Exotic Trees: Identity, Personhood and Exchange among the Iraqw of Tanzania': *Ethnology*, 41 (2): 155–73.

Stambach, A., 2000, 'Curl up and dye: Civil society and the fashion-minded citizen', in Comaroff , J.L. & Comaroff, J. (eds), *Civil Society* and the Political Imagination in Africa: Critical Perspectives, Chicago, IL, University of Chicago Press, 251–66.

Star, S., 1985, 'Scientific Work and Uncertainty', *Social Studies of Science* 15 (3): 391–427.

Star, S. & Griesemer, J., 1989, 'Institutional Ecology, "Translations" and Boundary Objects: Amateurs and Professionals in Berkeley's Museum of Vertebrate Zoology, 1907–39', *Social Studies of Science*, 19 (3): 387–420.

Stillerman, J. & Salcedo, R., 2012, 'Transposing the Urban to the Mall: Routes, Relationships and Resistance in Two Santiago, Chile, Shopping Centres', *Journal of Contemporary Ethnography*, 41 (3): 309–36.

Stirrat, R.L., 2000, 'Cultures of Consultancy', *Critique of Anthropology*, 20 (1): 31–46.

Strahl, H., 2003, 'Cultural Interpretations of an Emerging Health Problem: Blood Pressure in Dar es Salaam, Tanzania', *Anthropology and Medicine*, 10 (3): 309–24.

Strathern, M., 1999, 'What is Intellectual Property After?' in Law, J. & Hassard, J. (eds), *Actor Network Theory and After*, Oxford, Blackwell: 156–82.

— 2000, 'Introduction: New Accountabilities', in her (ed.), *Audit Cultures. Anthropological Studies in Accountability, Ethics and the Academy*, London: Routledge: 1–18.

— 2006, 'Bullet-Proofing: A Tale from the United Kingdom', in Riles, A. (ed.), *Documents: Artefacts of Modern Knowledge*, Ann Arbor, MI, University of Michigan Press: 181–206.

Sundet, G., 1994, 'Beyond Developmentalism in Tanzania', *Review of African Political Economy*, 21 (59): 39–49.

Svendsen, K.V., 1974, 'Development Administration and Socialist Strategy: Tanzania after *Mwongozo*', in Rweyemamu, A.H. & Mwansasu, B.U. (eds), *Planning in Tanzania: Background to Decentralisation*, Nairobi, East African Literature Bureau: 23–44.

Swantz, L, 1990, *The Medicine Man*, Uppsala, Scandinavian Institute of African Studies.

Swantz, M.-L., Ndedya, E., Masaiganah, M.L., 2001, 'Participatory Action Research in Southern Tanzania with Special Reference to Women', in Reason, D and Bradbury, H (eds), *Handbook of Action Research: Participatory Inquiry and Practice*, London, Sage: 386–96.

Swantz, M-.L., & Green, M., 2009, 'Bureaucracy Kills So Many Things': interview with M.L. Swantz, *Suomen Antropologi: Journal of the Finnish Anthropology Society*, 34 (3): 68–76.

Swidler, A., 2009, 'Dialectics of Patronage: Logics of Accountability at the African AIDS-NGO Interface', in Hammack, D. & Heydemann, S. (eds), *Globalization, Philanthropy and Civil Society, Projecting Institutional Logics Abroad*, Bloomington, IN, Indiana University Press: 192–221.

Swidler, A & Watkins, S.C., 2009, 'Teach a Man to Fish: The Sustainability Doctrine and Its Social Consequences', *World Development* 37

(7): 1182–96.

Tanzania National Archives, 1949, Proposals for the Development of the Social Welfare Department, Letter from Social Welfare Organiser to the Honorable Member for Social Services, Secretariat, Dar es Salaam, 18 August 1949, Item 3 in File DC32999 Development Commission Social Welfare, Tanzania National Archives, Dar es Salaam.

— 1951, Development Commission Social Welfare Development DC 32999, Item 12 Minor Development Projects, 1951, Tanzania National Archives, Dar es Salaam.

— 1954, Circular from Provincial Office Morogoro to all District Commissioners, regarding District Development Plans, 28 July 1954, Item 281 File D3/1 vol. III PC Office Morogoro, Development Schemes Eastern Province, Tanzania National Archives, Dar es Salaam.

— 1961a, Letter from Treasury to Ministries, dated 4 December, File PM/182/04 Prime Minister's Office, Colonial Development and Welfare Funds, Tanzania National Archives, Dar es Salaam.

— 1961b, 573 File IRA 2/14 Community Dev Iringa, Community Development Policy and Plans, Tanzania National Archives, Dar es Salaam.

— 1962a, Letter from Provisional Commissioner Bukoba to All District Commissioners 20 March, regarding regional Commissioners, Regional Development Committees, District Development Committees, Item 2 in File D/3 vol. V District Development Committee, Station Biharumulo, Tanzania National Archives, Dar es Salaam.

— 1962b, Circular from West Lake Region Local Treasury Office to all Councils Regarding *Mipango ya Kujisaidia Vijijini*, 9 May, Item 12, File D/3 vol. V District Development Committee, Station Biharamulo, Tanzania National Archives, Dar es Salaam.

— n.d., File 573/CD1/77A Community Development Assistant Iringa, Evaluation Questionnaire First Year of the Five Year Development Plan 1971–1976, Tanzania National Archives, Dar es Salaam.

Thomas, N., 1994, *Colonialism's Culture: Anthropology, Travel and Government*, Cambridge, Polity.

Thompson, C.B., 2012, 'Alliance for a Green Revolution in Africa (AGRA): Advancing the Theft of African Genetic Wealth', *Review of African Political Economy*, 39 (132): 345–50.

Thrift, N., 2000, 'Performing Cultures in the New Economy', *Annals of the Association of American Geographers*, 90 (4), 674–92.

Tripp, A., 1997, *Changing the Rules: The Politics of Liberalization and the Urban Informal Economy in Tanzania*, Berkeley, CA, University of California Press.

Tsing, A.L., 1993, *In the Realm of the Diamond Queen: Marginality in an Out of the Way Place*, Princeton, NJ, Princeton University Press.

— 2000, 'The Global Situation', *Cultural Anthropology*, 15 (3): 327–60.

— 2005, *Friction: An Ethnography of Global Connection*, Durham, NC, Duke University Press.

Turner, M., 2000, 'UN Presence Keeps Kenyan Economy Afloat', *Financial*

*Times*, London, 16 January.

United Republic of Tanzania (URT), 1969, Tanzania Second Five Year Plan for Economic and Social Development July 1969 to June 1974, vol. 1, General Analysis, Dar es Salaam, Government of Tanzania.

— 2001, The National Policy on Non-Governmental Organizations, Dar es Salaam, Vice President's Office.

— 2007, Joint Government Development Partner Programme Evaluation, Dar es Salaam, Local Government Reform Programme, Prime Minister's Office Regional Administration and Local Government.

— 2011, The Tanzania Five Year Development Plan 2011/2012–2015/2016: Unleashing Tanzania's Latent Growth Potentials, Dar es Salaam.

— n.d. Tanzania Development Vision 2025, Planning Commission, Dar es Salaam.

Uzoigwe, J., 1988, '*Ujamaa*: Perceptions and practices in the Tanzanian experiment with Socialism', *West African Journal of Archaeology*, 18: 125–40.

van der Riet, M., 2008, 'Participatory Research and the Philosophy of Social Science: Beyond the Moral Imperative', *Qualitative Inquiry*, 14 (4): 546–65.

van Ufford, P.Q., 1988, 'The Hidden Crisis in Development: Development Bureaucracies in Between Intentions and Outcomes', in van Ufford, P.Q., Kruijt, D., Downing, T. (eds), *The Hidden Crisis in Development: Development Bureaucracies*, Amsterdam, Free University Press: 9–38.

Varley, A., 2013, 'Postcolonialising Informality', *Environment and Planning D: Society and Space*, 31 (1): 4–22.

Verdery, K., 1991, 'Theorizing Socialism: A Prologue to the "Transition"', *American Ethnologist*, 18 (3): 419–39.

— 1996, *What Was Socialism and What Comes Next?* Princeton, NJ, Princeton University Press.

Wallace, T., Bornstein, L., Chapman, J., 2006, *The Aid Chain: Coercion and Commitment in Development NGOs*, Rugby, Intermediate Technology Publications.

Walley, C., 2002, '"They Scorn Us Because We Are Uneducated": Knowledge and Power in a Tanzanian Marine Park', *Ethnography*, 3 (3): 265–98.

— 2004, *Rough Waters: Nature and Development in an East African Marine Park*, Princeton, NJ, Princeton University Press.

Wangwe, S., 2010, 'Changing Aid Modalities and Tanzanian Development Assistance Partnerships', in Havnevik, K. & Isinika, C. (eds), *Tanzania in Transition: From Nyerere to Mkapa* , Dar es Salaam, Mkuki na Nyota: 207–22.

Warren, D., Slikkerveer, L., Brokensha, D., 1995, 'Introduction' to their (eds), *The Cultural Dimension of Development: Indigenous Knowledge Systems*, London, Intermediate Technology Publications.

Weiss, B., 2002, 'Thug Realism: Inhabiting Fantasy in Urban Tanzania',

*Cultural Anthropology*, 17 (1): 93–124.

West, H., 2001, 'Sorcery of Construction and Socialist Modernization: Ways of Understanding Power in Postcolonial Mozambique', *American Ethnologist*, 28 (1): 119–50.

West, P. 2006, *Conservation is Our Government Now: The Politics of Ecology in Papua New Guinea*, Durham, NC, Duke University Press.

White, Howard, 1995, 'Import Support Aid: Experiences from Tanzania and Zambia', *Development Policy Review*, 13: 41–63.

Whitehead, R., 2012, 'Historical Legacies, Clientelism and the Capacity to Fight: Exploring Pathways to Regime Tenure in Tanzania', *Democratization*, 19 (6): 1086–1116.

Wildavsky, A.B., 1986, *Budgeting: A Comparative Theory of Budgetary Processes*, 2nd edn, New York, Transaction Publishers.

Wilk, R., 1995, 'Consumer Goods as Dialogue about Development: Colonial Time and Television Time in Belize', in Friedman, J. (ed.), *Consumption and Identity*, Chur, Switzerland, Harwood Academic: 97–118.

— 1996, 'Learning to Be Local in Belize: Global Systems of Common Difference', in Miller, D. (ed.), *Worlds Apart: Modernity Through the Prism of the Local*, Routledge: 110–33.

Williams, G., 2004, 'Evaluating Participatory Development: Tyranny, Power and (Re)Politicisation', *Third World Quarterly*, 25 (3), 557–78.

Willis, R., 1968, 'Kamcape: An Anti-Sorcery Movement in South-west Tanzania', *Africa*, 38 (1): 1–15.

Wilson, M., 1963, *Good Company: A Study of Nyakyusa Age Villages*, Boston, MA, Beacon Press.

Wright, S. & Nelson, N., 1995, 'Participatory Research and Participant Observation: Two Incompatible Approaches', in Nelson, N. & Wright, S. (eds), *Power and Participatory Development: Theory and Practice*, London, Intermediate Technology Publications: 43–59.

Yakura, E., 2002, 'Charting Time: Timelines as Temporal Boundary Objects', *The Academy of Management Journal*, 45 (5): 956–70.

Yang, M.M., 1988, 'The Modernity of Power in the Chinese Socialist Order', *Cultural Anthropology*, 3 (4): 408–27.

Yeager, R., 1982, *Tanzania: An African experiment*, vol. 2, Boulder, CO, Westview Press.

Zanasi, M., 2007, 'Exporting Development: The League of Nations and Republican China', *Comparative Studies in Society and History*, 49 (1): 143–69.

# INDEX

accountability, 8, 14, 34–5, 39, 47, 81, 101–2, 116, 119, 122–4, 126, 132, 150, 176

acting (standing in for), 105

agency, 37–8, 45, 54, 60, 136, 155
  collective, 40
  illusion of, 91

agency staff. *See* development professionals and staff

agricultural modernisation, 19, 29, 43, 158, 163–5, 169, 181
  Indigenous Agricultural/ Technical Knowledge paradigms (IAK/ITK), 40
  mobile technologies and, 170–2, 177
  Southern Agricultural Growth Corridor (SAGCOT) initiative, 20

agriculture and agricultural workers, 43, 46–7, 158, 161, 164
  cultural devaluation of, 167
  middle class and, 159, 167–8, 177–8

allowances *(posho)*, 34–5, 67, 128
  participation in development and, 83, 93, 95

Amin, Ash, 121, 160

Amin, Idi, 7

anthropology, 12
  development as failure and, 57–60
  economic transformation in Africa in 90s, 176
  local knowledge and, 42
  witchcraft and modernity and, 137–9

anticipatory development, 117–18, 130–3

Arusha Declaration (Nyerere), 164

Askew, Kelly, 104 n.5

assistance or aid *(msaada)*, 50–5, 114, 152

auditing, 62, 64, 70, 113

Augé, Marc, 72–3

Bagomoyo District, 119, 132

Belgium, 22

*Big Brother Africa* (TV show), 167

*boda boda* (motorcycle taxis), 169, 171

boundary objects, 13, 76–8, 92, 94–7

British colonialism, 5–6, 13, 17–19, 23–5, 27, 29, 52, 181
  in Ulanga District, 46–7
  village resettlement and, 109
  witchcraft shavers and, 142

Bryceson, D., 166 n.18

by-laws, 27, 49, 76, 110, 122

Lightning Source UK Ltd.
Milton Keynes UK
UKOW05f1222230317
297349UK00008B/233/P